THE IMPACT OF AMERICAN RELIGIOUS LIBERALISM

Second Edition

Kenneth Cauthen
Crozer Theological Seminary

UNIVERSITY
PRESS OF
AMERICA

LANHAM • NEW YORK • LONDON

University Press of America,® Inc.

4720 Boston Way
Lanham, MD 20706

3 Henrietta Street
London WC2E 8LU England

Library of Congress Cataloging in Publication Data

Cauthen, Kenneth, 1930-
　The impact of American religious liberalism.

　Reprint. Originally published: 1st ed. New York :
Harper & Row, [1962]
　Bibliography: p.
　Includes index.
　1. Liberalism (Religion)—United States.　2. United
States—Church history—20th century.　I. Title.
BR1615.C35　1983　　230'.044　　82-23902
ISBN 0-8191-2762-0 (pbk.)

All University Press of America books are produced on acid-free
paper which exceeds the minimum standards set by the National
Historical Publications and Records Commission.

TO MY PARENTS

Mr. and Mrs. J. W. Cauthen

AND

TO MY WIFE

Eloise

without whose combined labors
this book would never have been

A NOTE FROM THE AUTHOR

I apologize to readers for the sexist language in the text. This book was written more than twenty years ago when that usage was universal. It is true but irrelevant in the context of today's new consciousness to say that the exclusive male language was generic in intention and fact. I cringe when I read my own words from that former time. It would be impractical to change it all for purposes of this reprinting. Let it stand as a reminder that the work of liberalism is never done, since new insights and sensitivities continually make ancient good uncouth.

CONTENTS

Part Four. CONCLUSION

FOREWORD

Titus Street Professor of Ecclesiastical History, Yale University

Religious liberalism in America, which began as a revolt against the dead hand of tradition, has itself become part of our theological tradition. Like other components of that tradition, it is in danger of being forgotten by a generation that reaps the benefits of the past without having passed through its conflicts.

For that reason Kenneth Cauthen's study is a useful introduction to the conflicts of American religious liberalism. The eight figures discussed in his central chapters spanned a great range of theological thought. As the individual chapters make clear, each of these men passed through various stages of doubt, controversy, and reformulation as he moved from a dated and obsolete conception of the Gospel to a theology that seemed relevant to the modern day. With genuine sympathy for the personal struggles behind the theological formulations, the author reviews some of the chief ways of being "liberal" that emerged from the situation of American Protestantism between 1900 and World War II. American religious liberalism was typically American, despite the stimulation it received from Continental, especially German, theological scholarship. Two of the features of liberal theology that mark it as American are its concern for ethical results and its preoccupation with the empirical.

In our time it has become fashionable to dismiss the theology of American religious liberalism as moralistic, and moralistic much of it certainly was. It is a shock to read some of the naïve declarations assembled in this book, and to be reminded of how drastically some of the liberals reduced the essence of Christianity to its moral imperatives. For if the basis of the Protestant Reformation was a recovery of the gift-character of salvation in opposition to the moralistic emphasis of Roman Catholicism upon human merit and the righteousness of works, then it must be conceded that some of the spokesmen for liberalism went far beyond medieval works-righteousness in their glorification of what man could do by his own efforts to win a right relation to God. The eternal qualitative difference between God and man, or between God and creation, or between God and natural process, seems sometimes to have been blurred into a merely temporary separation, soon to be transcended by man's moral progress.

Yet Cauthen shows that it is bearing false witness against one's neighbor to lump all of liberalism under the convenient smear word "moralism." The critical theology of the mid-twentieth century was not the first to discover that the moral improvement of man is a fragile and an ambiguous thing, distorted by the self-aggrandizement of the morally respectable poseur. Few have seen this self-righteousness more clearly, or diagnosed it more tellingly, than Walter Rauschenbusch or Harry Emerson Fosdick. Even today, if we are forced sometimes to smile rather superciliously at the naïveté of their moral preachments, we still find their prophetic power strangely moving, their ethical commitment permanently challenging.

The other hallmark of the theologians discussed here is their empirical orientation. This, too, was often quite simple-minded and reductionistic. Sometimes it represented a pathetic effort to bring Christian theology up-to-date by conforming its method to that of the natural sciences, that is, to the method espoused by the natural sciences of the generation that had preceded, the method that was gradually being surrendered by sophisticated scientists just at the time when theologians were adopting it. At the same time, the empiricism of the liberals was a continuation—and a legitimate continuation—of the seriousness about religious experience that has always belonged to Protestant theology. There is a line, however attenuated it may have become, from Luther's insistence that the power of the Holy Spirit *experiendum est* to the analysis of religious experience that figured so prominently in the theological methodologies of Macintosh and Wieman.

In opposition to an orthodoxy that was embarrassed by the Reformation's experiential validation of religious truth, American religious liberalism believed, with its mentors, Schleiermacher and Rudolf Otto, that a part of the uniqueness of religious faith was to be found, not in a sacred subspecies of intellectual knowledge nor yet in the moral life as such, but in the experience of the Holy. By some sort of Gresham's law whose operation in the history of Christian thought would deserve separate investigation, the simplistic theology of religious experience reflected in much of the literature of Protestant religious education has driven from the market place of ideas the profound and incontestably valid insights of American religious liberalism into the structure of man's life in God.

In Dr. Cauthen's presentation, many of these problems fall into place. Historical perspective, theological insight, and biographical information combine to cast new light upon many of the issues and figures of American Protestantism during the first half of this century. Anyone who relives the development of liberalism as represented by these seven thinkers will also understand better the nature of the reaction they evoked in the churches, as well as the role some of them played within the churches. We can see from the pastoral work of a Fosdick or from the interdenominational work of a Mathews that the title "churchman" dare not be reserved for those who fought against the liberals. Although some of the figures described here did lose most of their connection with the empirical Church and articulated their doctrines of the Church (if any) in abstraction from the great tradition, this was not necessarily a part of their liberalism. Indeed, one of the most interesting features of the present situation in American theology is how churchly American liberalism has become. Running throughout Dr. Cauthen's narrative are subtle suggestions of the ways by which liberalism has moved from the classrooms and pulpits of the *avant-garde* into the thought and life of most Protestant churches themselves.

Dr. Cauthen's researches suggest also the extent to which the liberalism of the 1920's was a product of its own time. Repeatedly he shows how uncritically the advocates of liberalism accepted the spirit of their time and incorporated it into their own theology. This illustrates one of the most touching ironies in the liberal movement. Among the permanent results of liberalism none is more important than the discovery that the Bible and the Church have been conditioned by history. The cosmologies underlying the thought and language of the biblical writers are not the product of the religious experiences and the revelations of Israel and early Christianity, but are the common property of believer and unbeliever in the ancient world. Similarly, many of the cherished beliefs and bitter controversies in the history of the Church owe their origins not to the Scriptural passages that were always being quoted or the doctrinal and moral concerns that were always being cited, but to the social, political, and cultural milieu in which the Church was living.

For our sense of this conditionedness and for the emancipation from "excess baggage" that this awareness has accomplished, we are everlastingly indebted to the work of liberalism. Yet those who discovered that the Bible and the Church have been conditioned by history were themselves historically conditioned—and did not seem to recognize that they were. What proved to be only the unexamined presupposition of their own epoch, they accepted as abiding truth; they demanded that the tradition of the Church be squared with "the facts," by which they meant the current (and quickly passing) intellectual or scientific fad. It is possible from Dr. Cauthen's account to multiply instances that prove to what extent American religious liberalism was a product of its own time.

But it was more than that, and it still is. It has, in fact, become an integral part of the way we see the history and message of Christianity. More perhaps than Dr. Cauthen's book indicates, liberalism was responsible for a new attitude toward the history of Christianity. Although liberalism in the United States did not produce an Adolf Harnack, its thought was shaped by the historical attitude toward the institutions and ideas of Christianity. Some of the moralism and naïve empiricism of the American liberals might have been tempered and deepened if they had been better historians, involved with the tradition even as they rejected it. After all, even Mathews put history behind him more completely than did his European counterparts. Yet liberalism did take "the historical" seriously, although it might have neglected the specific work of history. Here, more perhaps than in its ethics or its psychology of religion, is the continuing legacy of liberalism. In this sense there is no going behind the insights of the liberals. Even when we go beyond them, we stand in their debt. And if we have forgotten them, a book like this can reintroduce us to our own recent ancestors, regardless of where we may locate ourselves upon the Christian family tree.

PREFACE TO THE NEW EDITION

The preface to the original volume noted that no one had yet written a comprehensive account of liberal theology in American Protestantism. My book was offered as an attempt to fill that gap. Two decades later it can be recorded that THE IMPACT OF AMERICAN RELIGIOUS LIBERALISM has become the standard work on the subject. It has, however, been out of print for a number of years. With this reprinting this description of the themes and types of liberalism that dominated the intellectual centers of main-line Protestantism during the first third of the twentieth century will once more be available to scholars and students.

During the interval between the first publication of this work and the present, another theological generation has passed into history. It is tempting to add another chapter bringing the story of American Protestant theology up to date. This temptation has been resisted. One summary chapter has already been added showing how liberal methods were continued while many themes of liberalism were rejected in the neo-orthodox theologies that prevailed from the advent of Franklin Delano Roosevelt to the Presidency of John F. Kennedy. We are now two generations away from the era of Rauschenbusch, Fosdick, Knudson, Mathews, and Wieman. Another chapter capsuling present trends in theology would not do justice to them, nor would it add sufficiently to the main story of the book to make the effort worthwhile. Neo-orthodoxy and the multifarious impulses of the last twenty years require their own telling in detail. They exist in their own right and not merely as addenda to previous eras. The present book has its own work to do.

Yet the very description of that past era has its own timeliness. The task of liberalism is never done. Liberalizing, by which let us mean stating the old truths appropriately for each new day, is a continuing necessity if religion is to remain vital. Recent years have seen a resurgence of orthodoxies in many forms. The courts are now deciding whether creationism is to be taught in the public schools along with evolution. The Moral Majority frequently presents a combination of reactionary politics and fundamentalist religion. Resurgent conservatism has created strains in many Protestant denominations. A "New Evangelicalism" has appeared which combines a deep commitment to the Gospel "once and for all delivered to the saints" with liberal to radical social ethics. We have learned that among Roman Catholics we have to distinguish between conservatives and liberals who may frequently feel more at home with their Protestant counterparts than with their ideological opponents in their own communion. Today, as a half century ago, multitudes of Christians find themselves between frozen orthodoxies and a vapid humanism. As different as they may be from each other, they march under a banner that has no better name than Christian liberalism.

With all these and other factors in mind, a number of writers have attempted to state the themes and task of liberal Christianity for the present. A decade ago John Cobb addressed the question of LIBERAL CHRISTIANITY AT THE CROSSROADS (Philadelphia: The Westminster Press, 1973). Donald Miller has recently made THE CASE FOR LIBERAL CHRISTIANITY (San Francisco: Harper & Row, 1981). A younger colleague of mine, Leonard Sweet, is writing about REVITALIZING LIBERALISM (forthcoming). Dr. Theodore Weeden recently shared with a seminary convocation in Rochester his conviction that the mainline liberal church is a "sleeping giant" with a vital future if only it will seize the opportunity. It is a tenet of liberalism that no settled formulas from the past can serve the present. Hence, the work of those early twentieth-century liberals cannot suffice for the challenges of today. But we can learn from them how they preserved the essentials of a Christ-centered religion in ways that made the Gospel both credible and pertinent to their own time. Our situation requires its own combination of the abiding and the changing, but our task can be made easier by learning both from their successes and their shortcomings. If we see further than they, it is only because we stand on their shoulders. Hence, their story can be instructive as we find our own truths and fall into our own peculiar errors.

Harry Emerson Fosdick said that though astronomies change, the stars abide. The fundamentalists are fearful that if the old dogmas are surrendered, the stars will fall. The humanists believe that there never were any stars above us, but only the light within us. This volume is the account of how one generation of liberals attempted to revise astronomies while pointing to the stars that have never ceased to shine.

June 23, 1982
Rochester, New York

Kenneth Cauthen

PREFACE TO THE FIRST EDITION

More than ten years ago Henry Steele Commager stated that no satisfactory history of religious thought in America had yet been written. That observation still holds true today. It is also true that there has been no comprehensive account of one of the most significant movements within that history: theological liberalism. This book is an attempt to contribute toward the filling of this second gap. The aim is to discover the essence of liberal thought through an investigation of its major types and its leading exponents. The heart of the book deals in some detail with the thought of eight major theologians. These chapters are intended not only to distinguish significant variations of the liberal theme but to reveal the presuppositions, methods, structure, and dominant content of the liberal movement as a whole. A final section assesses the validity and permanent value of liberal theology and traces the persistence of liberal motifs in later theologies which have been highly critical of liberalism.

This book began as a doctoral dissertation at Vanderbilt University. Two motivations lie behind the offering of the revised work to a wider audience. The first is the conviction that there is a need for a sympathetic but critical presentation of what liberalism was during the days when it prevailed in the high places of the clerical and theological worlds. Those who, like the author, grew up being told that liberalism was a bad word may profit from a comprehensive survey of liberal thought presented through the writings of the greatest, or at least the most representative, exponents of this outlook. The younger reader may still be critical, but perhaps he will understand it better. Older adherents of liberalism should rejoice to see their convictions in print once more, and those who came through liberalism and later turned against it will be able to remind themselves of what they have rejected. There is need on all sides to re-examine this version of the faith which once saved many from unbelief or agnosticism. But the second and more important motivation is the growing conviction that much of the structure of liberalism has been carried over into those theologies which have been most critical of liberalism. Those who rebelled against liberalism in the thirties and forties of this century were very conscious of their points of disagreement with liberal thought, but they perhaps did not break as fully with this perspective as they may have believed at the time. There are important continuities as well as discontinuities between liberalism and post-liberal theology, making it incorrect to speak of liberalism simply in the past tense. To what extent are liberalism and neo-orthodoxy basically alike despite certain fundamental differences? This is a question which needs attention at the present time, particularly as we begin to think about the direction in which American theology needs to move in the future.

Others will doubtless need to correct, modify, and add to what is said here, but it is hoped that a substantial beginning has been made toward the understanding and evaluation of liberal theology with reference both to its past meaning and to its present significance. Certainly liberalism constitutes one of the most important chapters in the complex total history of American religious thought—a history which still awaits the writing.

Expressions of gratitude from an author to those who have been of great assistance in bringing a book into being are difficult to conclude once they are under way, for many debts accumulate over the years. Yet, never to begin at all is inexcusable. Let it be said, then, that there are many names in my mind which do not appear here, and to whom private tribute is hereby promised. First of all, I am grateful to Professor Roger L. Shinn, formerly of Vanderbilt and now of Union Theological Seminary in New York, and to Professor Langdon Gilkey of Vanderbilt Divinity School for their skill in directing the study which lies behind this book and for their continuing interest and assistance. I am indebted to the Administration of Mercer University, particularly to President Rufus C. Harris, for releasing me from some of my teaching duties to allow me to prepare this manuscript for publication. Professors Willis B. Glover, Ray Brewster, Joe Hendricks, Robert Otto, and James L. Clegg, former colleagues at Mercer University, are due gratitude for offering valuable suggestions with regard to the last chapter. Many insights were also contributed to the last chapter by an unpublished lecture of Professor L. Harold DeWolf of the Boston University School of Theology entitled "Themes of Continuity and Discontinuity in Recent Thought and in the Christian Faith." I appreciate very much the assistance of the staff of Harper & Brothers and their consultants for substantial help in clarifying matters of fact and judgment. Mr. Ralph Skipper of Macon, Georgia, did an excellent job of typing numerous drafts of the manuscript, often under the pressure of time, and never complained of my early deadlines.

Finally, I must thank my wife and two children for giving up many hours of family life in order that the task could be completed. In addition, my wife has contributed many hours of labor with pencil and typewriter and is therefore due public as well as private praise.

KENNETH CAUTHEN

Crozer Theological Seminary
Chester, Pennsylvania
February, 1962

PART ONE

INTRODUCTION

CHAPTER 1

FORMATIVE FACTORS
IN AMERICAN LIBERALISM

In 1901 Henry Churchill King wrote, "A new constructive period in theology, it may well be believed, is at hand."[1] The constructive movement to which he referred was the maturing of American theological liberalism. In 1933 John Bennett wrote, "The most important fact about contemporary American theology is the disintegration of liberalism."[2] The years circumscribed by the dates of these two writings define the approximate period during which liberalism was at the height of its influence in America. There had been, of course, important reactions against Protestant orthodoxy previous to this time. One thinks immediately of deism in the eighteenth century and unitarianism in the nineteenth century.[3] But it was not until about 1850 that the liberalism which was destined to overcome orthodoxy began to emerge in this country. Liberalism has continued to have many important representatives among the clergy and professional theologians since its displacement by newer modes of thought in recent years and is still, though largely in a modified form, one of the leading parties in contemporary American theology. However, it was during the first thirty-five years of this century that liberalism achieved its most pervasive influence among the leading thinkers of the day.

The liberal theology which was propounded in America during this span of time constitutes the subject matter of this book. The thought of a number of representative liberal theologians has been investigated in order to discover the essence of liberalism and to set forth the most important concrete forms in which this essence appears. The purpose, then, is to describe the major types of liberalism.

3

I. THE PROBLEM

Of the classical types of Protestantism Calvinism has been the most influential in America. The Puritans who settled in New England adhered to the tenets of the Westminster Confession. In the middle of the eighteenth century Jonathan Edwards incorporated the spirit of the Great Awakening and some of the newer currents of thought in Europe into a version of Calvinism which became the beginning of what was later to be identified as the New England theology.[4] In the ensuing years the impact of a strong Arminian tradition, the distinctive emphases of revivalism, and the Unitarian revolt led to further changes in the Calvinistic outlook. But while the successors of Edwards moved gradually toward a position which relaxed some of the sterner aspects of the older Calvinism with respect to such issues as original sin, the salvation of infants, limited atonement, the doctrine of the double decree, and freedom of the will, the basic orientation of their theology was still Calvinistic. This modified Calvinism dominated the theological enterprise until late in the nineteenth century, although in the middle of that century the work of such men as Lyman Beecher and Horace Bushnell had already set in motion some of the influences which eventuated in a triumph of liberalism over orthodoxy by about 1900. Most of the early liberals came directly out of the Edwardian school and were reacting most immediately against it. Thus, when Protestant orthodoxy is referred to in the following pages, the reference is primarily to the Calvinistic modes of thought embodied in the theology of Edwards and his successors, although most that is said about orthodoxy would refer equally well to other types of classical Protestantism represented in America.

It was during the last quarter of the nineteenth century that liberalism made its most rapid advance in overcoming Protestant orthodoxy in America. Frank Hugh Foster writes that in 1880 the New England theology was dominant in every Congregational seminary, with one possible exception, and was in control of many of the Presbyterian seminaries. Park at Andover, Harris at Yale, Fairchild at Oberlin, and Boardman at Chicago—all of these men held chairs of theology in outstanding seminaries, and all of them adhered basically to the tradition which had dominated New England since the time of Edwards. Fifteen years later all of these men had been replaced by thinkers who represented a different perspective. Speaking of the sudden demise of the New England theology, Foster says, "It had endured more than 150 years; it had become dominant in a great ecclesiastical denomination; it had founded every Congregational seminary; and, as it were, in a night, it perished from off the face of the earth."[5] The school of thought which replaced the modified Calvinism of Jonathan Edwards, Samuel Hopkins, Nathaniel Emmons, Timothy Dwight, Nathaniel W. Taylor, and Edward A. Park in the last quarter of the nineteenth century was the theological perspective which is now called liberalism, but which was then called "the new theology."

How did it happen that the Protestant, and largely Calvinistic, orthodoxy which had dominated American theology since the very beginning should suddenly disintegrate? Or, to say it differently, what were the principles and the problems which gave rise after approximately 1875 to a new theology which was successful in winning its way among the leading thinkers and seminaries of the country where previous attacks had failed? It is to these questions that attention must now be directed.

II. THE FUNDAMENTAL CONSIDERATION

The basic reason why liberalism overcame orthodoxy was stated by Henry Churchill King at the turn of the century. He argued that reconstruction in theology was necessary not because of a rationalistic or irreligious tendency in the church but rather because of the compelling demand that living faith come to terms with the modern world.[6] Previously orthodoxy had been able to maintain itself in the face of sharp attack because the climate of opinion in which it then operated was still favorable enough to make its basic principles credible to men of great intellectual ability. Such was not the case during the last half of the nineteenth century. New ways of thinking and feeling were permeating the minds of sensitive men in such a way that they gradually became alienated from the older modes of thought. Orthodoxy perished, then, for the basic reason that it could no longer serve as an appropriate vehicle for the intellectual expression of the faith, and liberalism arose in order to adjust the ancient faith to the modern world.

III. THE UNDERLYING PRINCIPLES OF LIBERALISM

But what were these new influences which gave rise to liberalism? Precisely what was it which alienated the minds of men from orthodoxy and led them to seek new modes of expression for their Christian faith? There grew up in the nineteenth century a climate of opinion in which many factors played a part. Its effects were felt in every realm of thought and in every area of life. Liberal theology arose out of, and in the midst of, these new intellectual, social, moral, scientific, philosophical, and religious developments. In a complicated movement of this sort it is extremely difficult to distinguish cause from effect, since the various factors which enter into the total situation interact upon each other in extremely intricate ways. Any exhaustive attempt to sort out these various influences and to trace them to their ultimate sources or to show in detail how and to what extent each operated upon the other is beyond the scope of this book. Yet, some attempt along these lines must be made in order to set the liberal movement in America in its proper perspective.

The complex factors which constituted the milieu in which liberal theology developed can be analyzed into three types of influences: (1) those factors which led to an emphasis on continuity rather than discontinuity in the world, (2) those influences which focused on the autonomy of human reason and experience rather than on an authoritative divine revelation, and (3) those forces which contributed to the stress on the dynamic rather than the static nature of life and the world.

A. *Continuity*

First of all, there were those influences which led to the stress on continuity. The older theology was characterized by many sharp contrasts and discontinuities. The most important of these contrasts was that made between the natural and the supernatural. The supernatural was a realm behind or above the natural. It was out of this supernatural realm that God acted upon the world and descended to become incarnate in the man Jesus. While God acted within the natural realm in terms of general laws, it was through miracles that many of the most significant divine actions occurred. Likewise, while certain truths could perhaps be known from the general revelation of God in nature, only through a supernaturally given revelation could saving knowledge of God be had. Similar discontinuities permeated the whole orthodox scheme, ranging from a radical distinction between the divine and the human natures of Jesus to the distinction between Christianity and other religions. These distinctions were based on a world view which antedated the modern world and which was antithetical to it.

1. SCIENCE

The impact of modern science in breaking down the orthodox scheme was decisive. Empirical investigation seemed to indicate that the reign of law was universal throughout nature. Mechanical causation appeared to be supreme, leaving little or no room for special divine activity. Thus, the gap between general and special revelation and general and special providence, in which miracle played an important role, was acutely called into question. The result was a conception of a unified world, everywhere subject to the inexorable sequence of natural cause and effect.

Moreover, the doctrine of evolution narrowed the gap between nature and man and, along with the developmental theories regarding the origin of the solar system and the earth, emphasized the fact that the whole natural world was characterized by a unity of process. The doctrine of evolution also operated to reduce the discontinuities which had dominated traditional theology between the creation and the fall of man, sin and salvation, and the flesh and the spirit. These distinctions now seemed out of place, since all of them are encompassed within the same unified process of human development.[7]

By virtue of these influences modern science had both a negative and a positive effect upon the development of theology. Its negative effect was to call into question the world view which had been believed for centuries upon the authority of the Scriptures and the Greek thinkers. It also called into question the possibility of miracles, upon which theologians had relied as proof of the special activity of God within nature and history. The positive effect of science was to prepare the way for a doctrine of God's immanence, in which divine activity was found not in miraculous intervention into the normal sequences of cause and effect but in the law-abiding evolutionary process of nature itself. Thus, science both helped to destroy the traditional supernaturalism and to establish in its place a view which stressed the continuity between nature, man, and God.[8]

2. OTHER MOVEMENTS OF THOUGHT

Other modern movements also stressed continuity in ways which affected theology. The whole thrust of the Enlightenment was to reduce or to eliminate completely the discontinuity between reason and revelation. Moreover, the Enlightenment rejected the ethical dualism between God and man and stressed the inherent goodness and perfectibility of human nature. The rights of man over against the sovereign God were emphasized, and the contrast between the comparative misery of the present life and the glories of the life to come was done away with on the assumption that the kingdom of God could be attained on earth.[9]

Other modern philosophies have also stressed the principle of continuity. There is a line in modern thought running from Spinoza to Schleiermacher and Hegel and throughout the nineteenth century which tends toward the pantheistic identification of God and the world. Absolute idealism, which dominated a large part of the nineteenth century, stressed the unity of God and man. Hegel's description of reality as Infinite Spirit unfolding itself through a dialectical process added a tremendous impetus to the emphasis on the immanence of God. Hegel's influence spread quickly to England and ultimately to this country, where Royce developed his own version of absolute idealism. McGiffert contends that the strong monistic tendency in nineteenth-century thought was due in large part to the influence which emanated from Hegel.[10]

Romanticism, which arose in the nineteenth century as a reaction against the sterile rationalism of the eighteenth century, also stressed the presence of God in nature and in man. The romanticists rebelled against the deistic picture of the world as a machine and of God as a machine-maker far removed from the world. As Randall points out, "This external deity completely disappeared for the romanticists and idealists: the world was no machine, it was alive, and God was not its creator so much as its soul, its life."[11] The stress of romanticism on the immanence of God can be seen making its way into theology through Schleiermacher in Germany, Coleridge in England, and Bushnell in America.

3. RELIGION

There were developments in the realm of religion itself which contributed to the stress on continuity in the world. The rise of the historical-critical method in Biblical studies made it possible to show the connections between the religion of the Hebrews and the beliefs and practices of surrounding peoples. The science of comparative religions, which developed in the nineteenth century, focused on the similarities between the various world religions. This raised the hope in some quarters that a universal religion might emerge at some time in the future to which all the major faiths would contribute.

More important than this, however, was the impact of a number of widespread movements which stressed the immediate presence of God in religious experience. Pietism in Germany, the Wesleyan movement in England, and revivalism in America, along with romanticism on the more secular side, all contributed directly or indirectly to the general revolt against the emphasis on the remoteness of God to experience in scholastic orthodoxy and eighteenth-century rationalism. These movements contended that God was not far off and unapproachable but immediately present and active in the inner life. Timothy L. Smith points out that the concept of "divine immanence" was expressed in radical terms by the holiness movement which swept America in the middle of the nineteenth century. God seemed near and active to those countless multitudes who had experienced the "tongue of fire" in revival meetings throughout the country.[12] A. C. McGiffert, Jr., refers to the "immanence of God in human personality" as one of the central principles of the theology of Horace Bushnell, who was a precursor of much of the liberal thought in this country.[13] The influence of Schleiermacher and Coleridge was also important in this regard for the developing liberal movement in America.

4. RESULTS

From all these directions came influences which created a cultural climate of opinion in which continuity was presupposed. It was in this climate that liberalism arose, and continuity was its dominating motif. This theme manifests itself in every area of thought and permeates all liberal theology. There is practically no end to its application. It reduces the distinction between animals and men, men and God, nature and God, reason and revelation, Christ and other men, Christianity and other religions, nature and grace, the saved and the lost, justification and sanctification, Christianity and culture, the church and the world, the sacred and secular, the individual and society, life here and hereafter, heaven and hell, the natural and supernatural, the human and divine natures of Christ, etc.

Continuity was, according to Henry P. Van Dusen, the "major positive principle of the liberal mind."[14] Taken in connection with the other two types of influences which are to be discussed, the principle of continuity was of utmost significance in the triumph of liberalism over orthodoxy. It was in connection with the doctrine of the immanence of God, which has been called the most characteristic doctrine of the nineteenth century,[15] that the principle of continuity had its most far-reaching effect on theology.

Some of the implications of this doctrine need to be noted specifically here. First of all, the distinction between the natural and the supernatural was reduced or reinterpreted. There is fundamentally one realm, one process, one world, in which God is present as its life or soul. God is a living force or spirit which permeates the whole. He is present everywhere and at all times. He is not so much the creator of the world as he is its preserver, not so much an occasional visitor as a permanent, pervasive influence which imparts a divine quality to all of existence. The tendency toward pantheism in this view of God is strong, and many liberals strove valiantly to avoid this conclusion.

Secondly, the importance of miracles disappeared. Miracle is typically defined in liberalism as the name for a religiously significant event (Schleiermacher).

Thirdly, the conception of revelation was affected in a vital way. If God is immanent in all things, he can be discovered in all things and known by all men. Elizabeth Barrett Browning expresses this liberal theme most effectively:

> Earth's crammed with heaven,
> And every common bush afire with God;
> But only he who sees, takes off his shoes.[16]

It is still true that God is most fully revealed in the life and teachings of Jesus. Nevertheless, revelation is seen to be continuous with other knowledge and to have its supreme focus within the self and not without in a book, a creed, or in the pronouncements of a church.

Fourthly, the goodness of man was stressed rather than his inherent depravity. The infinite worth and goodness of personality became a central principle of liberal thinking. If God is present within him, man needs no miraculous regeneration but only to be awakened to the divine impulses within.

Fifthly, striking changes have resulted in the conception of the person of Christ. With the breakdown of the radical distinction between the natural and supernatural and with the establishment of the potential divinity of all men, the doctrine of the two natures of Christ fades into insignificance. In the words of Dillenberger and Welch, "The perfection of humanity *is* the fullest embodiment of deity. The divine and the human in Christ are not alien to each other but are one."[17] The Jesus of history, not the supernatural Christ, is the focal point of liberalism's concern.[18]

In the sixth place, there emerged a stress on the solidarity of men. Individuals are not discrete units like rocks on a pile but are organically related to each other as the members of the physical body. This means that the individualistic methods of evangelism and social service which were characteristic of nineteenth-century Protestantism were inadequate. The social order as well as the individual must be dealt with. This principle was of vital importance in the emergence of the social gospel.

In the seventh place, the contrast between the good life here and the life beyond was reduced. Liberalism was concerned with the development and perfection of moral personality in the present life. Eternal life was seen to be continuous with the process of moral growth already begun on earth.

In the eighth place, the rigid distinction between the twofold destiny of the saved and the lost was abandoned. The difference between the sinner and the saint is one of degree. The doctrine of everlasting punishment was seldom heard, and a belief in the ultimate salvation of all was widely held.

Finally, the principle of continuity reduced the distance between the church and the total society. Liberals were more interested in the transformation of the whole society into the kingdom of God than in the church itself as a distinctive community of faith. The church was widely regarded in an instrumental and pragmatic sense. Its purpose was to co-operate with other social agencies in promoting the ends of justice and brotherhood. As a result the doctrine of the church fell into serious neglect among many liberal thinkers.

B. *Autonomy*

Closely connected with those influences which resulted in a stress on continuity were those factors which led to an emphasis on the autonomy of human reason and experience with respect to religious knowledge. The principle of autonomy will refer throughout this volume to the way the problem of revelation and reason is dealt with in liberal theology. A distinction can be made between a concept of religious knowledge based on human reason and experience and one based on a given revelation of God which stands over against the reasoning, experiencing subject. These two approaches to religious knowledge are by no means mutually exclusive, and theologians generally have tried to include both reason and revelation in one way or another. Nevertheless, the emphasis usually falls on one side rather than on the other, and liberalism differs significantly from Protestant orthodoxy in the way it deals with this issue. Within this context the principle of autonomy means that liberal theologians rejected any arbitrary appeal to external authority and insisted that all religious affirmations must be grounded in, or at least subject to confirmation by, the data of religious experience or the conclusions of reason. All liberals adhered to this general principle, although they varied considerably in the extent to which they retained belief in a normative historical revelation. Some contended that there was to be found in the teachings and in the personality of the historical Jesus a permanent, universally valid standard of religious truth which validated itself by its appeal to the highest and best in man's moral and spiritual nature. Others virtually gave up any appeal to historical revelation and relied exclusively upon the findings of reason and the data of experience, although they insisted that their conclusions were in harmony with the permanently valid essence of historic Christianity. All agreed, however, in affirming the autonomy of human reason and experience over against the orthodox stress on an authoritative revelation of God contained in Biblical propositions.

Another contrast must now be introduced. Within the liberal perspective a distinction needs to be made between those thinkers who stressed the subjective factors in human knowledge and those who stressed objective factors. Some liberal thinkers were subjectivistic in that they pointed to certain inner experiences as being the most relevant source of religious knowledge. These men emphasized feeling, intuition, and the immediate awareness of the divine presence and power. By comparison some liberals were objectivistic in that they stressed the role of sensory observation, scientific method, speculative reason, and other such factors. The polarity here has to do with the distinction within reason and experience between knowledge based on a study of what occurs within an experiencing subject and that based on a study of what is objectively present to the receiving subject.[19]

The former emphasizes the immediate apprehension of God within the soul and involves a report of internal experience. The latter stresses empirical investigation or rational inquiry or both and involves a report on what is discovered to be real without. This distinction is subtle, since both subjective and objective factors are involved in knowledge and in religious experience. Moreover, most liberal thinkers reflect a variety of influences in their thinking, some of which led to a stress on one side of this polarity while others led to the opposite emphasis. Nevertheless, when all of these qualifying considerations are taken into account, it is still possible to discern a relative distinction between those who focus attention upon *experience* and those who focus attention upon *the experienced*. The further elaboration of this distinction and of the complex ways in which it operated in liberalism must wait upon the more detailed examination of the thought of the individual thinkers under consideration.[20] It should be kept in mind, however, that the principle of autonomy will refer in every case to the reliance of liberals upon reason and experience, whether interpreted subjectivistically or objectivistically, rather than upon an authoritative divine revelation which must simply be appropriated and interpreted.

The attempt must now be made to point out those influences which led to the emphasis on reason and experience in religious knowledge and to the abandonment of the belief in Biblical infallibility. Protestant orthodoxy was based upon an objectively-given, authoritative revelation of God found in the Bible. The Bible was believed to contain a body of material made up of factual data and propositions of doctrine which were completely reliable and without error. In short, the Bible was the infallible source of all beliefs and practices which were necessary to salvation. These truths were simply to be received and acted upon. Since man's nature was depraved by virtue of the corruption inherited from Adam, reason and experience were not safe guides to religious truth. God's Word given in the Bible must enlighten the mind, and the Holy Spirit must validate this truth in the heart and convert the soul. Thus, theology and the religious life were based upon a Biblical authoritarianism.

This does not mean that human factors were neglected altogether.[21] Experience could confirm portions of the Scriptures, especially those dealing with the nature and effects of sin and the results of salvation, and reason could demonstrate or show the inherent reasonableness of certain doctrines regarding God and his relation to the world. But, in the last analysis, reason and experience had to conform to what was given. Whatever in the Scriptures seemed to be irrational or morally repugnant was simply believed on divine authority and justified on the basis that what is mysterious to finite, sinful men is somehow rational and good in God's perfect judgment. Objectors were silenced with the admonition that it is not appropriate for human beings to judge God.

The Protestant orthodoxy which dominated America until the last quarter of the nineteenth century was based upon this kind of authoritarianism. However, there arose in the modern world a series of influential movements which called the infallible authority of the Bible into question. It became necessary for theology to find a new basis for Christian belief within the soul and in harmony with reason. An examination of these forces will help to make it clear why liberalism arose.

1. SCIENCE

One of the most influential forces which led to the destruction of the authoritarianism of orthodoxy was modern science. This influence operated in at least three ways. First of all, the discoveries of a succession of scientists from Copernicus to Darwin had demonstrated the falsity of the world view of the Bible. This made it impossible any longer to claim infallible authority for the Scriptures in the realm of science. Moreover, it raised the possibility that if the Bible were wrong in matters of fact, it might also be wrong in matters of faith. In this way science gave impetus to the search for a foundation for faith which did not depend on an external authority.

Secondly, the search for a foundation of faith within experience and in accordance with reason was strengthened by the effectiveness of the empirical method, which stressed observation and experimentation rather than reliance on authority. This influence of science furthered the principle of autonomy largely in the direction of an objectivistic interpretation of experience which sought to make of theology itself an empirical science. The attempt of these empirical theologians was to get away from a reliance on inner experience and feeling and to attain knowledge of the Object of religious experience through the employment of scientific method.

Thirdly, the mechanistic and materialistic view of the world, which was the outcome of seventeenth-century science, posed an immense problem for faith. Whitehead has pointed out with great clarity the nature and seriousness of this problem. There persists, he says, throughout the last three centuries

. . . the fixed scientific cosmology which presupposes the ultimate fact of an irreducible brute matter, or material, spread throughout space in a flux of configurations. In itself such a material is senseless, valueless, purposeless. It does just what it does do, following a fixed routine imposed by external relations which do not spring from the nature of its being. It is this assumption that I call "scientific materialism."[22]

This view of the world has made for a radical contradiction in the thinking of the modern world. Whitehead says:

A scientific realism, based on mechanism, is conjoined with an unwavering belief in the world of men and of the higher animals as being composed of self-determining organisms. This radical inconsistency at the basis of modern thought accounts for much that is half-hearted and wavering in our civilization. . . . For instance, the enterprises produced by the individualistic energy of the European peoples presuppose physical actions directed to final causes. But the science which is employed in their development is based on a philosophy which asserts that physical causation is supreme, and which disjoins the physical cause from the final end. It is not popular to dwell on the absolute contradiction here involved. It is the fact, however you gloze it over with phrases.[23]

In the eighteenth century this mechanistic materialism was embodied in the view of the world as a vast impersonal machine, which view seemed to be the inevitable outcome of Newtonian science. This world machine seemed to be dead, void of purpose, and indifferent to the most precious values of men. God seemed to have no relation to this world except that of having created it in the beginning to let it operate henceforth according to its own inexorable laws.

2. REACTIONS AGAINST MECHANISM

This exclusion of God, freedom, purpose, and value from the world produced a number of widespread reactions in the nineteenth century which insisted that this scientific mechanism had left out what was most important in life. This was part of a general reaction against eighteenth-century tendencies.[24] There was in the nineteenth century an intense concern with the realities of the inner life, of personal experience, of feeling and intuition. It was felt that whatever science might mean for the external world, there was a sure foundation for freedom, morality, and religious faith within the moral and spiritual consciousness. This effort to distinguish between the inner spiritual world and the external mechanistic world of science can be seen in the distinctions which have been made by a number of important thinkers in Germany, England, and America between the pure and practical reason (Kant), understanding and reason (Coleridge), the natural and the supernatural (Bushnell), and nature and moral personality (Ritschl).[25] This attempt to distinguish between the realm of moral and religious values and the realm of empirical fact and to find in the immediate intuitions of the inner self a basis for religious faith is typical of the nineteenth-century liberal reconstruction of theology.[26]

The whole romantic movement was also part of this protest against the exclusion of God from the world of nature. The romanticists spoke of the immanent presence of God as the soul of the world, now conceived of as an organism rather than as a machine. They asserted that God is known immediately through feeling and intuition and not through the speculative intellect, which examines the world dispassionately to find evidences of divine activity, or through science, which reduces everything to lifeless mechanism.[27]

3. THE ENLIGHTENMENT AND OTHER PHILOSOPHICAL MOVEMENTS

The Enlightenment also contributed to the breakdown of authoritarianism in religion by insisting that all beliefs must be reasonable, that is, in harmony with universal rational principles which were independent of special revelations and external authorities such as the Bible, the church, and creeds. Whatever is based on mere arbitrary authority and not verifiable by the autonomous reason must be rejected. The Enlightenment, then, is one of the primary sources of the principle of autonomy in liberal theology. It should be noted that the impact of rationalism tended to further the emphasis on objectivity in religious knowledge. The deists sought to establish a kind of natural religion based on universal truths. They affirmed that there were certain moral and religious principles which could be discerned by men everywhere by the cool and clear light of impartial reason. Nature is so structured that reason by examination can arrive at proof of the existence of God as a benevolent creator and ruler, distinguish between right and wrong, adduce reasonable grounds for believing in immortality, and, in general, furnish a sound basis for religious belief and practice.[28] Thus, the objective findings of reason, not the inner experiences of the pious, were taken to be the main source of religious truth. Objectivism, in this sense, entered strongly into the heritage of liberalism, and many liberal theologians sought to show by rational argument that the essentials of the Christian religion could be accepted by reasonable men.

It would be impossible to ignore the influence of Immanuel Kant in connection with the principle of autonomy. Kant is a towering figure in the history of thought, and in a real sense it can be said that all subsequent developments both in theology and philosophy can be traced back to him. His impact on the world of thought has many facets, and his influence in theology is a complex phenomenon which can only be treated in summary fashion here. Kant concluded that it is impossible to attain metaphysical truth about the soul, the world, and God through the theoretical reason. He had, he said, destroyed knowledge in order to make room for faith. The faith which he advocated is based, not on truth discerned by the intellect by an inspection of the objective world or on an external religious authority, but on the immediate certainty of moral obligation. The voice of conscience from within subjects all men to the demand that their action proceed from respect for duty and not from natural interests or hedonistic impulses. Man's sense of obligation to obey the moral law has its origin in the structure of the practical reason and is a necessary and universal principle of thought. The demands of the moral imperative lead to the postulation of freedom, God, and immortality and give a practical basis for religious faith. While the postulates of the practical reason cannot be thought of as knowledge in the same sense as scientific knowledge based on sensory experience, they are morally and practically necessary if reality is to be thought of as rational and good.

This revolution in religious thought whereby the moral needs of the self become the determinative and active ground on the basis of which religious realities are postulated has been of tremendous importance for all subsequent theology. His thought is one of the major influences which gave rise to the principle of autonomy in theology. Kant showed that it is possible to ground religion in reason without reference to supernatural revelation and that it is philosophically permissible to justify faith in God on the basis of man's moral nature.

Thus, he succeeded in making ethics and religion into self-sustaining realms, free from Biblical authoritarianism, on the one side, and from philosophical skepticism and scientific materialism, on the other side.[29] In the light of the complex impact of Kant upon later thinking it is probably safe to say that his influence fostered both subjectivism and objectivism with reference to the interpretation of religious knowledge, but the major impact seems to have been in the direction of the former.[30]

4. RELIGIOUS MOVEMENTS

Finally, there were religious movements which helped to break down the Biblical authoritarianism of orthodoxy and to re-establish religious faith on autonomous grounds. The rise of the historical-critical method in the Biblical studies helped to destroy confidence in the infallible authority of the Scriptures. Not only literal contradictions in specific matters of fact and doctrine but also basic differences in theological perspective were shown to be present in the Biblical documents. The recognition that the writers were fundamentally conditioned by historical and social factors magnified the prominence of the human element in the Bible and ruled out the possibility of verbal inspiration. Literary and historical research showed the falsity of many of the traditional views relating to the authorship and date of the Biblical writings. Moreover, the findings of modern scholarship, along with the results of science, revealed the deep, irreconcilable differences between the world view of the Bible and that of the contemporary world. This, of course, raised the crucial question as to the relevance of this ancient document to the religious life of the contemporary man. In short, modern methods of Biblical study made the older views of the Bible impossible and necessitated the elaboration of an alternative view of its authority and relevance. This alternative took the form of seeing the Bible as the most illuminating record of the progressive stages through which the human experience of God had come to reach its climactic height in the historical Jesus, whose life and teachings have given to mankind the supreme revelation of religious truth.

Pietism, which expressed itself in America as revivalism, stressed the human side of conversion and religious faith. The great revivals which swept through the nation during the nineteenth century with their emphasis on an intense conversion experience and on the immediate personal knowledge of God had the effect of weakening the orthodox insistence on correct belief. The focusing of attention upon feeling and personal experience significantly shifted attention from doctrines to life, from past, written revelation to present, experiential knowledge. A line from a contemporary Gospel chorus makes the point well: "You ask me how I know he [Christ] lives; he lives within my heart." Thus, at the end of the century when it became apparent that the results of Biblical criticism and empirical science had completely undercut the doctrine of Biblical infallibility, a foundation had already been prepared by the great revivals for the liberal shift of authority from inherited dogma to religious experience. The grounding of religious knowledge in the soul's own apprehension of the divine presence and power which is so prominent in liberalism stands in direct continuity with the major thrust of revivalism, although it should be recognized that liberal theologians thought of religious experience within a theological and philosophical context which distinguishes them from the revivalists in certain important respects. Nevertheless, the importance of revivalism in preparing the way for liberal modes of thought should be clearly recognized.

5. RESULTS

The impact of these influences was twofold. Some of them operated to break down the former view of theology as a discipline grounded in an infallible revelation of God in the Scriptures, while others worked to establish a new foundation for religious knowledge in experience. The connections between the negative and the positive sides of these influences are intricate[31] and are of no vital concern here. Suffice it to say, the end result was a profound reorientation in theology from reliance upon the authority of the Bible to a dependence upon the authority of religious experience and the findings of reason.

These tendencies in the modern world are embodied in striking fashion in the thought of Schleiermacher and Ritschl, both of whom were tremendously influential in the shaping of American liberal theology. Schleiermacher grounded religion in the feeling of absolute dependence and described theology as the articulation in systematic form of religious experience. Ritschl spoke of theological doctrines as value judgments made with reference to the revelation of God in

Christ. These value judgments express the significance of God and Christ for the believing subject. Religion thus centers in personal convictions and subjective evaluations, not in metaphysical speculations or theological dogmas. This grounding of religion in the practical reason puts Ritschl in the direct line of Kant. Schleiermacher and Ritschl represent superbly the two main forms which the emphasis on religious experience took: the mystical and the moral, Schleiermacher representing the former, Ritschl representing the latter. Various combinations of these emphases appeared in American liberalism.

This stress on reason and experience affected theology in at least five basic ways. First of all, religion was given an independent foundation in religious experience. Thus, religious faith was not dependent on, or destroyed by, any objective rational criticism or by any possible result of Biblical criticism.

Secondly, theology became secondary to, and dependent on, religious experience. The task of theology was to express in meaningful categories the significance of religious experience, not to systematize the religious teachings of the Scriptures.

Thirdly, reason was made equal to, or dominant over, revelation. Present experience, not ancient dogma, became the final criterion of theological truth. Whatever conflicted with present knowledge was rejected. Revelation was no longer thought of as supernaturally disclosed truth and tended to become synonymous with insight, special moments of intuition, or human discovery.

Fourthly, theology was defined as a practical and not as a speculative discipline. Theology may legitimately dismiss those theoretical concerns which have no direct relevance to the religious life. Pragmatic rather than intellectual interests became dominant.

Finally, basing theology on experience rather than on dogma reduced the significance of doctrinal disputes. Men may have the same basic experience of God but yet express this experience in diverse ways because of differences in their intellectual background or temper of mind. Moreover, in the light of the primacy of experience over doctrinal correctness or denominational affiliation, liberals urged Christians to forget past disagreements and join together in the accomplishment of the common evangelistic, ethical, and social aims of the church in the world. In this sense the emphasis upon experience rather than on doctrine and tradition helped to provide a basis for the movement toward church unity which many liberals favored.

C. Dynamism

The third set of influences which went into the construction of the climate of opinion which made orthodoxy impossible and a new theology necessary were those which stressed the dynamic factors in the religious life and in the world. Orthodoxy was characterized by a variety of static categories. Religious truth was conceived to be a body of propositions derived from the complete and perfect revelation of God in the Bible. The task of theology was to set forth in systematic form the faith once delivered to the saints, the content of which remains the same from age to age. The historical and social conditioning of the Biblical writers was largely unknown to the orthodox divines, or at least was not recognized as being of significance for theology. Likewise, the world and society were thought of in static terms. The world was thought to have been created at a definite time a few thousand years before and to be in all essential respects the same now as it was then. Man was thought to have been created originally in the form in which he now exists. The same was held to be true of all the varieties of plant and animal life. While enough was known about past history to make it clear that certain changes had occurred, the ideas of process and social change were not central to orthodox thinking. The institutions of society, for all practical purposes, were taken for granted in their present state.[32]

There arose in the nineteenth century a way of viewing the world which was incompatible with these static notions. Randall insists that since the eighteenth century the "one conception that all sorts and conditions of thinkers have accepted is that, whatever else the world may be, it is not a static and finished thing, but is itself, as a whole and in each of its parts, in a process of change and growth."[33]

1. THE ENLIGHTENMENT

Prominent among the forces which are associated with this dynamic view of things was the idea of social progress, which dates from the Enlightenment. Locke, Helvetius, Bentham, Fontenelle, Condorcet, Buffon, Lessing, and Herder[34]—to list only a few of the important names—were all imbued with the idea of progress and helped to communicate it through their writings. The spread of reason and the results of science were thought by the eighteenth century to make possible an unending ascent toward individual and social perfection. Crane Brinton contends that

. . . the basic idea and the striking novelty of the Enlightenment—the idea that makes it a cosmology—*is the belief that all human beings can attain here on this earth a state of perfection hitherto in the West thought to be possible only for Christians in a state of grace, and for them only after death.*[35]

This idea of progress, based on faith in reason and science, combined with, and was reinforced by, the growing belief in the evolutionary development of nature, man, and society to create a climate of optimism which thoroughly permeated the thought of the nineteenth century.[36]

2. SCIENCE

The results of modern science also helped to establish a dynamic view of the world. LaPlace set forth in 1755 the nebular hypothesis regarding the evolution of the solar system; Lyell published a book in 1830 presenting evidence for the gradual development of the state of the earth's surface;[37] and Darwin in 1859 propounded the theory of organic evolution with reference to the biological world. These theories completely ruled out the traditional notion that God had created the world and its inhabitants in their present form by divine fiat at definite moments of time. They also gave a tremendous impetus to the tendency to explain social origins as well as natural phenomena in terms of evolutionary process. The doctrine of organic evolution gave scientific evidence for a notion that had long been prominent. It would be difficult to overemphasize the influence of the doctrine of evolution in all of its forms on theology. The combination of evolution and immanence goes a long way toward providing the basic context out of which liberalism came and in which it grew.[38]

3. LITERATURE AND PHILOSOPHY

Meanwhile, movements in literature and philosophy were also emphasizing the importance of growth and process. A fundamental tenet of the whole romantic movement in the nineteenth century was that the world is alive and growing. This means that time and history are of fundamental importance, since human institutions and ideals realize themselves through an evolutionary process.[39] Further impetus to the emphasis on development came from the philosophy of Hegel. History, according to Hegel, is a dynamic process whereby the Absolute realizes itself in time. Human thought, social institutions, the world, the totality of things—all are a process of becoming.[40] This notion of history as the arena for the self-realization of God aroused an intense fascination for the processes of history and was one of the most influential factors which led to the prodigious amount of historical research which was carried out in the nineteenth century. This changed conception of history as a process of evolution increasingly took possession of the nineteenth century, and the older static notions were almost completely ruled out. Nature and history were now seen as processes of development. In the minds of most this process carried with it the implication of progress.[41] More recent philosophies have been even more emphatic than those which were prominent in the nineteenth century in stressing the priority of becoming over being. Pragmatism, the process philosophies of Bergson, Alexander, Morgan, Whitehead, and others have made their influence felt in some of the liberals who did their thinking and writing well on into the twentieth century.

4. BIBLICAL STUDIES

Evolutionary notions were also taken up by Biblical scholars. Historical research during the nineteenth century indicated that the religious ideas of the Hebrews had undergone a long period of development from primitive polytheism to the lofty heights of the ethical monotheism of II Isaiah and had come to its climax after many centuries more in the religion of Jesus. Thus, it became evident that there was not one complete, perfect, and static body of religious truth contained within the Bible. Rather, the Bible was seen to contain a developing religion which embraced many stages from its primitive beginnings to its maturity in the New Testament. There were many theologies and points of view in the Bible. Different levels of truth and value were seen to exist side by side. The Bible came to be thought of as a record of the progressive discovery of God in human experience, not as a static body of theological dogmas all equally inspired and all of equal religious value. This application of evolutionary ideas to the study of the Hebrew religion by the Wellhausen school of thought came to dominate Biblical studies in the latter part of the nineteenth century.

5. RESULTS

In short, developments in the modern world have brought about a triumph of dynamic categories in every area of life. Randall contends that "if we are justified in entitling the eighteenth-century world essentially the Order of Nature, we are right in calling the universe in which men have lived since that time a Growing World."[42] Such a basic reorientation was bound to have repercussions on theology.[43] Some of the changes which have come about in theology as a result of this new climate of opinion may be briefly noted. First of all, there developed a tentativeness with regard to particular theological formulations. What is basic in religion is experience, but ideas change as the social and intellectual climates change. The recognition of this has the effect of reducing the seriousness of doctrinal differences between denominations and theological parties. Moreover, this tentativeness is, in part, the source of the "liberal spirit"—that flexible temper of mind, openness to new truth, broad-minded toleration of differences of opinion, and spirit of humility which has been characteristic of liberal thinking.

Secondly, the idea of social progress has stimulated the belief that society as well as the individual can be redeemed. The social gospel, which played such a large part in twentieth-century American liberalism, was imbued with this optimism with regard to the possibility of realizing the kingdom of God on earth.

Thirdly, the theory of evolution broke down the older theories with regard to the creation and fall of man and gave rise to new ideas regarding the origin and nature of sin. A whole new perspective developed, characterized by an emphasis on the process by which man had emerged slowly and painfully from his animal ancestry to progress gradually but surely toward moral perfection. He was thought to be hindered mainly by the drag of animal passions from within and the impersonal mechanisms of nature from without. Needless to say, this notion of man embodies an optimistic confidence which is alien to orthodox views of original sin and inherited corruption.

Fourthly, as has already been mentioned, the dynamic view of the world process gave a tremendous impetus to the doctrine of immanence, by which God is taken from without the world and placed within the process itself as its dynamic ground and immanent spirit.

Fifthly, all religions, both Christian and non-Christian, were seen to be subject to internal development as they evolved from lower to higher stages. Christianity was viewed simply as the highest stage to which religion had thus far developed and different only in degree from other religions.

In the sixth place, revelation ceased to be thought of as a body of truths given once and for all in the Biblical record and came to be interpreted in terms of a gradual process in which the accumulated insights derived from religious experience are progressively purified.

In the seventh place, the employment of dynamic categories affected both individual and general eschatology. The life beyond was seen to consist in a process of growth toward moral perfection. It was hoped by most liberals that all men could finally be won to repentance by a gradual process of discipline and training under intensified circumstances. Moreover, it was no longer felt that history would suddenly be ended by the return of Jesus on the clouds, but a long process of historical development was thought to lie ahead in which the kingdom of God would be realized on earth.

Finally, the emphasis on history and on the development of ideals within the historical process which came from Hegel and the romanticists gave a powerful impulse to the study of the New Testament origins of Christianity and to the search for the historical Jesus, who became the focal point of liberal Christology. In short, in every area of theology the dynamic categories of growth, process, and evolutionary continuity replaced the static, rigid discontinuities of orthodoxy, resulting in profound revisions of basic theological doctrines.

IV. SUMMARY

These three motifs, then—continuity, autonomy, and dynamism— are the formative principles of American liberalism. They are seen most clearly in the emphasis on the immanence of God, on the centrality of religious experience, and on the evolution of nature and history. Wherever the combination of these three motifs became the determining principles of the thinking of late nineteenth- and early twentieth-century theologians in America, some type of liberal theology emerged.

CHAPTER 2

TYPES OF AMERICAN LIBERALISM

I. THE PERENNIAL PROBLEM AND AMERICAN LIBERALISM

The theological enterprise in every generation moves between the poles of Christ and culture.[1] On the one hand, the theologian stands within a tradition which accepts as normative for the understanding of human existence the revelation of God in Christ. The meaning of this revelation is discovered by the Christian in the authentic witness of the Bible, in the commentary of creeds and previous Christian thinkers, in his own personal experience, and in the total life of the church both past and present. On the other hand, the theologian stands within a particular historical situation, with its own peculiar needs, problems, presuppositions, and categories of thought. In the art, literature, science, philosophy, and other forms of cultural expression of a people there appears an understanding of the nature of the world and the meaning of life which is characteristic of that particular era. To use Tillich's terms, each "situation" has its own "creative interpretation of existence."[2] This does not mean that the Christian tradition and secular culture are two parallel streams which develop independently without ever interacting upon each other. Every theological witness to the act of God in Christ that has ever appeared, including the Bible, bears the marks of some particular culture. Moreover, the influence of the Christian understanding of life is profoundly reflected in every aspect of Western civilization. Nevertheless, it is still true that there is a duality between the Christian revelation, given once and for all in Christ, and the cultural reason

26

which prevails at a given time, regardless of whether or not this cultural reason has been influenced by Christianity. The theologian moves between these two poles, and it is of the essence of his task to make the Christian interpretation of reality both credible and relevant to his own age. Moreover, since history is a dynamic process, it is necessary to wrestle afresh in every succeeding generation with this problem.

The liberalism which emerged in this country at the beginning of the twentieth century is one phase in this continuing struggle of the church to relate the enduring Christian message to a constantly changing cultural situation. One of the central concerns of theology since the eighteenth century has been the compatibility of Christianity with the modern mind.[3] Thoughtful persons became increasingly conscious as the decades passed of the gulf between the ancient faith and the newly developing view of the world. Liberalism arose in an attempt to bridge this chasm. The central aim of liberal theology was to make it possible for a man, to use Fosdick's phrase, "to be both an intelligent modern and a serious Christian."[4]

Liberalism, then, can best be understood in terms of its effort to harmonize Christ and culture under the conditions set by the late nineteenth and early twentieth centuries. However, not all liberals went about this task in the same way. Diverse forms of liberalism appeared. A fundamental difference between two groups of liberals can be specified in terms of the way each related the Biblical faith to modern culture. Thus, there are two basic types[5] of liberalism. One will be called evangelical liberalism, and the other will be referred to as modernistic liberalism.[6]

A. *Evangelical Liberalism*

The evangelical liberals can appropriately be thought of as "serious Christians" who were searching for a theology which could be believed by "intelligent moderns." They stood squarely within the Christian tradition and accepted as normative for their thinking what they understood to be the essence of historical Christianity. These men had a deep consciousness of their continuity with the main line of Christian orthodoxy and felt that they were preserving its essential features in terms which were suitable to the modern world.[7] One of the evidences of the loyalty of the evangelical liberals to the historic faith is the place which they gave to Jesus. Through his person and work there is mediated to men both knowledge of God and saving power. He is the source and norm of the Christian's experience of God. In short, evangelical liberalism is Christocentric. In the words of William Adams Brown, "the new theology raises the old cry, 'Back to Christ.' Let no theology call itself Christian which has not its center and source in him."[8]

This estimate of the centrality of Christ is closely related in the thought of the evangelical liberals to their way of dealing with the problem of revelation and reason. These men believed in special revelation in the sense that through the history and experience of Israel recorded in the Bible there has been given to mankind a unique and normative disclosure of the nature and will of God. The high point of this revelation is to be found in the life, work, and personality of the historical Jesus. His teachings were thought to be of universal and permanent relevance to the moral and religious quest of mankind, and it is to him that even modern men must look for the highest insights into the meaning of human existence. The revelation of God in Christ, then, is the norm of religious truth.

However, this revelation stands in direct continuity with reason and experience. The affirmations which Christianity makes about the existence and nature of God were seen to be fundamentally reasonable and in harmony with the available evidence. The high claims concerning Christ were thought to be validated by the moral and religious fruits which resulted from the impact of the personality of Jesus upon the believer. The Bible could be seen as the record both of God's progressive revelation of himself and of man's growing discovery of God in experience. It is not to be appealed to arbitrarily as a source of authoritative doctrine. Rather, the teachings of the Scriptures are to be accepted because of their intrinsic worth as measured by the mind and conscience of man. Thus, while the norm of religious truth was found in the act of God in Christ witnessed to by the Bible, this revelation was thought to validate itself in experience by virtue of its own inherent reasonableness and practical value.

The wide gulf between the thought patterns of the Bible and those employed in the modern world made it necessary to reinterpret many of the doctrines of orthodoxy in order to avoid intellectual embarrassment. One widely employed method of overcoming this hiatus was to set up a distinction between the religious experiences of men and the categories which gave expression to them. The experiences may remain the same from age to age while the categories change. Fosdick's phrase—"abiding experiences and changing categories"—attained wide currency among liberals as the means by which the permanent truth of the historic faith could be reinterpreted to fit the idiom of the contemporary world.

In short, evangelical liberalism represents the attempt of men who were convinced of the truth of historic Christianity to adjust this ancient faith to the demands of the modern era. The theologians to be discussed who fall into this category are William Adams Brown, Harry Emerson Fosdick, Walter Rauschenbusch, A. C. Knudson, and Eugene W. Lyman.[9]

B. *Modernistic Liberalism*

The modernistic liberals can best be thought of as "intelligent moderns" who nevertheless wished to be thought of as "serious Christians" in some real sense. They are called "modernistic" because they were basically determined in their thinking by a twentieth-century outlook. They had no real sense of continuing in the line of the historic faith. Rather, they were conscious that they were introducing something new. Nevertheless, they believed that there were elements of permanent significance in the Christian tradition which ought to be retained. However, the standard by which the abiding values of the Christianity of the past were to be measured was derived from the presuppositions of modern science, philosophy, psychology, and social thought. Nothing was to be believed simply because it was to be found in the Bible or Christian tradition.[10]

The loose connection of the modernistic liberals with the traditional faith can be seen clearly in their estimate of Jesus. The thinking of these men was not Christocentric. Jesus was important—and even unique—because he illustrated truths and values which are universally relevant. However, these truths and values can be validated and even discovered apart from Jesus. He is not so much the *source* as he is the *exemplar* of the religious norm. Jesus might be psychologically helpful, but he was not usually thought to be logically necessary for the highest experience of God in human life.

One characteristic feature of modernistic liberalism was its intense concern with methodology. Having abandoned belief in revelation, these men, unlike the evangelical liberals, had no norm in the Bible, Christ, or tradition to which they could appeal. This made it necessary for them to discover a source and standard of religious truth independent of the historic faith. Hence, the search for a new methodology became a prime consideration and often overshadowed the efforts to define the content of religious truth. The most promising source of help along these lines was found by the modernists in empirical science. Here was a distinctly modern method of attaining and testing truth, the practical worth of which had already been demonstrated in the natural sciences. If the methods of observation and experimentation which had been so effective in unlocking the secrets of nature could be adapted for use in the realm of religion, the way seemed open to restore theology to a respectable place in the modern world. It would no longer be necessary to appeal arbitrarily to some external authority which had to be accepted on faith. Rather, it seemed possible to build up a body of religious truth which could take its place on an equal basis alongside the knowledge attained in physics, chemistry, biology, and the other empirical disciplines. All of the modernistic liberals to be considered in this undertaking found in the empirical method of science the surest way of attaining for theology a hearing in the modern scene.

In short, modernistic liberalism represents the attempt of men who were thoroughly immersed in contemporary culture to reinterpret what they felt to be of permanent truth and value in the Christian tradition in terms of the methods and categories of early twentieth-century science and philosophy. Modernism developed slightly later than evangelical liberalism and was strongest in the last fifteen years of the period under consideration. Men in this category to be discussed here are Shailer Mathews, D. C. Macintosh, and Henry Nelson Wieman.[11]

II. OTHER RELIGIOUS PERSPECTIVES

There were two other types of religious thought which were prominent in America between 1900 and 1935. They can also be classified according to the way they related themselves to the two poles of Christ and culture.

A. *Fundamentalism and Conservatism*

To the right of the liberals were the fundamentalists and conservatives who were primarily interested in being "serious Christians" and who were much less inclined to revise traditional beliefs in the face of modern ways of thinking. Fundamentalism as a theological movement is a distinctly twentieth-century phenomenon.[12] It represents the reaction of the older orthodoxy against the new theology. These men defended what they believed to be the true faith against the onslaughts of science, Biblical criticism, and the liberal reinterpretation of Christianity. They believed that Christianity did not need to come to terms with modern thought, since there was to be found in the Bible an infallible source of religious truth. Those conclusions of science, philosophy, or liberal theology which contradicted what they believed to be the plain and literal teaching of the Bible were immediately rejected. An explicit, thoroughgoing supernaturalism was reaffirmed, along with a stern insistence on the miraculous nature of revelation. As a result of this movement theological attention was directed to a few "fundamentals" thought to be essential to the faith and which were often being denied by the liberals. The outcome, for the most part, was a rigid, dogmatic outlook largely negative in effect and lacking the creativity which many of the older orthodox thinkers had.

Others of a conservative bent, however, were more positive and restated for their own day a perspective which was thought to contain the unchanging essentials of Christian belief. They were firm in their convictions and in their opposition to liberalism, but many of them did make an effort to come to terms with some of the newer currents of thought. A. H. Strong is a good example of the theologians who fall into this category. He affirmed the doctrine of evolution, accepted higher criticism in principle, denied verbal inerrancy, and asserted that the Bible is not a book of science. However, his conservative orientation is evident in that he accepted the Mosaic authorship of the Pentateuch, asserted the historicity of Adam, employed a prooftext method, denied that the Bible had ever been shown to contain scientific error, maintained that the progressive disclosure of truth in the Bible never involved the contradiction of any doctrine given earlier, and insisted generally on the supernatural, miraculous nature of the Biblical revelation. Strong asserts his firm belief in "the old doctrines of holiness as the fundamental attribute of God, of an original transgression and sin of the whole human race, in a divine preparation in Hebrew history for man's redemption, in the deity, pre-existence, virgin birth, vicarious atonement and bodily resurrection of Jesus Christ our Lord, and in his future coming to judge the quick and the dead."[13] E. Y. Mullins and J. Gresham Machen are also examples of men of great intellectual ability and wide learning who engaged in theological debate at a high level with the liberals and made many incisive criticisms of the newer developments in theology.[14]

B. *Humanism*

To the left of the liberals were the humanists.[15] The humanists were interested only in being "intelligent moderns" and rejected Christianity outright. They insisted that the liberals were timid and lacked the courage to follow their own presuppositions to their logical conclusions.[16] They pointed out, for example, that the appeal of the liberals to reason and present experience was not compatible with their commitment to the authority of the historical Jesus. The humanists, of course, rejected absolutely an appeal to a historical revelation and saw all religions as the expression of the "quest for the good life."[17] These men believed that modern science, technology, philosophy, and social thought, when properly employed by human intelligence, were sufficient to enable man to attain his highest moral possibilities. They denied that there was any cosmic support for human values, asserting that man was totally dependent on his own resources of knowledge and moral drive for working out his own salvation. Thus, this man-centered religion was set within the context of a naturalistic world view. Two main types of humanism appeared: the optimistic (E. A. Haydon, John Dewey) and the pessimistic (Walter Lippmann, Joseph Wood Krutch).[18]

III. SUMMARY

The theological spectrum in America between 1900 and 1935 consisted, then, of three major parties: conservatism, liberalism, and humanism.[19] These three groups formed a continuum between the two poles constituted by Christ and culture.[20] At one extreme, fundamentalism erected a theology on the basis of an infallible, propositional revelation of God found in the literal teachings of the Bible and resisted all modern tendencies which were thought to call this revelation into question. At the other extreme, humanism rejected outright any appeal to a historical revelation and elaborated a naturalistic religious philosophy centering on man's self-directed quest for values. Liberalism stood between these two extremes and tried in various ways to harmonize the historic faith with the currents of modern thought. The evangelical liberals began from within the Christian tradition and sought to make contact with the contemporary situation from that perspective. The modernistic liberals took their stand self-consciously within modern scientific culture and attempted to preserve those elements of historical Christianity which seemed to be in harmony with contemporary patterns of thought.[21]

IV. Subtypes of Liberalism

In addition to the basic types of liberalism which have been defined, it is possible to specify subtypes for each of them. Various ways of grouping these subdivisions are open to the interpreter. One might make a classification based on denomination, on epistemology,[22] or on certain philosophical traditions such as pragmatism, idealism, realism, or naturalism.[23] The subtypes to be employed here are set up in terms of certain broad theological interests having to do with the nature and function of theology. Generally speaking, a division is to be made between those theologians whose primary interest is in elaborating a theology which will serve the practical moral and spiritual needs of men and those whose interest in theology is of a more theoretical nature. This classification involves the problem of religious knowledge but includes other matters. A division of this kind is applicable both to the evangelical and to the modernistic liberals. It is, of course, a relative distinction and by no means excludes theoretical interest on the part of the one or a practical interest on the part of the other. It is intended simply to point to a broad orientation and to certain primary tendencies manifested by each. A more specific distinction be-between the subtypes to be included in each major perspective must now be made.

The evangelical liberals will be divided into two groups: the ethical-social liberals and the metaphysical liberals. Likewise, the modernistic liberals will be divided into two groups: the ethical-social modernists and the empirical modernists.

A. *Ethical-social Liberals*

The ethical-social liberals were men within the evangelical wing of liberalism whose primary interest was in relating the Christian message to the ethical and social needs of men in the modern world. Religion to them is primarily a practical concern, and it is centered in the moral life. William Adams Brown, for example, operated on "the assumption that it is through the practical needs of the ethical and religious nature that we gain our insight into the highest truth."[24] Theology is a way of expressing in appropriate categories the meaning and value of the moral experience of God. This involves, of course, some concern with theoretical problems and systematic analysis. Nevertheless, the engagement of these men in theological discussion was, first of all, at the point at which it touched the concrete problems of human living.

This orientation is partly a matter of intellectual conviction and partly a matter of vocation. All the men in this group were strongly influenced by Kant and Ritschl and were thus skeptical about the possibilities of attaining metaphysical knowledge of God. Moreover, these men felt that their primary calling was to interpret for their generation the relevance of the redemption accomplished through the impact of Christ on human personality. This concern overshadows whatever interest they may have had in philosophy. Fosdick was primarily a preacher and Rauschenbusch a social prophet and reformer. Brown, who was professionally a systematic theologian, devoted more attention to the theoretical aspects of Christian theology, yet he shared the same broad interests and theological concerns which are found in the others. He insisted that religious beliefs are to be validated ultimately by their practical results in experience and not by conformity to some metaphysical scheme. Whatever metaphysical assumptions these men may have had are largely implicit rather than explicit.

B. *Metaphysical Liberalism*

The metaphysical liberals were men within the evangelical wing of liberalism who combined with a strong interest in the practical side of theology a fundamental concern to relate Christian beliefs to some systematic theoretical framework. They explicitly wanted to state a Christian world view in connection with some philosophical or metaphysical scheme. The liberals of this type recognized with Ritschl the importance of the moral approach to religious knowledge, but they insisted that the practical reason must not be separated from the theoretical approach to reality. Theology is not complete until it grounds itself solidly in some overall philosophical world view.[25]

Both Knudson and E. W. Lyman were self-conscious about their philosophical orientation and worked out their theology in the light of an explicit metaphysics. They took pains to make clear their metaphysical assumptions and to distinguish their position from other alternatives. Knudson, standing in the idealistic tradition, found in personalism a system of thought which is rationally convincing and in harmony with the Christian revelation. He combined a belief in the metaphysical competence of human reason with a strong emphasis on religious experience. Lyman began his career as a pragmatist. He saw in this approach to reality a way of avoiding both the Ritschlian dualism between the practical and the theoretical reason and the abstractions of absolute idealism. At the same time, pragmatism enabled him to construct a positive empirical metaphysics which justified the theological contentions of ethical Christianity. At a later period Lyman moved from pragmatism to a kind of realism which took into account the contributions of the emergent evolutionists and philosophers like Whitehead.

C. *Ethical-social Modernism*

The ethical-social modernists were men standing within the modernistic wing of liberalism who, like their evangelical counterparts, viewed religion primarily from a practical standpoint. Here again there appears an intense interest in Christianity as a workable solution to ethical and social problems, along with a relative unconcern with metaphysics and technical philosophy. The fundamental nature of this perspective can be seen clearly in the thought of Shailer Mathews. His practical interest was revealed in his devotion to the social gospel. Mathews falls into the ethical-social category primarily, however, by virtue of his understanding of the nature of theology. He affirmed that religion arises in experience and is given theological expression in categories which are derived from the prevailing social patterns. Theology is transcendentalized politics. The background of theology is social experience, not metaphysics. Thus, the theologian is more like a social analyst than a metaphysician. The present-day task of theology, according to Mathews, is to discover by a study of history the functional significance of the previously employed socio-theological patterns and to set forth the modern equivalent in twentieth-century language.

D. *Empirical Modernism*

The empirical modernists were men within the modernistic wing of liberalism who distinguished themselves by their resolute attempts to

erect a theology on the basis of a method suggested by modern empirical science. They, like the metaphysical liberals, combined both
a practical and a theoretical interest in theology. They followed as
closely as possible the procedures of the natural sciences, using as
raw data the facts of religious experience. By employing the techniques
of observation and testing, they attempted to arrive at a theoretical
scheme which interprets the human experience of God. They were
convinced that by such a method, and only in this way, it is possible
to attain valid religious knowledge. Both Henry Nelson Wieman and
D. C. Macintosh fall into this category, although there are important
differences between them regarding both method and content.

V. CONCLUSION

American liberalism, then, was made up of at least four fairly distinct
groups—ethical-social liberals, metaphysical liberals, ethical-social
modernists, and empirical modernists. However, this by no means
exhausts the possibilities of classification and typing. At least two
more possible types come readily to mind.

Within the evangelical wing one could certainly add Rufus Jones
under the heading of mystical liberalism. Here is a distinctive emphasis on the direct knowledge of God in mystical experience which
incorporates a strong emphasis on moral action, human individuality,
and historical revelation.[26] This additional type has not been included
for the reason that the centrality of religious experience is basic to
all of liberalism, while the distinctive mystical type of religion espoused by Jones is not so widespread as the other types. Moreover,
some attention will be devoted to mysticism in connection with E. W.
Lyman and Henry Nelson Wieman.

Under the modernistic heading it would be possible to add a type
which could be labeled metaphysical or rationalistic modernism. In
this group are men who shared the theoretical interests of the empirical modernists but whose approach put more emphasis on the
power of reason to discover and validate truth. One thinks immediately in this connection of E. S. Brightman, a personalist, and W. E.
Hocking, who holds to a type of absolute idealism.[27] This type has
not been included since both of its best-known representatives are important primarily as philosophers of religion rather than as theologians, although the thought of Brightman and Hocking is positively

oriented toward Christianity and the church. Moreover, one person-alist has already been included, while absolute idealism was not widely adhered to among twentieth-century American liberals.

It is quite possible that a more refined typology would substitute other perspectives or add to the types described here. However, the foregoing typology offers a legitimate way of interpreting the main concrete forms of American liberalism in the period from 1900 to 1935.

PART TWO

EVANGELICAL LIBERALISM

CHAPTER 3

THE OLD GOSPEL AND
THE NEW THEOLOGY:
WILLIAM ADAMS BROWN

With the background provided by the preceding chapters clearly in mind, it is possible now to show how the fundamental principles of liberalism manifest themselves concretely in the thought of various individual theologians and to demonstrate how each reflects the tendencies of a particular subtype of liberal theology.[1] The first to be considered is William Adams Brown (1865–1943), who was one of the most influential and widely read American theologians of his time. Brown, a native of New York City, received his undergraduate education at Yale University and his theological training at Union Theological Seminary in New York City. After spending two years abroad at the University of Berlin, he returned in 1892 to join the Department of Church History at Union. A year later he was transferred to the Theology Department, assuming the position of Roosevelt Professor of Systematic Theology in 1898. Brown held this post until 1930, at which time he became Research Professor in the field of Applied Christianity. After six years in this post he became an Emeritus Professor. He was a member of the Presbyterian Church and took an active part in its life in many capacities. Brown was perhaps best known as a teacher of Systematic Theology, and it is significant that he entitled his autobiography *A Teacher and His Times.*

Brown was clearly an evangelical liberal. He was thoroughly convinced that the Christian message had to be reinterpreted in terms which were meaningful to twentieth-century men, but he felt that he

41

was not altering the essentials of the historic faith. He believed that "underneath all differences of theological expression, there is a gospel which makes the Church, in fact, one."[2] In this regard Brown saw himself in the role of a mediator. He tried to maintain a connection between the old theology and the new or, as George Hammar put it, between "American revivalistic Christianity and German liberal theology."[3] He addressed his volume on systematic theology to those who value the Christian heritage but who are perplexed because they do not know how to relate this ancient treasure to contemporary modes of thought.[4] His pronounced tendency to retain traditional theological language is an expression of his attempt to hold together the old and the new.[5] Brown was perhaps nearer to the orthodoxy of the immediate past than any other theologian to be considered.

Closely related to this mediating role is his eclecticism. He is best described as a neo-Ritschlian. In his definition of Christianity, in his grounding of religion in the practical reason, and in his emphasis on historical revelation, for example, Brown followed the familiar lines laid down by Ritschl. Brown went beyond Ritschl, however, and insisted on the Christ of faith as well as the Jesus of history.[6] He believed that it is possible to verify the value judgments of the believer regarding Jesus on the basis of the actual results which flow from contemporary faith in him. Thus, Brown "has not only been influenced by German Ritschlianism but also by William James' pragmatism."[7] Moreover, Brown moved in a later period to take some account of the neo-orthodox movement in American theology which developed around 1930 and after. This tendency is reflected in *God at Work*, published in 1933, which emphasizes the objective side of religion and characterizes it as "man's answer to God's approach."[8] This eclecticism is perhaps doubly grounded in his self-chosen role as a mediator and in his basing of religion on experience, both of which allow him to employ interpretative patterns drawn from a variety of sources.[9] The theology of Brown, then, is a kind of Ritschlianism modified by evangelicalism, on the one hand, and by a kind of pragmatic realism, on the other hand, and later influenced mildly by American neo-orthodoxy.[10]

The most important book for the study of Brown's thought is his *Christian Theology in Outline*, published in 1906. It should be noted that this volume was largely a revision of William Newton Clarke's

Outline of Christian Theology, published in 1898. At first Brown used Clarke's *Outline* in his classes in theology but decided that it needed rewriting because it neglected the doctrine of the church and contained very little historical material. These two volumes were the most widely used textbooks of liberal theology and constitute the best sources available for the study of evangelical liberalism in America during the period under consideration.

A. *Christianity and Theology*

1. THE ESSENCE OF CHRISTIANITY

One of the fundamental ingredients of nineteenth-century thought was its sense of history, i.e., the conviction that any social movement or system of ideas must be understood in terms of historical development.[11] In theology this historical consciousness gave rise to the notion that the nature of Christianity must be determined by a study of its New Testament origins. Historians soon began to ask the question as to whether there was a continuing essence present in all the various historical forms which Christianity had assumed in the process of its development.

Brown shared the historical consciousness of his time and wrestled with the problems raised by it. He followed his famous teacher Harnack, who "argued that the essence of an historical manifestation is present in unique and normative fashion in the original form of that manifestation, and that other and later forms may be judged to represent accretions, distortions or returns to the original."[12] Brown gave his most detailed answer to this problem in *The Essence of Christianity*.[13] He says that he is searching for a scientific definition of Christianity arrived at on inductive grounds which will include the idea of its absoluteness. He discovers the essence of Christianity in the teachings and in the person of the historical Jesus. In him there is to be found a unique revelation of God which makes Christianity the final form of religion. The fatherhood of God, the brotherhood of man, the worth of the individual soul, greatness through service, salvation through sacrifice, the kingdom of God as the goal of humanity —these truths are the unique contribution of Jesus to the religious thought of the human race. Despite the many departures from the original teachings of Jesus and from the religion which he espoused, one principle can be found which holds true of every age and of every type of Christianity. This principle is "the progressive realization, in thought as in life, of the supremacy of Christ."[14]

2. THE TASK AND METHOD OF CHRISTIAN THEOLOGY

In a symposium in 1910 dealing with the task and method of systematic theology, to which Benjamin B. Warfield and Gerald Birney Smith also contributed, Brown asserted that theology, like all thought, deals with three questions: the question of definition, the question of value, and the question of cause.[15] In answering these questions, Brown (1) defines Christianity in terms of the life, teachings, and personality of the historical Jesus, (2) finds its supreme value in the practical effects which Jesus Christ has had in transforming human life, and (3) concludes that it requires for its cause and explanation belief in the existence of a Christlike Supreme Being. In these answers Brown reveals his connection respectively with the historical emphasis of Ritschl, the pragmatism of James, and a kind of objectivistic metaphysical concern which transcends both of them.[16] This article gives an excellent insight into his eclecticism.

It will help to clarify Brown's position in American theology at that time as an evangelical liberal to contrast his views with the other two contributors to this symposium. Warfield was a representative of the older Calvinistic orthodoxy, now centered at Princeton University. Theology for him consisted in the exposition and systematization of the verbally inspired propositions of doctrine contained in the Bible. Smith was a modernistic liberal who belonged to the Chicago school of empirical theology. He insisted that the task of theology was to search for pragmatic religious truth by confronting modern human needs with the historical Christian tradition. Convictions arrived at in this way are purely relativistic and can claim no divine authority. Their only guarantee of validity is that they are workable in practice. Brown, then, represents a middle position between the right- and left-wing extremes.

Brown's theology clearly stands within the modern tradition. As Karl Barth has pointed out, the chief characteristic of theology since the nineteenth century has been the transformation of dogmatics into *Glaubenslehre,* teachings about faith.[17] This is the strain of autonomy or theological subjectivism in modern theology, and it dates from the time of Schleiermacher.[18] In this tradition theology becomes "the science of religious experience as it takes place in the church" (Barth).[19] Brown is taking this point of view when he affirms that theology is the interpretation of the religious life. Theology has to do with convictions which can be appropriated and verified in experience. Brown, however, qualifies this view in two ways.[20] On the theological side he states that theology is not concerned with religious experience in general but with Christian experience which has its source in a historical revelation of God in Christ. On the epistemological side he maintains that "through the practical judgments of the moral and religious life we gain knowledge of objective reality, and insight into ultimate truth."[21] In short, Christ-centered religious experience yields beliefs about the nature of ultimate reality which verify themselves by their practical results in life. These beliefs are the subject matter of theology. This position may be referred to a kind of Christocentric pragmatic realism, and it is reiterated throughout Brown's writings.[22]

While a critic may contend that the principle of continuity overcame the Christian dogmatic tradition in liberal theology to the extent that revelation "was more or less dissolved,"[23] this was certainly not the intention of the evangelical liberals. Brown, of course, insists on the direct continuity of revelation with reason and experience, yet he does find in the historical Jesus a norm for religion to which theology must adhere. By revelation is meant the disclosure of the nature and will of God in the person and work of Jesus Christ. In the narrow sense revelation is identical with Christ. In a wider sense revelation includes the preparation for the revelation in Christ and the results of his influence in the lives of individuals and in the church since the time of Christ. This shift of the focus of revelation from the Bible to Christ is typical of the liberal reconstruction of theology. This made it possible for the liberals to retain a belief in a normative disclosure of God in history and yet, at the same time, to appropriate the results of the higher criticism of the Bible and the findings of modern science, which together had destroyed the older basis of theology.

The relationship between Brown's view of revelation to contemporary interpretations in terms of personal encounter between God and man rather than in terms of doctrine is not immediately clear.[24] Similarity may be found in the fact that Brown speaks of revelation as the self-manifestation of God. Moreover, he has shifted the focus of revelation from Biblical propositions to the historical Jesus, from doctrines to a person. However, Brown puts more emphasis on the

teachings of Jesus than is often the case among contemporary thinkers. The teachings of Jesus seem to have for Brown a kind of normative significance. The fatherhood of God, the brotherhood of man,
the worth of the soul, etc., which Brown took to be central to the
thought of Jesus, appear to be truths to which all later theology must
conform. This at least raises the question as to whether Brown considers these teachings as revealed propositions. Many contemporary
theologians tend to neglect the historical Jesus and point rather to the
Incarnation as an Event in which God encounters man. For the believer this confrontation of God in Christ takes on revelatory significance. There are no doctrines given in this encounter, but they may
be distilled from the encounter by reflection upon it. Thus, the emphasis is on the meaning of the Christ-Event and not on the personality and teachings of Jesus of Nazareth. In short, a comparison of
Brown with present-day thinkers such as William Temple and Emil
Brunner reveals both similarities and differences. However, the issues
about which contemporary thinkers debate regarding the "divine-
human encounter" are not focused upon sharply enough in Brown's
Outline to make possible a precise interpretation of his position in
regard to them.

In this new interpretation offered by Brown the Bible becomes the
supreme witness to the revelation of God, which is now centered in
the historical Jesus. It presents in authoritative form the contents of
Christian belief and is the primary source of theology. The Bible is
at the same time a witness to man's growing experience of God in
history and the record of God's progressive self-disclosure to man.
To say that the Bible is inspired means that the Bible appeals to the
reason and conscience of man as an authority because of its own intrinsic qualities. While it is not infallible either in matters of science,
philosophy, or religion, the Bible has permanent value for the church
because it is the most ancient, direct, and reliable source of the knowledge of the historic Jesus and is the most effective means of awakening
and stimulating the present Christian life.

B. *The Doctrine of God*

1. THE PRINCIPLE OF CONTINUITY

There are a number of themes which will appear again and again
throughout this survey, but none will occur with more frequency than

the principle of immanence. Brown is very conscious that his convictions regarding God's immanence set him apart from the older view represented so well in Catholicism and Calvinism. In an article in *The Harvard Theological Review* entitled "The Old Theology and the New," Brown points out his divergence from these orthodox traditions. According to the older view, he says, the world is divided into two separate parts, nature and the supernatural. The former is the realm of law and natural knowledge. The latter is the realm of grace, miracle, and revelation. God dwells in the supernatural realm far removed from the world, from whence he arbitrarily interferes from time to time with nature and with the affairs of men. He acts on these occasions by granting revelations and causing miracles for the benefit of his favorites. His justice and love are inscrutable, and his will is arbitrary, mysterious, and sovereign.

In the new theology, Brown says, all of this is changed, and nature and the supernatural are now thought of, not as different kinds of reality, but as two aspects of one and the same reality. Nature refers to law and to cause in the process, while the supernatural has to do with the meaning and value of the process and the end toward which it moves.[25] Brown is here giving expression to the pervasive liberal principle of continuity in the most fundamental area to which it was applied. The result is that the dualism between two orders of being is reduced to a duality within one order. The distinction which Brown makes between the natural and the supernatural sounds very much like Bushnell,[26] and it is typical of a number of attempts to make similar distinctions between the realm of necessity and freedom, fact and value, the realm of science and the realm of ethics and religion, pure and practical reason, etc.[27] These modern thinkers felt compelled to reject the older supernaturalism with its transcendent God. Yet, within the natural order they confronted the materialistic determinism of modern science, which threatened to rob reality of value and purpose. In order to avoid the ethical and religious nihilism of this scientific determinism, it became necessary to distinguish between the mechanistic world of nature open to the inspection of the senses and the world of freedom, value, and purpose apprehended through moral intuition, feeling, mysticism, etc. This procedure, of course, works against the principle of continuity, but it was unavoidable in the light of the dominating influence of scientific materialism. The problem of finding value in a world of fact constitutes the wider context of

Brown's distinction here between the natural and the supernatural within the framework of the principle of continuity.

When the principle of continuity is applied to the doctrine of God, the result is immediately apparent. God is not separate from the world, living in a distant heaven, but rather is an ever-present Spirit guiding all that happens to a good end. He discloses himself in nature, in history, in the lives of great men, in the Bible, and supremely in Jesus, through whom he has given us the clearest revelation of himself.[28] God in this view is not arbitrary and inscrutable. His character and will are ever the same. Wherever we meet him, he has but one purpose, and that is to make all men like Jesus and to unite them in brotherly service in the kingdom which he founded. An immanent Spirit, Christlike in nature—this is the heart of the liberal doctrine of God.

2. KNOWLEDGE OF GOD

It is typical of liberalism that knowledge of God is said to rest on experience rather than on rational argument. This is the line that Brown takes. Brown is an "ethical intuitionist"; i.e., he affirms that moral experience is the surest source of insight into the nature of ultimate reality.[29] Knowledge of God, he insists, begins with the experience of moral value and moves to belief in the objective source of that value.[30]

However, it is of fundamental importance to notice that for Brown the moral experience in which knowledge of God is rooted is not a generalized experience of universal values available to all men everywhere. Here, as elsewhere, Brown's method is Christocentric. The Christian's experience of value is mediated through Christ. In him is found a supreme moral and spiritual ideal which leads to the postulation of a Christlike God as its source. It is in this way that Brown unites the experiential and revelational approaches to knowledge of God. Christ is both the source of the Christian's experience of God and the norm of religious truth. Brown, however, has no difficulty in making moral experience Christocentric, since he is convinced that revelation and reason stand in direct continuity. In other words, there is no great gap between man's general experience and appreciation of moral values and the moral ideals of Christ. Thus, Brown insists that belief in a Christlike God is fundamentally reasonable. It is reasonable, not in the sense of being demanded by, or conforming to, some metaphysical system, but because it appeals to the highest and best in man's moral nature.

In Brown's thought, as the above analysis indicates, the grounds on which belief in the Christian God rests are found in the area of what Kant called the practical reason. Brown's connection with Kantian modes of thought can also be seen in his interpretation of the traditional arguments for the existence of God.[31] Brown apparently agrees with Kant that as arguments in the realm of theoretical reason, the traditional proofs are failures, since they never get beyond the experience that brings them forth. They are analytical and not synthetic; i.e., they simply spell out in detail the content which is implicit in the assumptions underlying them. Brown does two things with these traditional proofs. First of all, he transfers them from the realm of theoretical argument to the practical reason and employs them as postulates of faith. Secondly, he bases them on data derived from Christian experience. Interpreted in Christocentric fashion the traditional arguments—the cosmological, the teleological, the moral, and the ontological—lead to the postulation of a Christlike Being who is the source of the world and its order and the ground of experienced moral values. Since these arguments yield only probability and not absolute metaphysical certainty, belief in a Christlike God remains in part an individual and subjective matter, but Brown affirms that faith in the Christian God continually verifies itself by its appeal to the moral consciousness and by the practical results which flow from such belief.

3. THE TRINITY

As Claude Welch points out, the Trinity became a doctrine of second rank in liberal theology.[32] Importance is often attributed to the experiential sources of the doctrine, but the orthodox formulations are generally viewed with suspicion. The doctrine of internal relations is virtually abandoned, and it is maintained that the principle of immanence solves many of the traditional problems associated with the classical versions of the concept. This description fits Brown perfectly. He insists that the doctrine of the Trinity is best understood as an interpretation of the Christian experience of God as revealed. God may be thought of (1) as the Absolute, beyond all human knowledge, (2) as the self-revealing One, progressively disclosed in nature and history, and (3) as the self-imparting One, experienced in the human consciousness as the source of the spiritual life. The Trinity sums up this threefold way in which God is known. The doctrine of the Trinity, then, does not have to do primarily with distinctions which are original to, and characteristic of, God's internal being or essence but with the Trinitarian form of man's cognitive relationship to God.[33] This is to say that Brown adheres to what has been called the economic Trinity or Trinity of manifestation in contrast to the immanent Trinity or the Trinity of essence.[34]

However, while Brown is agnostic about the possibility of describing God's internal being, he is not willing to forego the ontological implications of the doctrine of the Trinity altogether. He maintains that Christian theology must go on to assert that there is an unseen reality behind the three-experience of God which is its source and ground. God *is* the self-revealing and self-imparting God. We can know God as he is only by unfolding the significance of the revelation in which he is known to us, and now, since God is sought within instead of without the world, "the antithesis between the Trinity of essence and that of manifestation disappears. The self-revealing God is the real God—the only God we either can or need to know."[35] Thus, we confess faith in a real God who is Father, Son, and Holy Spirit, for no "other terms express so adequately that basis in unseen reality which is implied in the Trinity of Christian experience and which is necessary to give it its fullest expression."[36] Brown, then, affirms that the doctrine of the Trinity does imply something for God's internal being, although it is impossible to specify precisely what.

4. GOD AND THE WORLD

In a system of thought in which the principle of immanence dominates, the doctrine of creation tends to be merged with the idea of the world's dependence on God. The most extreme example of immanentism, of course, is pantheism in which the distinction between God and the world disappears altogether. While William Adams Brown did stress the immanence of God, he nevertheless maintained his connection with the historic Biblical and Christian tradition in affirming a genuine doctrine of creation. The world is real existence, objective to God, which originates in his deliberate activity. The world is completely dependent on God and is adapted to realize the ends which he has ordained. Supreme among these ends is the realization of the kingdom of God. Brown's view of the relation of God to the world is indicated in summary fashion in the following statement in which he defines his view of God:

God is "the personal Spirit, perfectly good," who creates, sustains and orders the universe according to the wise, holy and loving character and purpose revealed in Jesus Christ; and who, through his Spirit, indwelling in man, is ever at work in the world, calling men out of their sin and misery into the kingdom of God, and, by his redemptive grace, transforming individuals and society into the likeness of Christ. The name which best expresses his character, and which, since Christ, has become the characteristic name for God, is Father.[37]

He notes that this definition includes three elements: (1) the concept of personality, taken from Israel; (2) the concept of absoluteness, derived from Greek thought;[38] and (3) the conviction that this absolute personality is Christlike, originating in the revelation which came through the historical Jesus. This last element is the central theme in liberalism's view of God.[39]

C. *The Doctrine of Man*

1. THE NATURE OF MAN

In the older orthodoxy man was viewed primarily as a creature who had inherited a corrupt nature from Adam. The outlook of this perspective, by and large, was pessimistic. Man is a sinner condemned before God and in need of redeeming grace. According to the Calvinists, only a few could hope to be delivered from this dreadful state. In liberal theology the interpretation of man proceeds from a different basis, and a more optimistic note is sounded. Man is no longer a helpless creature burdened with a corrupt inheritance from Adam but a struggling spirit progressively overcoming the drag of nature. Man is a moral personality whose spiritual capacities tower above the natural world in which they are embedded.

Within this context Brown affirms that man has a dual origin and a dual constitution. Man is a creature of nature and a child of God. As a creature he is a dependent being who shares all the limitations of finite existence. As a child of God he is a moral personality with capacities of reason and freedom who contrasts himself with nature as he becomes conscious of his dominion over it.[40] He consists of a union of body and spirit and is destined for immortality. Man is free only in the sense that his choice is based on nothing outside himself and is the expression of his character at the moment.[41] Man does not have the power of contrary choice. Rather, he is determined spiritually by all of the personal and social relations in which he lives and moves, the totality of which are ultimately grounded in the sovereign will of God. This limitation of freedom to the power of self-determination reflects Brown's Calvinistic and Presbyterian inheritance and stands in some contrast to the general liberal tendency to stress rather than to restrict the capacities of man.

2. THE DOCTRINE OF SIN

Man is a child of God, but he is a sinner. Brown's divergence from the older orthodoxy can be seen clearly in his insistence that sin is not a foreign intruder making its appearance at one moment in history and bringing an abrupt corruption of human nature as a whole from that point on. Sin, he urges, is the inevitable result of certain tendencies in the very structure of man's personality. It is the expression and the survival of the animal in man and indicates his failure to rise to the higher capacities in him.[42] Here is a theme which will be repeated by every liberal theologian to be considered. Sin emerges out of the conflict between nature and spirit. Man is a creature who has kinship with the brutes beneath him, and sin is the failure of his nascent spirit to impose its ideals upon his animal impulses. This way of putting the problem is an inheritance from Kant and Ritschl. What concerned Ritschl, says Richard Niebuhr,

. . . as a moral thinker and as a Kantian was the effort of the ethical reason to impress on human nature itself the internal law of the conscience; to direct individual and social life toward the ideal goal of virtuous existence in a society of free yet interdependent virtuous persons. In the ethical realm man faces a double problem: he needs not only to subdue his own nature, but also to overcome the despair which arises from his understanding of the indifference of the external natural world to his own lofty interests.[43]

In one way or another this view of man's basic problem dominated liberal thinking and is here being affirmed by William Adams Brown.

In his account of the nature and origin of sin Brown reveals clearly his comprehensiveness and his eclecticism. He tries to find the particle of truth in every competing theory. Sin has both a formal and a material dimension and an individual and a social aspect. On the formal side sin is the failure to realize fellowship with God, while on the material side it is the failure to realize the moral ideal revealed in Christ. For the individual the ideal is unselfish love, and for society it is the organization of social life in accordance with the moral principles of Jesus. In order to account for the origin of sin, Brown finds it necessary to refer to three different views, each of which is partially true. Sin originates in part from the conflict in man between his higher spiritual nature and his lower animal nature, in part from the influence of immoral social patterns and institutions, and, in the final analysis, from the identification of the self through choice with these inner tendencies and outer forces which incline the self toward evil.[44] Ultimately, however, sin is mysterious. It arises in the depths of the human spirit in a way that defies complete analysis. Sin, then, according to Brown, does not originate in a corrupt nature inherited from Adam (orthodoxy) or in a self-chosen, prideful rebellion against the sovereignty of God (neo-orthodoxy). Rather, it has its source in the victory of the lower nature and the adverse influence of society over an essentially good but weak spirit, a capitulation to which the will gives consent. Other liberals reject Brown's determinism and insist on the reality of metaphysical as well as moral freedom, but the essential structure of Brown's view of sin is widely affirmed.

3. THE DOCTRINE OF SALVATION

If sin is interpreted in liberalism as the triumph of nature over spirit, it follows that salvation will be viewed as the victory of spirit over nature. This is the background of the thought of William Adams Brown, although it does not appear as clearly in him as in some other liberal thinkers. The essence of salvation in liberal thought is moral transformation whereby the personality is integrated around the ideals of Christ rather than around the natural impulses of the lower animal self. The emphasis in liberalism is clearly on the ethical rather than the religious side of redemption. However, in line with the liberal principle of continuity, the ethical and the religious tend to merge, so that the older distinction between justification and sanctification generally loses its importance. Brown's interpretation is recognizably liberal, but his effort to maintain a connection with the older evangelicalism can be seen in his retention of this distinction. Justification by faith describes the religious side of salvation and refers to a relationship of personal trust between the self and God. Sanctification refers to the moral side of salvation and has to do with the transformation of character toward the ideal revealed in Christ. The significance of this analysis is that the religious aspect of reconciliation with God precedes and makes possible the power and joy of the converted moral life.

One basic theme in liberalism—and one which represents another aspect of the principle of continuity—is the insistence on the organic connection between the individual and society. This emphasis has already been seen in Brown's doctrine of sin. Sin is socially mediated and transmitted, and the individual is caught up in these environmental influences. This is the experiential meaning of the doctrine of original sin. Salvation, likewise, has a social as well as an individual dimension. Social salvation is related to the process of history and consists in the gradual triumph of the ideals of Christ in all aspects of man's cultural life.[45] The kingdom of God becomes the dominant concept in this regard. It was for the purpose of establishing a community of love between all men and God that the world was created, and it was for the purpose of initiating the kingdom in history that Jesus was called of God to his ministry. Individuals are saved only as they enter into, and participate in, this kingdom dominated by the spirit of love and sacrificial service. This kingdom is being gradually realized and will ultimately embrace all men.

It is interesting to note that both individual and social salvation have been defined primarily as a process. Here it is possible to see the dynamic principle at work in liberalism. This emphasis on gradual growth and progressive attainment is most prominent in the concept of social salvation. The faith that history is a process of redemption is fundamental in modern thought[46] and receives Christian expression in the idea of the gradual triumph of the kingdom of God. However, Brown does not believe that complete perfection is possible either for the individual or for society. His outlook as expressed in *Christian Theology in Outline* is optimistic but not utopian. Individual and social perfection are, in principle, attainable, and no limits can be put on the extent to which progress can be made. However, perfection is never actually attained on earth either by individuals or by society. The complete realization of the kingdom of God lies beyond this dimension of history.[47]

In Brown's eschatology both the principle of continuity and the dynamic principle come into play. The former is seen in his contention that the future life is a direct continuation of this life. All men will take up the process of growth toward moral perfection where they left off at death. Thus, there is no radical distinction between the saved and the lost, between heaven and hell. The difference between the present life and the future life, on the one hand, and the advanced and the retarded souls, on the other hand, is simply one of degree. He expects that ultimately all will come under the domination of Christ and his ideals. The dynamic principle is seen on the emphasis on gradual growth for all toward ultimate perfection, rather than an instantaneous sanctification at death for the righteous or a fiery hell for the wicked.[48]

D. *The Meaning of Jesus Christ*

1. THE JESUS OF HISTORY AND THE CHRIST OF FAITH

William Adams Brown did his theological thinking in an atmosphere which was dominated by an intense concern with and enthusiasm for the Jesus of history. He stood at the end of a long period during which Biblical research had devoted itself assiduously to the recovery of the man Jesus. Brown commends this movement heartily.[49] The Jesus of history movement, he says, has recovered the humanity of Jesus, given a better understanding of his Gospel, offered new insight into the greatness of his character, and has set forth with greater clarity the nature and significance of his claim to uniqueness.[50]

However, Brown recognizes that this development in theology raises new and difficult questions regarding the validity of the traditional Christian claims about Jesus. Jesus Christ has always been for Christian faith both the ideal man and the incarnate God. Is the Christ of faith a valid interpretation of the Jesus of history? Or is the Christ of the theologians and the Messiah of the Gospels a figment of the pious imagination which will not bear the close scrutiny of the Biblical critic? These questions cannot be answered by historical means alone, says Brown, for the effort to move from the Gospel picture of Jesus back to Jesus himself inevitably involves a subjective element in the imagination of the interpreter.[51] Historical criticism can discover many things about the life of Jesus and the environment in which he lived, but it cannot answer the question as to the consciousness of Jesus or the question of the perfection of his moral character. Brown recognizes that, at these points, the objective approach ceases to be of value, contending that "when it comes to the deepest secrets of personality, the methods of science break down, and the last word must always be spoken by the human spirit."[52] Thus, the decision as to whether or not the Christ of faith is a true picture of the historic Jesus is an act of the will which is in part individual and subjective.[53]

Brown is writing at a period in which the confidence of recovering a completely accurate and objective portrait of the first-century Jesus of Nazareth had already been called into serious question by the work of Albert Schweitzer and others.[54] This new development introduces an element of relativity into theology and forces a gap between objective historical study of Jesus and the Christian's subjective evaluation of him.[55] If left at this point, the continuity between faith and reason would be sundered. However, as a liberal, Brown is not willing to accept this consequence. He believes that on the basis of a kind of pragmatic realism it is possible to bridge the gap between the subjective decision and the objective fact. The effects which the life and character of Jesus have had in transforming human life, both individually and socially, are cogent evidences of the truth of the claims which Christians make about Jesus.[56] Thus, Brown is enabled to believe that the Christ of faith is indeed a true interpretation of the real Jesus of history. This conviction that the proof of the value judgments which the Christian makes regarding Jesus is to be found in the redemptive results of faith is a consistent answer which Brown gives throughout his career.[57]

2. THE PERSON OF CHRIST

It has been pointed out previously that Brown intends at every point to construct a Christocentric theology. His Christology, therefore, is of supreme importance. Brown intends to affirm with the historic tradition that God was in Christ. However, given a background of thought informed by a doctrine of the immanence of God, this assertion takes on new meaning. God is no longer believed to be revealed by an appearance from without the world in the incarnation of the divine Logos. Rather, God is seen to be revealed from within the world in the moral and spiritual excellence of the man Jesus. God manifests himself not in a vertical intrusion into history but in an immanent development within the horizontal process of history in the emergence of the historical Jesus. In the perfection of the human is seen the clearest revelation of the divine. Thus, a continuity is established between man and God, a continuity which, by the same logic, also extends to the relationship between Christ and other men. This principle of continuity underlies every liberal estimate of the person of Christ.

Brown finds the significance of Jesus to be threefold: he is true man, unique man, and God in man. Jesus was completely human, a man of his times completely like other men. Yet, Jesus was a unique man. This aspect of his significance for Christian faith is expressed in the concept of Messiahship, which means two things: authority and saving power. His authority rests in his moral and spiritual excellence, and his saving power lies in his capacity to mediate that excellence to us. This view of the supremacy of Jesus does not depend, as does the older view of Jesus' divinity, on miracles and physical manifestations of power. To say that in Jesus we find God in man means that God is everywhere and always like Jesus in character. Jesus reveals the true nature of ultimate reality. Jesus Christ is God in man; yet Jesus is at the same time a representative man. Jesus is seen as the type and ideal to which all men should conform and, in God's time, will conform. He represents the goal of all history. In this reconstruction of the person of Christ the vast gulf which the older theology posited between the divine and the human natures of Jesus and between Christ and other men is clearly rejected. As an alternative Brown has presented a scheme consisting of a gradually ascending scale which moves smoothly from ordinary men to the human Jesus to the divine Christ.

3. THE WORK OF CHRIST

Brown's connection with the older evangelicalism can be seen in his preservation of the traditional way of interpreting the work of Christ in his threefold role as prophet, priest, and king. However, his liberalism is manifested in the content with which he fills these categories. Here, again, Brown is playing the part of a mediator between the old theology and the new. As a prophet Jesus reveals both by word and deed the holiness and love of God to men, makes known the ideal to which all men should aspire, and sets forth the goal toward which society should move. In his interpretation of the role of Christ as priest Brown sets forth what is commonly known as a subjective or moral influence theory of the atonement. The death of Christ in no way satisfies the justice of God in such a manner as to make the mercy of God operative or alters the objective situation in which man exists by overcoming the evil powers which hold him captive.[58] Rather, the atonement is effective from the manward side in creating a community of faith. As a king Jesus exerts authority over men in his role as the founder of the kingdom of God. His kingship is seen in the transformation of men and societies under his redemptive influence. The ideals of Jesus will by spiritual conquest ultimately win consent from all men, and his spirit will dominate the world. This is the meaning of the doctrine of the second coming of Christ. Here again the principles of continuity and dynamism combine to alter radically the traditional eschatology. No longer is there a radical gulf between this age and the future age marked by the catastrophic intervention of God at the moment of Christ's return. Instead, Brown sees the coming of the kingdom of God as a gradual process of growth in which evil is progressively defeated.

E. *The Church*

As a general rule the doctrine of the church was neglected in liberalism. It was usually subordinated to the kingdom of God and made instrumental to it. This neglect is evident in Brown's *Outline of Christian Theology*. The church is dealt with in less than twenty pages. In his definition of Christianity in *The Essence of Christianity* Brown makes no mention of the church. However, in spite of this scant attention to the church in his earlier works, it would not be fair to say that Brown had little concern with it. In later years Brown devoted two complete books to the church—*The Church in America* (1922) and *The Church, Catholic and Protestant* (1935)—and numerous articles as well. Perhaps even more important than this is the fact that Brown was amazingly active in the practical life of the church throughout his career. He was a promoter of the settlement house movement and was for a long time associated with the home mission work of the Presbyterian Church. In addition, he was one of the leading figures in the earlier stages of the ecumenical movement. If deeds count for anything, William Adams Brown considered the church to be of supreme importance.[59]

In *Outline of Christian Theology* the church is defined as

. . . the religious society, tracing its origin historically from Jesus of Nazareth, and finding in him its bond of union in common worship, work, and life, in which the revealing and redeeming influence of Christ is per-petuated; and through which, under the influence of the divine Spirit, the Christian life is mediated to the world.[60]

The church is the social expression of the Christian life and serves as the agent by which the kingdom of God is revealed and realized in history. The church in carrying out this task has a double function. It exists as a means of training Christians in the knowledge and serv-ice of God, and it is the organ by which the influence of Christ is mediated to those outside the church. In line with liberalism generally Brown stresses the continuity between the church and other social institutions. The church is not against the world but rather it is one institution among many through which God is working to establish his kingdom. He rejects the view that the church should be an in-clusive agency which undertakes all sorts of charitable and philan-thropic activities in isolation from other institutions. On the contrary, the church should co-operate with the home, school, factory, and the state to Christianize society as a whole.[61] The goal of the church will be reached when the line between the church and the world is oblit-erated by the victory of the former.[62]

This conviction regarding the continuity of the church and the world can be seen clearly in *The Church in America,* written in 1922. In this volume Brown investigates the question of the place of the church in a democratic society and with regard to the great democratic experiment which was then being undertaken. It is his conclusion that the purpose of the church is to supply "the unifying spiritual influence needed in a democracy" and "so make possible under the conditions of our modern life the coming of a new social order called by our Maker the Kingdom of God."[63] The church, then, according to Brown is to promote the ends of democratic culture. This is a clear example of what H. Richard Niebuhr has called culture-Protestantism.[64]

This practical task of transforming the world for Christ, urges Brown, requires the unity of the church. He suggests that the best way to overcome denominational barriers is for the churches to join to-gether in common enterprises.[65] By working together, understanding and good will can be generated between Christians of different intel-lectual and institutional backgrounds which will ultimately lead to greater doctrinal and institutional unity. In *The Church, Catholic and Protestant* Brown imagines "the ultimate possibility of a rich synthesis of Christian experience in which the Catholic and the Protestant views will be found to be supplementary rather than contradictory."[66] This is a good illustration of the ecumenical sympathies of Brown.

F. *Conclusion*

To summarize briefly, it may be said that the result of the theological reflections of William Adams Brown was a moderate evangelical liberalism of the ethical-social type which had broad sympathies and wide appeal. Since his volume on systematic theology appeared early in the twentieth century, he was a strong and continuing influence in American theology throughout the period under consideration. Many of his students were themselves to become in later years outstanding leaders of theological thought in America. No one of them, however, attained any greater eminence than did Harry Emerson Fosdick, to whom attention will be turned in the next chapter.

CHAPTER 4

PERSONALITY-CENTERED
CHRISTIANITY:
HARRY EMERSON FOSDICK

Born in Buffalo, New York, Harry Emerson Fosdick (1878–   )
attended Colgate University and, after one year at Colgate Seminary,
went to Union Theological Seminary in New York City, where he
completed his theological education. In 1904 he was called to the
pastorate of the First Baptist Church, Montclair, New Jersey. After
eleven years there he was called back to Union Seminary as Morris
K. Jessup Professor of Practical Theology. Shortly after World War I
Fosdick became "guest preacher" in the First Presbyterian Church of
New York, while at the same time he continued his seminary duties.
This relationship ended in sharp controversy in 1925 in the height of
the fundamentalist-modernist struggle. Forced to resign from this pulpit by reactionary elements in the denomination, Fosdick soon was
called to the Park Avenue Baptist Church of New York. In order to
meet his demands, this church agreed to give up all sectarian restric-
tions on membership and to build a new structure capable of providing a wide variety of community services to an inclusive constituency.
This new structure was the Riverside Church, completed and dedicated in 1931. Fosdick continued his relationship with Union Seminary and Riverside Church until 1946, at which time he retired from
both.[1]

Fosdick was primarily a preacher and not a technical theologian.
His first aim was to communicate to persons struggling with life prob-

61

lems a practical Christianity grounded in a Christ-centered experience of God. In his autobiography Fosdick states that at the beginning of his career his aim was to make "a spiritual contribution to my generation."[2] In pursuing his life purpose, Fosdick became the most eminent preacher of his time. The practical intent and unsystematic nature of Fosdick's writings impose a somewhat different task upon the interpreter than in the case of William Adams Brown. The structure of Fosdick's thought is often implicit rather than explicit and has to be extracted to a large extent from sermons and essays, although he did write certain books which deal in a more formal way with theological issues. It is to be questioned whether or not Fosdick ever worked out even in his own mind anything like a systematic theology. He operated in his writing and preaching from a set of basic convictions which expressed themselves as the occasion arose. These convictions are distinctly liberal and add up to a perspective which can be described best as a version of the ethical-social type of evangelical liberalism.

Fosdick is one of the four men considered in this book who are Baptists, Rauschenbusch, Mathews, and Macintosh being the other three. In addition William Newton Clarke, whose *Outline* was the foundation of Brown's textbook, was also a Baptist. Clarke was also the man who first showed Fosdick the way to a theological outlook which avoided literalism but was yet distinctly Christocentric. The Baptist influence on twentieth-century liberalism in America, then, is of great significance. One suspects that there is an important connection between some of the theological emphases of Baptists and the development of liberalism. Baptists have always shied away from any creedal statements which would enforce strict doctrinal conformity and have stressed the freedom and competency of the individual under the leadership of the Spirit to interpret the New Testament for himself. Moreover, Baptists were among those most affected by revivalism in the nineteenth century. The stress of revivalism on conversion and Christian experience shifted attention away from concern with correctness of belief and the significance of dogma to the authority and importance of personal experience. In the light of this background it is not surprising that some of the most influential leaders of liberal thought in America came out of a Baptist, pietistic environment which had already laid the groundwork for some of the most distinctive liberal emphases.

Fosdick's most important theological writings appeared after 1920. He felt himself caught during these years between two extreme groups, and his writings give evidence of his double struggle with his opponents on either side. On his right were the fundamentalists, who held to a static orthodoxy which defied advances in modern knowledge. Fosdick remarks that he was unable to be a theological reactionary because it seemed to him that "the fact that astronomies change while stars abide is a true analogy of every realm of human life and thought, religion not least of all. No existent theology can be a final formulation of spiritual truth."[3] On his left were the modernistic liberals and the humanists, who in varying degrees abandoned the historic Christian tradition, even to the point of denying theism in some cases. Fosdick writes that he could no more be a theological radical than a reactionary. The radicals seemed to feel that because the old astronomy had gone, belief in the stars must be surrendered as well. Fosdick's own position was that of an evangelical liberal. He believed that the Christian tradition contained abiding, universal religious truth, but he was just as firmly convinced that this ancient truth had to be restated in modern categories. He summarized his position in his own words as follows: "What I have done I would do again and try to do better: believe both in abiding stars and changing astronomies."[4]

A. *Religion, Christianity, and Theology*

1. RELIGION

Like Brown, Fosdick is an ethical intuitionist. Religion is grounded in moral experience. In his autobiography Fosdick says that one factor in his "struggle for a convinced faith has been emphasis on direct, immediate personal experience as the solid ground for assurance."[5] In *As I See Religion*[6] Fosdick asserts that religion is not primarily a matter of believing certain theological doctrines or of participating in an ecclesiastical institution. Instead, it is, first of all, an individual, psychological experience. Here is an expression of the familiar strain of autonomy in liberal theology. Religion begins in the experience of the subject and not in the imposition of doctrines or a code of ethics from without.[7]

There are, Fosdick believes, two aspects to religion, one active and the other passive. On the active side religion is devotion to spiritual values. This commitment to the morally good is the pathway to truth about ultimate reality and leads inevitably to faith in the Conserver of those values. This is the essential meaning of God for religion. However, religion also involves a passive element, consisting of inward communion with God which brings to the believer peace, power, and joy. Thus far Fosdick has said nothing about religion as a response to revelation, and he has made no distinction between the experience of moral values in general and Christian values. The presupposition is that there is no radical distinction between the values of culture or reason and the values of Christ or revelation. Neither is there any real gulf between the Conserver of experienced moral values and the Father of Jesus Christ. Fosdick will proceed to unite the believer's present experience of value with the historical revelation by centering Christian experience in Jesus' reverence for personality. This way of uniting the experiential approach to religion is a procedure which has already been seen in Brown. However, what is of importance to note now is the principle of continuity which underlies Fosdick's interpretation of religion.

2. CHRISTIANITY

One principle which was of supreme importance for liberalism was the emphasis on the development of personality. Salvation meant largely the fulfillment of the potentialities of the human person in both his individual and social existence. The moral and spiritual growth of the individual and the evolution of society into the kingdom of God were prime goals in the liberal version of Christianity. In Jesus the liberals found both a revelation of the ideal of personality and the power to attain this ideal. This concern with the value of personality manifests itself with perfect clarity in Fosdick's definition of Christianity. The uniqueness of Christianity, thinks Fosdick, is to be found in its reverence for personality.

Take it or leave it, that is what Christianity is about. That is its guiding star and its dynamic faith. Personality, the most valuable thing in the universe, revealing the real nature of the Creative Power and the ultimate meaning of creation, the only eternal element in a world of change, the one thing worth investing everything in, and in terms of service to which all else must be judged—that is the essential Christian creed.[8]

This creed involves picturing God in personal terms, and it leads to faith in immortality. In short, religion within the Christian context consists of devotion to spiritual values conceived of in terms of enrichment to personality, involves belief in a Conserver of values pictured by personality at its best, and issues in communion with an Unseen Friend which will last forever.

Liberalism was infused with a fresh enthusiasm for the historical origins of Christianity. It is in the moral teachings and the religious experience of Jesus himself that the essence of Christianity is to be found. Liberals began to make a distinction between the religion *of* Jesus and the religion *about* Jesus. This gulf began to evidence itself even within the New Testament in the thought of Paul and John, some claimed. The present task of theology, according to this way of thinking, is to strip off the secondary accretions which have polluted the original Gospel and get back to the pure essence of Christianity with its locus in the historical Jesus. This point of view is reflected in Fosdick's analysis of the two types of historical Christianity.[9] One, he says, is the religion which Jesus himself had, and the other is the religion about him consisting of creeds, theories, and theologies. Fosdick makes it clear that he, like most liberals, wants as much of the former and as little of the latter as can be had. Christianity, for Fosdick, centers in the life, teachings, and—above all—in the personality of the historic Jesus. One is not really a Christian until he begins to share the ideals, attitudes, personal character, and religious experience which Jesus had. Creeds, rituals, ecclesiastical organizations, denominational affiliation—all of these are secondary to the sharing of Jesus' reverence for persons.[10]

3. THEOLOGY

Liberals were fond of saying that religion is prior to theology in the same way that flowers are prior to botany. Theology is secondary to experience and arises from it. Fosdick shares this position but, nevertheless, believes theology to be important. Its role, he insists, is to formulate, clarify, and interpret religious experience. In *The Modern Use of the Bible*[11] Fosdick shows in detail, in connection with the use of the Bible, the method by which theology should operate in interpreting experience. Since the method suggested by Fosdick in this book is typical of liberalism's approach to the Bible, it will be worthwhile to examine the thesis of the book at some length.

Modern critical study, says Fosdick, has made it possible to arrange the books of the Bible in chronological order and to trace a development from very primitive beginnings to the lofty religion of Jesus in the New Testament. The results of the new study of the Bible are considerable. The critical approach avoids the futility of trying to harmonize the Bible with itself, makes it unnecessary to apologize for the more immature portions of the Bible, and—most important of all—restores the whole book in its unity as a progressive revelation of God. However, the new view of the Bible raises a serious problem. The Bible uses thought forms and categories which are utterly strange to men influenced by modern science and philosophy. How can the Bible be made relevant to modern men? The solution to this problem is suggested by Fosdick in the phrase "abiding experiences and changing categories." There are certain basic human experiences which are ever the same, but the mental framework in which these experiences are expressed changes from one time and place to another. The task of the theologian is to search out the abiding experiences which lie underneath the categories of the Bible and then to reinterpret and restate the meaning of these experiences in modern terms.[12]

This approach to the Bible exhibits two of the basic underlying principles of liberalism: autonomy and dynamism. The continuity of Christianity is to be located not in a body of static, objective propositions of doctrine enshrined in a book or in a system of theology. Neither is it to be found in the life of an institution which overarches the centuries. It is to be found, rather, in the abiding experiences of believers which are repeatable in every generation. This is the element of autonomy. The dynamic factor is found in the belief that doctrine is a growing, changing, developing thing. The discovery of religious truth is a constant process of interpretation and reinterpretation. Both factors are contained in the formula of "abiding experiences and changing categories."

In connection with Fosdick's conception of the Bible and its use, one other book should be mentioned. *A Guide to Understanding the Bible,* published in 1938, is the outcome of a long personal study of the Bible and is widely recognized as being one of the best summaries available in English of the results of nineteenth-century critical scholarship. In this work Fosdick traces the growth of ideas relating to six major themes—God, man, right and wrong, suffering, fellowship with God, and immortality. He employs the familiar pattern of evolutionary development which is so characteristic of the liberal approach to the Bible. However, he is cautious in his use of this pattern and warns against what he calls the chronological fallacy, i.e., "the illusion of constant ascent, as though being posterior in time always meant being superior in quality."[13] Nevertheless, in general he does find that a rising curve of spiritual insight characterizes the development of Hebrew religion from its most primitive beginnings to the sublime heights of the religion of Jesus.

This book reveals two important things about Fosdick. First of all, it reveals the pre-eminent place which the Bible had in Fosdick's own thinking. The modern approach to the Bible does not imply for him any diminution of its importance, and it does not release the preacher and Christian thinker from the obligation of mastering the Scriptures. The years which Fosdick himself spent at the task of trying to understand the Bible substantiate the genuineness of his conviction that "the central ideas of Scripture, in whatever changing categories they may be phrased, seem to me the hope of man's individual and social life."[14] Secondly, this book indicates that the practical task of ministering to the needs of ordinary men and women was uppermost in his mind. He made no claims to technical competency in the field of Biblical scholarship, although he produced an able work. The book was written, he said, to make available the work of Biblical scholars for a wider public, to mediate the findings of the experts to the average minister, the intelligent layman, and the college student. This is but another illustration of the fact that Fosdick was interested in theology primarily at the point at which it made contact with the moral and spiritual needs of people in the modern world.

4. THE DEVELOPMENT OF FOSDICK'S THOUGHT

The theology of Harry Emerson Fosdick took its shape within the context of the fundamentalist-modernist struggle, and between 1920 and 1930 he became the very center of that controversy. In his autobiography he remarks that his problem from his youth on was the endeavor to be both "an intelligent modern and a serious Christian."[15] Liberalism made that possible by providing the only way that he could be a Christian at all. It was not a choice, he says, of liberalism or the traditional faith. It was a choice between liberalism and no faith at all. He could not honestly believe in an inerrant Bible, the virgin birth, the traditional view of miracles, substitutionary atonement, Jesus as the second hypostasis of the Trinity, a fiery hell, the second coming of Jesus from the clouds, and all the other staple beliefs of traditional orthodoxy. Unless Christianity could be harmonized with the established truths of modern culture, he felt he could not be a Christian. He pleaded for harmony and good will between fundamentalists and modernists, but when the battle lines were drawn, he wielded his considerable influence and intellectual powers on the side of the modernists.[16]

Thus, at the beginning of his career he conceived the task of contemporary theology as being that of making Christianity intelligible to modern men. However, by the middle of the 1930's Fosdick was adding a somewhat different note to his preaching. Like William Adams Brown, Fosdick was sensitive to the rising tide of what has variously been called neo-supernaturalism or neo-orthodoxy in this period, and the effect of this new perspective is reflected in his thought. A new emphasis on the transcendence of God, the importance of revelation, the sinfulness of man, and a rejection of the continuity between Christ and culture now become evident. In the year 1935 Fosdick preached a sermon entitled "The Church Must Go beyond Modernism." In this sermon he contended that modernism had been "excessively preoccupied with intellectualism," "dangerously sentimental," had "watered down and thinned out the central message and distinctive truth of religion—-the reality of God," and had "too commonly lost its ethical standing-ground and its power of moral attack."[17] Modernists, he said, have won the intellectual battle in the church, but now a new battle cry must be sounded. No longer is the task to accommodate and adjust. The new task is to challenge culture from the standpoint of the Christian revelation.

While the changes in Fosdick's thought after 1930 are significant, it ought to be noted that as far back as 1922 in *Christianity and Progress,* Fosdick had a note of realism in his writing that was often lacking in other liberals. In this book Fosdick speaks of the sinfulness of man with a seriousness which anticipates in many ways developments in American theology a decade later. Thus, the sermon of 1935 is rooted to a significant degree in his own insights and in his heritage from Rauschenbusch and not simply in criticisms derived from the growing neo-orthodox movement. This changing note in his thinking and his correction of himself in the light of new situations is consistent with his belief that the "one utter heresy in Christianity is thus to believe that we have reached finality and can settle down with a completed system."[18] In his autobiography Fosdick, while for the most part defending his liberal convictions against neo-orthodox attack, makes further admissions that he and other liberals were guilty to some measure of many of the things of which neo-orthodoxy accuses them—an excessive confidence in reason, not enough emphasis on the transcendence of God, too much optimism about man, for example.[19]

5. CONCLUSION

Basic, abiding moral and religious experiences mediated to Christians by the impact of the personality of Jesus interpreted in tentative, changeable categories—such is the foundation of the theology of Harry Emerson Fosdick. This is a thoroughly liberal methodology, and on the basis of this methodology Fosdick erected a theology which was equally liberal in content. The result was a practical, non-technical religious perspective designed to serve the spiritual needs of modern men.

B. *The Doctrine of God*

1. THE DEFENSE OF THEISM

In developing a methodology, Fosdick's main concern is to discover what the modern use of the Bible should be in opposition to fundamentalism. With regard to the doctrine of God, however, he seems to feel most keenly the challenge of humanism. He is concerned to vindicate the claims of Christian theism, with its doctrine of a personal, Christlike God, against the atheism of the naturalistic humanists. Fosdick defends belief in God in double fashion by appealing to religious experience and by employing a version of the teleological argument.[20]

The primary source of knowledge about God, Fosdick holds, is man's experience of moral value. Man is a being who distinguishes between right and wrong, who suffers remorse when he violates the inner voice of conscience, and who struggles ceaselessly for a more abundant life. This struggle is not simply the outcome of natural necessity but has been made in response to a cosmic pull. Values are grounded in the very nature of reality, and in devotion to them man enters into communion with God.[21]

In Fosdick's argument thus far the familiar liberal combination of autonomy and continuity is plainly in evidence. The locus of revelation is not in an objective body of Biblical propositions (orthodoxy) or the events of Israel's sacred history (the *Heilsgeschichte* theme of much recent theology) but in the experience of the believing subject. Moreover, God is not known in any special or revealed set of moral values but in every experience of truth, goodness, and beauty. There is a direct continuity between the values of Christ and the Platonic triad. Thus, revelation is not a contradiction of all natural knowledge or a judgment upon even the best human values (Barth) but is a continuation and sanction of the universally available knowledge of God in moral experience. Given the liberal doctrine of immanence, it obviously follows that God can be experienced everywhere, although supremely in the realm of the personal.

In addition to this argument from religious experience Fosdick also engages the humanists in philosophical argument. He attempts both to show the logical fallacies involved in non-theistic humanism and to demonstrate the cogency of the theistic position. First of all, he contends that the pose of nonchalance which the humanist has in regard to the existence of God cannot be logically maintained. The humanist assumes that as long as men have their values, they need not worry about cosmic support for them. Fosdick employs here the same argument as Walter Marshall Horton, who points to the contradiction between "the pessimistic, naturalistic conception of cosmos and the optimistic anthropology of humanism."[22] Fosdick, like Horton, insists that humanism "must either give up its faith in *man* by adopting a rigid naturalism or come to a more positive appreciation of *cosmos*."[23] Loss of faith in the God who creates, sustains, and forever preserves personality has an inevitable effect on morale and morals. A mechanistic philosophy will sooner or later lead to cynicism and moral degradation.

Furthermore, Fosdick urges, the philosophy of humanism is itself faulty. It assumes that dead matter and blind energy can elaborate a universe which involves everything from solar systems to Christ. Such a philosophy cannot long survive, Fosdick thinks, when men seriously examine its foundations and implications, since it cannot give a reasonable account of the spiritual reality and moral values which do, in fact, exist. One can be sure that

. . . no theory which represents the universe as merely *pushed up* from below by its own component energy-units without *pull* akin to intelligent purpose to supply pattern or structure can ever permanently hold the philosophic field.[24]

Fosdick argues against his humanistic opponents that if there were no God, then personality would never have emerged out of the evolutionary process, and there would be no way of accounting for enlarging truth, creative beauty, and expanding goodness in the world. He does not explicitly set forth the epistemology upon which this argument is based, but apparently he offers it as a cogent theoretical proposition to be taken realistically, i.e., as applying directly to the objective world of being.[25]

Two things are worthy of note here with regard to these arguments against the humanists. First of all, they demonstrate how strongly theologians in the period from 1920 to 1935 felt the challenge of the naturalism which was making such a headway during that time in the universities and among the intelligentsia. Secondly, they show how liberals based their defense of theism primarily on reason and experience rather than on revelation. The liberals had given up an arbitrary appeal to authority and insisted on the primacy of present experience and the autonomy of the human reason. Moreover, in making his appeal to reason Fosdick adds an objective note to his thinking. He is now not appealing to inner experience or intuition but is maintaining that humanism cannot be defended in the light of general philosophical principles. He seeks to refute humanism by reference to universal rational considerations which he feels are objectively convincing to the clear light of human reason. One may see here a remnant of the idea present in the Enlightenment period that religion is a reasonable affair and can be defended without recourse to supernatural revelation.

Although Fosdick rejects the philosophy of the humanists he shares one presupposition with them—the rejection of supernaturalism. Fosdick abandons this sort of dualism altogether and assumes a philosophy based throughout on the principle of continuity. Supernaturalism, he urges, is an obsolete concept. The history of thought reveals a process by which all phenomena have been reduced to regular, discoverable patterns which leave no place for the intervention of supernatural causes and powers. The universe is law-abiding. "The partition of the world into a natural order overlaid by a supernatural order which keeps breaking through is to a well-instructed mind impossible."[26] But, he continues, when the humanist goes on to assert that religion can get along without cosmic support, the theist must demur, for basically theism is a value judgment about the worth of personality which humanism cannot maintain. In Fosdick's own picturesque phrase humanism "sucks the egg of personality's value and then tries to hatch a high religion out of it."[27]

2. THE BEING AND CHARACTER OF GOD

Fosdick presents a non-technical, unsystematic description of the being and nature of God which can be designated as symbolic, personal, and Christocentric. The first thing to be said, admits Fosdick, is that God in his full reality is incomprehensible to the human mind. Just as we cannot catch the sun in a butterfly net, so we cannot capture God in our thoughts. All thought about God is symbolic and pictorial. Yet, if we are to think about God at all, we must use some analogy drawn from experience. Thus, the real problem is that of discovering the place in man's experience which provides the best symbol of God. The most reasonable view is that man touches the "near end of God"[28] in the spiritual life at its best. God, then, must be pictured in spiritual terms. Furthermore, since God is known best in man's highest experience of spiritual values within personal life, God must be symbolized in personal terms. Therefore, the Christian

. . . will not take a by-product of experience as physical energy, not a section of personality such as mind; he takes the full orb of personality, *self-conscious being that knows and purposes and loves,* and he affirms that God is most like this. Such in its simplest form is the Christian assertion of God's personality.[29]

Finally, since the highest personal life is found in Jesus Christ, Christians have always thought of God as being in character like Jesus.[30]

With regard to the doctrine of the Trinity Fosdick says only that the metaphysical theories used to explain the three persons constituting one Deity are not in the Bible. There is, however, a Trinitarian experience—"the grace of our Lord Jesus Christ, the love of God, and the Fellowship of the Holy Spirit."[31] Theoretical speculation about the nature of God in himself, he feels, is a waste of time, since it has no practical relevance for man's moral life. This is a more thorough rejection of a Trinity of being than that of William Adams Brown.

3. SUMMARY

Briefly, then, these are the main elements which go into Fosdick's thought about God. Nowhere in his writings does he give a systematic treatment of his doctrine of God as a technical theologian would do.

He apparently has no interest in this sort of thing or feels that this is a job for theologians, while he is a preacher. Yet, in his books and in his sermons there emerges a definite outlook and attitude regarding God's existence and nature. Fosdick is primarily interested in the doctrine of God from the standpoint of man's practical life, his moral struggles, and his spiritual needs. His aim in speaking of God is to assert that there is beyond man and beyond the natural world an ultimate power and value which is friendly, purposeful, personal, and good. This cosmic Friend is the guarantee of the real worth of personality and its values here and now and of the persistence of personality beyond death. Ultimate reality as personal, spiritual, and Christlike—this is the essence of Fosdick's doctrine of God.[32]

C. *The Doctrine of Man, Sin, and Salvation*

1. THE CENTRALITY OF PERSONALITY

It is already becoming clear that the foundation stone of Fosdick's theology is the infinite worth of personality. Let him say it now in his own words.

Let me tell you my philosophy. I can put it in a few words. Everyone who follows this ministry will recognize it. All my thinking starts from and comes back to it. Here it is: *the key to the understanding of all life is the value of personality.*[33]

This is the central theme which unifies all his thinking and gives the clue to the rest of his thought. He goes on in this same sermon to point out that the infinite value of personality is the source of man's sense of moral obligation, the test of man's moral obligation to others, the standard of judgment on social questions, the highway to truth about God, and the source of man's faith in immortality. He defines Christianity's uniqueness in terms of reverence for personality. The divinity of Christ consists in the perfection of his humanity. He begins with man—his experiences, his values, and his worth—not with God—his will, his revelation, and his actions. God is understood in terms of man, not man in terms of God. This anthropocentric tendency is widespread in liberalism. It is related closely to the principle of autonomy and the principle of continuity. Since God is immanent within the world and within the experience of man, the liberal can begin with man and move easily to God—from man's discovery to God's revelation, from man's moral consciousness of value to God's ethical will, from man's long upward struggle to God's redemptive action in history. Thus, the liberal is not conscious of any vast gulf between anthropocentrism and theocentrism. Yet, the actual starting point with Fosdick, and with liberals in general, is man and not God.

2. THE NATURE OF PERSONALITY

Fosdick's doctrine of man, as well as his doctrine of God, was developed in the context of his opposition to naturalism. Much recent theology has been in rebellion against the optimistic view of man and his possibilities affirmed in liberalism. American liberals of Fosdick's generation found themselves in quite a different situation. The error they were conscious of was not a too exalted opinion of human nature but a scientific naturalism which robbed man of the *imago dei* and reduced him to the status of an unusually gifted animal. Their task, they felt, was to oppose this reductive philosophy and to defend a Christian estimate of man's nature and destiny. Thus, Fosdick argues that man is more than matter. He is a moral personality, whose spiritual capacities tell of his divine origin. The philosophy of mechanistic naturalism would have us believe that man "is a physical machine made by the fortuitous self-arrangement of matter, with interesting mental and spiritual by-products."[34] If this be so, Fosdick insists, man is a queer kind of machine. He is a machine who sets high ideals for himself and his fellows, grieves with remorse when he violates them, and struggles constantly to make life better for himself and his children. To suppose that matter by accident could arrange itself in such a way as to produce everything from the brain of Plato to the character of Christ is to believe in sheer magic. Far more reasonable, he urges, is Christianity's postulate that personality has a divine origin, an infinite worth, and an immortal destiny.[35]

What sort of being is this moral personality which Fosdick assumes? Fosdick's approach in this connection, as elsewhere, is untechnical and unsystematic. His terminology has more connections with modern psychology than with traditional theological anthropology. Yet, implicit in his books and sermons are three convictions which are of basic importance for his understanding of the nature of man. In the first place, personality is dynamic. Within man there are many competing impulses, desires, drives, and interests.[36] There is conflict between the law of man's mind and the law of his flesh, between the sense of moral duty and the impulse to satisfy his selfish desires. Secondly, it follows from this dynamic concept of the self that human nature is plastic. No one ought to stay as he is, for no one lives at the highest level of his moral capacity, and no one needs to stay as he is. The self can operate at the lowest moral level, or it can be transformed into sainthood.[37] Implicit in what Fosdick has said here is a principle which had wide currency in liberalism—the idea of the higher self (spirit) struggling with a lower self (the animal nature). The thrust of man at the center of his personality is toward the good, but the upward climb of the spirit is hindered by the drag of natural tendencies. The preference of the animal self for the pleasurable passions and the natural desire for self-enjoyment make it difficult to integrate the self around the higher ideals. Given the competing tendencies of spirit and nature, a dynamic situation emerges. On the one hand, the self can be natural drift and inertia gravitate toward the lower end of the scale of moral attainment. Or, on the other hand, by disciplined struggle within and by the influx of spiritual influences from ideals and persons from without, the self can rise indefinitely toward moral perfection.

In the third place, the sources of human behavior are complex and stem from forces embedded deep within the personality. This conviction of Fosdick's grew out of his wide experience in personal counseling and his study of modern psychology. For many years Fosdick set aside time in his schedule for conferences with individuals who desired his help as a Christian pastor. Soon, he says, he began to confront problems, "the like of which I had not even known existed, whose genesis and diagnosis I could not guess, and before which I stood helpless, fearing rightly that I might do more harm than good."[38] His subsequent study of psychotherapy and his continuing role as a counselor added a note of realism to his understanding of human nature and of the plight of human beings which otherwise he might have missed. In dealing with a succession of disturbed personalities, he became very conscious of the hidden depths from which attitudes and actions spring. He saw the sordid messes into which people get, the guilt and anxiety from which they suffer, and the rationalizations, evasions, and projections people use to escape the truth about themselves. In short, he became aware of the profound complications within human personality which lead to moral failure, neurotic behavior, and intense inner suffering. Too, it should not be forgotten that

Fosdick himself suffered a severe nervous breakdown in his youth which at one point almost led to suicide.[39] All of these factors together made it impossible for him to believe that simple moral persuasion could get at the roots of human difficulties and mend broken lives. An easy recommendation of love and brotherhood to be attained merely by more strenuous moral effort was inadequate to make over human beings in the image of Christ. What was needed was a Gospel which could relate persons to a power not their own sufficient to change the personality from within. This evangelical note was repeatedly sounded in Fosdick's writing and teaching.

3. SIN AND SALVATION

Within the context of Fosdick's understanding of the self as dynamic and plastic, the doctrines of sin and salvation can now be approached. The self can be organized around its lowest motives. This is what sin means. The essence of sin can be simply defined. It is contempt for personality. Whatever hurts, hinders, degrades, destroys, or in any way prevents the growth, development, and highest expression of personality either in oneself or in others or in society at large is sin.[40]

Sin is defined here in typical liberal fashion in horizontal terms. Sin is primarily against man. It is contempt for persons, not rebellion against God. However, here again the principle of immanence reduces this distinction, so that the liberal can move easily from one to another. Sin against man *is* rebellion against God. Nevertheless, it is significant that the point of orientation is man and not God.

Fosdick has room in his thought for the doctrine of original sin. Beneath this doctrine is the abiding experience that all men are bound up together across the generations in wrongdoing. However, the category in which this experience is expressed is changed radically from the older orthodoxy. No longer is original sin viewed as the inheritance of a corrupt nature which inevitably issues in rebellion and disobedience, a corruption rooted, in the first instance, in Adam's defection (orthodoxy). Rather, original sin is interpreted as the solidarity of men in sin, a solidarity rooted in the continuity between individual and society and between one generation and the next. The doctrine informs us that

. . . humanity's sinful nature is not something which you and I alone make up by individual deeds of wrong, but that it is an inherited mortgage and handicap on the whole human family.[41]

Man, then, is a sinner, but he can be transformed. Salvation, according to Fosdick, is primarily the renewal of man's moral nature so that henceforth his personality is organized around the moral ideal represented by the character of Christ. One is saved to the extent to which he comes to share Jesus' reverence for, and service of, personality. However, sin cannot be overcome by sheer force of will power or simply by trying. Man must be renewed from within by a power from without. Transformation of character and progress in goodness "must be achieved by grace of some power which can give us the victory over our evil nature."[42] Inner renewal, conversion, transformation by the influx of spiritual power from above—this is the clue to goodness. Now what can he mean by this? He certainly does not mean to imply any supernatural operation of grace in the older sense. By the influx of power from without, Fosdick seems to mean what is implied in the phrase, "the expulsive power of a greater affection." There is a burst of moral energy which invades the self in the psychological process of conversion, which consists of a reorganization of the dynamic tendencies of the self. The powers of the self are now all integrated and harmonized around a new center of personal aim. The guilt and conflict which formerly raged within are no more. It is this sort of psychological readjustment which results from the attainment of a "greater affection" through the impact of the personality and ideals of the historic Jesus upon the believer which Fosdick seems to have in mind. Again, since God is immanent in all experience and supremely in Jesus, Fosdick can refer to Christian conversion as the work of God and yet understand the whole process in the terms of contemporary psychology.

Yet, Fosdick is sure that it is Christ who saves. Christ transforms men by his attractive excellence and by the inspiration of his moral example. He saves by his ability to bring men to their knees in confession of their wrongdoing, to mediate God's forgiveness of sins, and to lead men into such confidence and trust in God that results in the remaking of character from within. When one has thus been renewed, he can be good without trying.[43]

It is worthwhile to note that according to this way of thinking the radical distinction which orthodoxy posited between saved and lost, regenerate and unregenerate, disappears. Instead, there is a graduated scale of attainment from the brutes at the lower end to the saints at the upper end. Continuity has overcome dualism. Men differ relatively from each other in terms of the extent to which they share Jesus' reverence for persons. There is no absolute difference between men in terms of their belonging either to the elect or the non-elect (Calvinism) or to the group which has or has not accepted the justifying grace of God (Arminianism). The principle of continuity has been presupposed throughout Fosdick's discussion of sin and salvation, and it permeates all liberal thinking about man.

Fosdick shares the universally held position among liberals regarding the inseparability of individual and social salvation. There is a continuity between the person and his social relationships. If one starts out, says Fosdick, to redeem society, he will soon discover that this is impossible apart from the spiritual renewal of the individual person. If one sets out to save the individual, he will soon discover that this is possible only as a social environment is brought into being in which personality can thrive and realize its fullest potentialities. Thus, while Christianity has a great stake in the social situation, it must move through the social gospel into personal religion; and while Christianity begins with the remaking of the individual, it must move out into the social gospel to complete the task.[44]

4. THE SERIOUSNESS OF SIN AND SOCIAL PROGRESS

To what extent are man and his societies perfectable on this earth? Fosdick shared the optimistic mood of the nineteenth and early twentieth centuries, and he confesses in his autobiography that he was overoptimistic.[45] The capacities of man and society for moral growth are endless. Fosdick is here giving voice to one aspect of the underlying liberal principle of dynamism, according to which life and history are subject to forward development and progressive movement. Progress has been made, says Fosdick, in every area of life, but it has not been easy in the past and will not be easy in the future.[46] In his Cole Lectures at Vanderbilt University in 1922, published in *Christianity and Progress,* Fosdick concerns himself with this problem.

Fosdick is certainly within his rights when he protests[47] that he was aware of the fallacies of the doctrine of inevitable progress and of the seriousness of sin long before neo-orthodoxy was heard of. He complains that the new theology (liberalism) has too often overlooked the depths of man's iniquity and that modern man needs to be reminded that he is a sinner.

The moral order of the world has not been trotting us on her knees these recent years; the moral order of the world has been dipping us in hell; and because the new theology had not been taking account of such possibilities, had never learned to preach on that text in the New Testament, "It is a fearful thing to fall into the hands of the living God," we were ill-prepared for the experience.[48]

Strange as it may sound to this modern age, long tickled by the amiable idiocies of evolution popularly misinterpreted, this generation's deepest need is not these dithyrambic songs about inevitable progress, but a fresh sense of personal and social sin.[49]

We do not need artificially to conjure up a sense of sin. All we need to do is open our eyes to facts. Take one swift glance at the social state of the world today. Consider our desperate endeavours to save this rocking civilization from the consequences of the blow just delivered it by men's iniquities. That should be sufficient to indicate that this is no fool-proof universe automatically progressive but that moral evil is still the central problem of mankind.[50]

Now Fosdick certainly means to take sin seriously. The accusation of "naïve optimism" which is often made of all liberals does not apply to liberals of Fosdick's persuasion. Not all liberals, of course, were this cautious. It should be remembered, too, that these statements of Fosdick were written after World War I, when the optimistic tide was already beginning to turn. The second edition of Barth's *Der Römerbrief* was published in Europe the same year of the Cole Lectures. However, the most important thing to remember is not how loud Fosdick talks about sin but what he means by it. Fosdick is not a forerunner of the neo-orthodox view of sin, with its rediscovery of Augustine. Rather, he is a modern Pelagian. Sin is not for Fosdick, as it is with neo-orthodoxy, an inevitable corruption of the will springing from pride, the essence of which is rebellion against the sovereignty of God. Rather, sin for Fosdick emerges out of the conflict of the higher and lower self. It is the victory of bodily impulses and adverse influences over the ideals and good intentions of an essentially pure self. It does not really touch the center of personality in such a way as to corrupt the essential self (reason, will, or spirit). Obviously, the neo-orthodox version of sin puts man in a much more serious position than that envisioned by Fosdick. In the same manner, salvation is the surcharging of the self with moral energy, which aids the spirit in its struggle with the recalcitrant lower self. In this case, the essence of salvation is moral transformation. Thus, while Fosdick certainly takes sin seriously on his own terms, the decision still has to be made as to whether or not he is able to discern the real nature of sin within his own framework of interpretation. This is the point at which the discussion between Fosdick and neo-orthodoxy must go on, not at the point concerning which perspective talks about sin most.

Fosdick holds an eschatological view with regard to the future moral progress of the race; i.e., he believes that only beyond this history can redemption be fully realized. However, it was not primarily his consciousness of the depths of sin that convinced him that the kingdom of God would never fully come on this earth. Rather, it was the scientific pronouncement that this planet would once again in the future become uninhabitable. This realization was also a major reason for his faith in immortality.[51] No final resolution of man's problem or consummation of divine purpose can be found within a temporary planet. Life and history must have some further dimension beyond what we know now in which the kingdom of God will be completely realized.

D. *The Doctrine of Christ*

1. THE DIVINITY OF CHRIST

The starting point of Christology for Fosdick is the human Jesus— a man with the same flesh and blood, the same emotional, mental, and spiritual needs and capacities as any other person. Nevertheless, the impact of the personality of Jesus has convinced the millions of his followers that he is more than human. What does the divinity of Christ mean?

Divinity is not something supernatural that ever and again invades the natural order in a crashing miracle. Divinity is not in some remote heaven, seated on a throne. Divinity is love. Here and now it shines through the highest spiritual experiences we know. Wherever goodness, beauty, truth, love, are—there is the divine. And the divinity of Jesus is the divinity of his spiritual life.[52]

It would be difficult to find a statement which indicates with more clarity the result of the application of the principle of immanence to the problem of Christology. The divinity of Christ is not something of God added to the human from above but the perfection of the human from within. The presence of God is equated with the presence of moral values—all moral values. The uniqueness of Jesus is simply that he represents the supreme instance of the immanence of God.

In *The Modern Use of the Bible* Fosdick elaborates on his conception of the deity of Christ. The New Testament speaks of Jesus as the Messiah and as the Logos. These were the loftiest categories available to the Jews and the Greeks respectively. What experiences do these most exalted of all titles represent, and what terms shall be used to express the same experiences today? Consider first the term Messiah. Jesus must have been the sort of person who could do what he has done. Jesus has given the world its most significant idea of God, immeasurably heightened man's estimate of his worth and his possibilities, made men believe in the reality of moral renewal, and given the world its loftiest set of ethical ideals and its most effective demonstration of vicarious sacrifice. Most important of all, his personality has supplied an object of the noblest devotions of men for generations since he came. If, facing these marvelous achievements, one says that Jesus was the divinely appointed agent to inaugurate God's kingdom on earth, he is saying precisely what the Jews meant by Messiah. It is this achievement which is indicated by the doctrine of his divinity. The category of Logos applied to Jesus intends to say that he represents the forthcoming of God into the world. When this category is reinterpreted, it has its place today. The concept of the Logos means that what Jesus taught and stood for is grounded in the power and goodness of ultimate reality. The divinity of Jesus does not primarily concern Jesus but has to do with the existence, nature, and purposes of the invisible God.[53]

What can be said about this interpretation of Christ? First of all, while Fosdick follows both Luther and Ritschl in interpreting the person of Christ in terms of his work, the content of Fosdick's doctrine has connections only with Ritschl. The accomplishments of Jesus mentioned are those which could be determined empirically by a historian using a Christian scheme of evaluation. Nothing is said about the cosmic result of his work, such as the satisfaction of the divine justice or the conquering of the demonic hosts. Secondly, the doctrine of the person of Christ has undergone a like transformation. The statement that God *was in* Christ has come to mean that God *is like* Christ. Not the incarnation of the second person of the Trinity is indicated by the Logos doctrine but only the revelation of a Christlike cosmic support for moral values. This tendency to interpret Christ's work in purely historical rather than cosmic terms and his person in revelational rather than incarnational terms is typical of the liberal revision of the orthodox tradition.

2. THE ATONEMENT

The tendency to interpret the work of Christ in immanental, historical terms can be seen more clearly in what Fosdick has to say about vicarious sacrifice. Fosdick has no concern for—and not much patience with—technical theology, but if he can be said to have a theory of the atonement, it consists in the conviction that the vicarious suffering of Christ is the supreme instance of a universal spiritual law. The cross of Christ is illustrative of at least two fundamental principles. First of all, it demonstrates that forgiveness is costly.[54] Secondly, it sets forth the truth that redemption is made possible only by the kind of love that stands behind vicarious sacrifice.[55] However, the work of Christ, he reminds us, is not centered primarily in his atoning death but rather in the impact of his total personality upon his followers. Through contact with him men have been led to forsake their sinful ways, to find God's forgiveness, and to appropriate the power and inspiration they need to enable them to follow his moral example. In this encounter of personality with personality, says Fosdick, men have found that new and more abundant life which the Savior came to bring.

E. *The Church*

In Fosdick's scattered writings about the church there appear both implicitly and explicitly many characteristic liberal convictions. The dominant view which emerges in Fosdick's case is that of an individualistic, voluntaristic institution grounded in present Christian experience, rather than in dogma or tradition, and oriented largely toward ethical concerns. Since the basis for membership is Christian experience, dogma and denominational traditions lose their importance—thus opening the way for reunion of Christendom for the sake of greater ethical effectiveness. Fosdick affirms what he calls an inclusive view of the church which stands over against the exclusive view of rigid sectarianism. In *Christianity and Progress* he maintains that the church ought to "be the point of incandescence where, regardless of denominationalism or theology, the Christian life of the community bursts into flame."[56]

The church, then, is a community of faith and action composed of individuals bound together by a common loyalty to Jesus of Nazareth and to the principle of reverence for personality. Its supreme task is to combat whatever hinders the development of personality and to promote those activities which bring about the fullest realization of personal life in the light of the life and teachings of Jesus.[57] This means, of course, that the sacramental, ritualistic, institutional, and doctrinal aspects of church life are necessarily subordinated to ethical matters.[58] This does not mean, however, that worship was not important to Fosdick or that he lacked altogether any concept of the church as an organic community which nourishes the spiritual life of its individual members. He points out in his autobiography that he felt that the sanctuary at Riverside Church should be centered upon the altar. This surprised many who expected that the church would have a pulpit at the center.[59] Moreover, he says that when he was young, he felt that Christians made the church but that later he came to see that it was equally true that the church made Christians.[60] In both these ways Fosdick modified to some extent his general tendency to describe the church primarily in individualistic and ethical terms.

F. *Conclusion*

As the preceding discussion has made clear, every doctrine touched by Harry Emerson Fosdick illustrates the nature of ethical-social liberalism. Fosdick was a preacher who was concerned at every point to relate an ancient Gospel to the concrete needs of those contemporary people who sat before him in the congregation. There was abiding truth in the Biblical revelation, but it was useless to twentieth-century men unless it could be framed in such a way as to make contact with flesh-and-blood people in the midst of their daily struggle to find the abundant life. It was this attempt to mediate the old Gospel to modern men that has motivated him throughout his life and kept his mind open to new insight from whatever source that would assist him to make, in his own words, "a spiritual contribution to my generation." One of the important influences on the life and ministry of Fosdick was a fellow Baptist, Walter Rauschenbusch, who illustrates with equal clarity the nature of evangelical liberalism motivated primarily by ethical, social concerns. The next chapter will consider his contribution to liberal thinking.

CHAPTER 5

THE SOCIAL GOSPEL:
WALTER RAUSCHENBUSCH

Like Brown and Fosdick, Walter Rauschenbusch (1861–1918) was a native of the State of New York. He was born in Rochester and educated at the University of Rochester, Rochester Theological Seminary, and in Germany. Rejected for a foreign missionary appointment for which he had prepared, owing to a suspected defect in his Old Testament theology, Rauschenbusch accepted the pastorate of the Second German Baptist Church on West Forty-fifth Street in New York City. For eleven years he ministered to a poverty-stricken neighborhood. From 1889 to 1891 he helped in editing *For the Right,* a monthly paper devoted to the interest of the working people of New York and written from the standpoint of Christian socialism. One of the great influences of his life was a cell group which he and a few other ministers organized "in order to realize the ethical and spiritual principles of Jesus, both in their individual and social aspects." This group, which called itself the "Brotherhood of the Kingdom," met for a week every summer for more than twenty years to discuss the social gospel. In 1897 Rauschenbusch accepted a position in the German Department of the Rochester Theological Seminary. Five years later he became Professor of Church History in the English division of the Seminary, a position which he held until his death.[1]

I. RAUSCHENBUSCH AND THE SOCIAL GOSPEL

A. *The Background*

The consuming passion of Walter Rauschenbusch's life was the social gospel. It will contribute to the understanding of the thought of Rauschenbusch to indicate very briefly something of the origin and nature of this movement. H. Richard Niebuhr contends that the dominant theme in American Christianity has been the idea of the kingdom of God.[2] However, the rule of God in human life has not always meant the same thing. Niebuhr finds that the idea has a trinitarian form and that American Christians have in successive periods of their history focused on one particular aspect of the idea and then another. In New England Puritanism the kingdom of God meant "sovereignty of God." In revivalistic evangelicalism it meant "reign of Christ." In a wide variety of movements in the nineteenth century, including liberalism, it came to mean "kingdom on earth." Niebuhr concludes, "The social gospel with its emphasis on the kingdom on earth was building on the work of previous generations with their different emphases—emphases which had implied but not expressed the ideas or the faith of the subsequent movements."[3] Thus, the idea of social redemption, which to Rauschenbusch was the essence of the Gospel, has roots deep in the history and nature of American Christianity.

1. INTELLECTUAL AND SOCIAL FACTORS

However, the more specific origin of social Christianity is to be found in certain intellectual and cultural developments which emerged after the Civil War. The social gospel grew out of the dynamic interplay of distinctly religious and theological factors, on the one hand, and secular ideologies and socio-economic factors, on the other hand. On the cultural side, according to Waldo Beach, the social gospel drew (1) from the Marxists and English socialists a realization of the power of social conditioning on personality, (2) from the Utilitarians the ideal of social reform to extend happiness to the greatest possible number, and (3) from Darwin and his followers the evolutionary theory of the progressive development of human affairs.[4] In addition, the Christian social thinkers were affected by the socialistic critique of *laissez-faire* capitalism, Spencerian social science, the Social Darwinism of Sumner, the social telesis of Lester Ward, the utopianism of Bellamy, the single-tax theories of Henry George, the radicalism of Tolstoi, the ethical economics of the American Economic Association, the philosophies of John Fiske and Henry Drummond, and Henry D. Lloyd's crusade against monopoly—to mention some of the more prominent of the intellectual currents which entered into the making of the social gospel.[5] All of these intellectual tendencies merged with the robust optimism, activism, and pragmatic temper of America, with its deep-rooted hope of a perfected social order in the new world (the American dream). In this complex interaction of forces the groundwork was laid for a new interpretation of the relevance of the Gospel to social reform.

The social gospel burst upon the scene more immediately, however, amidst the painful throes of social crisis. Henry F. May's thesis is that, while the new doctrines of social Christianity arose partly in response to intellectual and theological developments, they were primarily a response to a "series of shocking crises."[6] "From 1877 through the middle nineties, it became more and more difficult," he says, "to believe that strikes, depressions, unemployment and bankruptcies were part of a Divinely-regulated and unchangeable social order."[7] Charles H. Hopkins, the foremost historian of the movement, agrees with May in stressing the importance of social and economic factors, urging that the social gospel was the response of American Protestantism "to the challenge of modern industrial society."[8]

2. RELIGIOUS AND THEOLOGICAL FACTORS

On the religious and theological side the social gospel was heir to the "expectation of the coming kingdom upon earth," which in the nineteenth century "became the dominant idea in American Christianity."[9] In a variety of movements which antedated the social gospel, American Christians turned increasingly "from the expectation of heavenly bliss to the hope of a radical transformation of life upon earth, without abandoning the former as though the two expectations were exclusive of each other."[10] From Unitarians on the left to the Millerites on the right Christians were confident in the expectation of the coming Christian revolution which was to remake the world.[11] Timothy L. Smith has documented the thesis that revivalism and the quest for perfection in mid-nineteenth-century America were powerful influences in generating social reform.[12] "Far from disdaining earthly affairs, the evangelists played a key role in the widespread attack upon slavery, poverty, and greed."[13]

Smith contends that more weight must now be given to the evangelical origins of the social gospel, owing to his discovery that, contrary to the long-standing opinion, "the doctrine of sanctification and the methods of mass evangelism played an increasingly important role in the program of the churches *after* 1842. . . ."[14] His thesis is that the "preoccupation with social problems which later dominated American Protestantism stems from the zeal and compassion which the mid-century revivalists awakened for sinning and suffering men. And it rests in large measure upon social theories which they originated."[15] At any rate, both Niebuhr and Smith are agreed that the blossoming hope for a new social order which so dominated nineteenth-century American Christianity prepared the way for what later, under liberal auspices, was to become the social gospel.

B. *The Place of Rauschenbusch in the Social Gospel Movement*

All of these intellectual, religious, economic, and social forces inter-acted upon each other and with a theology which was moving increasingly toward liberalism to give rise to the social gospel about 1880 and afterward.[16] Liberal theology and the social gospel developed together and are inseparable.[17] Washington Gladden, who has been called "the father of the social gospel," was also one of the most prominent of the earlier liberal theologians. By 1900 such men as Gladden, Josiah Strong, Richard Ely, Francis G. Peabody, and George Herron had already brought the movement to its maturity. In 1907, with the publication of *Christianity and the Social Crisis,* Rauschenbusch became the undisputed leader of Christian social idealism. He was by far the most outstanding proponent of the social gospel during the period of its greatest influence. According to Walter Marshall Horton, "The Social Gospel, with its hope of Christianizing the social order and building the Kingdom of God on earth, was the main positive message of American liberalism before and during the First World War."[18] And Hopkins maintains that the works of Rauschenbusch "were undoubtedly the most significant religious publications in the United States if not in the English language in the first decades of the new century."[19]

Rauschenbusch was very much aware of the dominant intellectual, theological, and social forces of his time, and he was alive to the issues of his day. He absorbed a warm evangelical piety from his early family life, and through his studies in Germany he came into contact with the latest developments in German liberal theology. Like Brown, he was in a real sense a mediator betwen the older evangelicalism and the new learning. A deep Christian piety was combined in him with influences from Schleiermacher, Ritschl, Harnack, and

German idealism. He had both the mystical tendencies of Schleiermacher and the ethical tendencies of Ritschl. On the social side he
had read the works of the critics of capitalism and was converted to
socialism. Thus, Rauschenbusch was a complex figure of wide learning and rich experience. In him a variety of complex influences came
to focus.

The most fundamental motivation behind Rauschenbusch's advo-
cacy of the social gospel was not his learning, however, but his Christian compassion.[20] It was his experience in "Hell's Kitchen" in New
York City more than anything else which gave him a passionate concern for social justice. This compassion and his deep evangelical
convictions combined with his knowledge of social criticism and liberal theology to enable him to give the classic statement to the social
gospel.

II. The Theology of Rauschenbusch

A. *The Social Gospel and Theology*

1. CHRISTIANITY AND THE SOCIAL GOSPEL

Christianity, the social gospel, and the message of the kingdom of
God—these three are names for the same religious reality.[21] To understand any one of them is to understand all three as they are interpreted by Rauschenbusch. It would be difficult to find a more
thoroughgoing statement of ethical-social liberalism. If H. Richard
Niebuhr is correct in contending that the idea of the kingdom of God
has been the central theme of American Christianity from its inception and that in the nineteenth century this idea came to mean kingdom on earth, then Rauschenbusch has not added anything new with
regard to these points. What is important in Rauschenbusch is the
completeness with which he identified Christianity with the message
of social redemption and the fact that he gave the classical statement
to the liberal version of this message.

a. *Biblical Religion*

With this understanding of Christianity it is only natural that
Rauschenbusch should find the essence of Christianity in the ethical
side of Biblical religion. He was influenced most by the teachings of

the Hebrew prophets[22] and the synoptic thought of Jesus.[23] The heart of Jesus' message was the kingdom of God, which means essentially the reign of God in human affairs. Jesus rejected the nationalistic, materialistic, militaristic, apocalyptic, and ritualistic elements which the contemporary Jewish concept contained and spoke of a gradual, universal, spiritual triumph of love as the motive and standard of all human activities in personal and social life. The essence of the religion of Jesus, then, was the message of "the social redemption of the entire life of the human race"[24] and the hope for "a divine social order established on earth."[25]

Rauschenbusch was clearly an evangelical liberal. As George Hammar says, "Rauschenbusch energetically strove for a Biblical foundation for his social gospel."[26] His aim was not to revise the ancient faith but to recover it in a modern form. Original Christianity as expressed in the New Testament, and particularly in the teachings of Jesus, constituted for him the norm of Christian thought. Thus, Rauschenbusch felt himself to be anchored solidly in the historic Christian tradition.

b. *Defection and Restoration*

It is typical of theologians in every new generation to feel that they are recovering essentials of Christianity which have been obscured or lost in previous theologies. Protestant theologians are particularly given to this tendency. A familiar sequence is employed in every case: the pure Biblical faith, defection, and recovery. The reformers believed that they were restating the original faith over against the corruptions of Catholicism. Liberals felt that they were recovering the religion of Jesus which had been obscured by the religion about Jesus. Many recent theologians are sure that they have now discovered the true Biblical faith which had been dissolved in liberalism.[27]

Rauschenbusch employs a similar pattern. He contends that the gospel of the kingdom of God did not long remain at the center of the Christian religion. For a number of reasons other ideas triumphed over the religion of Jesus, and the social gospel was replaced by the doctrine of the church[28] with very unfortunate consequences.[29] It is the great accomplishment of modern theology, Rauschenbusch feels, that it has restored the kingdom of God to the central place which it held in the primitive church. In *A Theology for the Social Gospel* Rauschenbusch offers a theological formulation of the doctrine of the kingdom of God which he hopes will be the foundation of a theology of the social gospel.[30]

2. A THEOLOGY FOR THE SOCIAL GOSPEL

The social gospel is a reality, and theology must take account of it—this is the central thesis of Rauschenbusch regarding the task and method of contemporary theology.[31] In this assertion there is involved the characteristic liberal assumption of the priority of ethics over theology. The practical message of social redemption and its appropriation come first. Theology exists to interpret this practical ethical Gospel in terms which are relevant to the age. Theology is the servant of the religious life, not its master.[32]

Rauschenbusch proceeds to say in this connection that theology arises out of experience, and it must change with new experiences and adapt itself to meet new situations.[33] A clear distinction may be seen here between orthodoxy and liberalism. In orthodox theologies of all varieties dogma is prior to experience and is relatively unchanging. The assumption is that the normative substance of religious truth has been laid down in the past in a given body of doctrine. This ancient truth may need to be applied and reinterpreted in some measure to meet new circumstances and to incorporate new experiences, but essentially it is thought to remain the same from age to age.[34] In liberalism doctrines are subsequent to experience and are subject to change. Evangelical liberals held to the position that the revelation of God in Christ constituted the universal norm of religious truth, but the patterns by which Christ was interpreted were thought to change with experience.

In line with the liberal approach to theology Rauschenbusch maintains that since the social gospel creates a new type of religious experience, it will create a new theology. The older Protestant theology, he says, concentrated on the needs of the isolated individual, whereas the social gospel connects religious experience with a consciousness of the solidarity of all people and with the needs of society as a whole.[35] Rauschenbusch contends that theology must be periodically rejuvenated to keep it from becoming stagnant and obsolete. To insist that modern men subscribe to the outdated formulas of an earlier age is nothing less than ancestor worship and has no justification whatsoever. In short, Rauschenbusch's thesis is that theology can become relevant to the modern world only by incorporating the insights of the social gospel into its doctrines. The social gospel is already a reality, and what is needed most is "a systematic theology large enough to match it and vital enough to back it."[36]

3. REVELATION AND INSPIRATION

Because of his democratic and immanent view of God, Rauschenbusch has not much place for a doctrine of special revelation. God is not remote from men and known only to a select few by miraculous means. God lives and moves within the experience of all people and can be felt and known by the masses of men. As an evangelical liberal Rauschenbusch does, of course, believe that Christ is normative for religious thinking. "For a Christian man the only sure guide in speaking of God is the mind of Christ. That is our logic and metaphysic."[37] However, the combination of the principle of immanence with his strong mystical inclinations tend to make the concept of historical revelation ambiguous. At the most Jesus represents only the high point within man's historical experience of God. He adds nothing to this experience from above or beyond the range of the human consciousness of God which all men share to a greater or less degree. Perhaps this tendency of immanence to dissolve revelation is no more acute in Rauschenbusch than in Brown or Fosdick, but his stronger Schleiermacherian overtones do sometimes make it seem so.

Rauschenbusch speaks more of inspiration than he does of revelation. Perhaps this is because the concept of inspiration seems to be more dynamic and experiential. The Bible is inspired because of the testimony of its writers to their experience of God within their own historical and social context. However, God's Spirit is at work at all times and among all men, and no doctrine which makes revelation into an infallible static body of truth revealed in the past is tenable. What is needed is a keen sensitivity to the inner light, the voice of the Holy Spirit, as it calls men to present tasks and inspires them to work for social redemption.[38] Rauschenbusch insists that the social gospel is the voice of prophecy for the modern age, the inspired message of God for the present.

B. *The Doctrine of God*

1. SOCIAL PATTERNS AND THEOLOGY

Rauschenbusch has been considerably influenced by the *religions-*

geschichtliche Methode. The history of religions school in Germany emphasized the influence of culture on religion and religious knowledge.[39] Recognizing the validity of this approach, Rauschenbusch affirms that knowledge of God is shaped by the historical context out of which it comes. Social experience more than theoretical and metaphysical considerations determine the patterns of religious thought.[40]

This emphasis on the social conditioning of Biblical doctrines further jeopardizes the concept of revelation. If the prophetic view of God is a social product, what part does the initiative of God have to do with this process? Would the democratic view of God which Jesus held have emerged in some other culture had the requisite social conditions prevailed by some coincidence, or do the teachings of Jesus in some way constitute a unique divine revelation? In short, to what extent is the factor of special revelation involved in the development of the religious ideas which Rauschenbusch holds to be normative? In a system of thought dominated by the principle of immanence the concept of revelation tends to be ambiguous in any case. However, Rauschenbusch's stress on the social basis of the Biblical view of God, in the absence of any real insistence on the unique activity of God in the events of Israel's history, further threatens the idea of any special divine self-disclosure. The principle of continuity has once again reduced and almost dissolved the distinction between human discovery and divine self-disclosure.

Sometimes the emphasis on the social basis of doctrines moves in the direction of social determinism. He indicates, for example, that the conflict of the religion of Jesus with autocratic conceptions of God in the modern world is part and parcel of the social struggle to overcome economic oppression and political tyranny. In another connection he says, "The triumph of the Christian idea of God will never be complete as long as economic and political despotism prevail."[41] Again, he observes that in the past under "tyrannous conditions the idea of God was necessarily tainted with the cruel hardness of society."[42] These statements seem to point to an inevitable causal relationship between social conditions and theological doctrines. He implies that a change in the social structure is prerequisite to a change in theology and that the reform of theology is as much the result of social change as of a renewed study of the Christian revelation.

On the other hand, however, he does point out that theologians can aid in the social struggle by stressing the democratic idea of

God and, in this way, provide a model for social organization. Too, Rauschenbusch believes that the teachings of Jesus constitute a universal and permanent norm to which theology in every age should conform. Supposedly, then, theologians are free in some measure to transcend their culture and to appeal to ideals which are in tension with the prevailing social patterns. Moreover, Rauschenbusch refers to divine providence in connection with the struggle for a theology untainted by autocratic conceptions. The social gospel, he says, is "God's predestined agent"[43] to purify the idea of God. Again, he observes that in the present world it takes a revelation to enable one to see that God is really on the side of the poor.

Rauschenbusch obviously means to say that social conditioning, human freedom, and divine activity are all involved both in the development of the Biblical idea of God and in the continuing process of theological development. However, he never makes any attempt to clarify the relationship between these factors. Rauschenbusch was not a technical theologian and made no attempt to deal with many of the questions in which a systematic thinker would be interested. As a result some of his convictions remain unclarified.

2. THE DEMOCRATIC VIEW OF GOD

In dealing with the doctrine of God, as in dealing with the doctrine of the kingdom, Rauschenbusch employs the sequential pattern of pure doctrine, defection, and restoration. The pure doctrine, of course, consists of the teachings of Jesus. The great contribution of Jesus was that he democratized the idea of God.[44] One can see in this democratic view of God a clear example of culture-Protestantism. Christ is represented as teaching a view of God which supports and furthers the movement of modern American culture toward democratic institutions. In fact, Rauschenbusch goes so far as to maintain that unless theology conforms to the democratic tendencies of society, it cannot survive. "The worst thing that could happen to God would be to remain an autocrat while the world is moving toward democracy. He would be dethroned with the rest."[45] Democracy is taken to be a normative value to which theological ideas must conform in order to be called Christian. Rauschenbusch, of course, believes that Jesus himself is the author of the democratized idea of God. This makes Jesus in this respect the hero of modern culture. In many ways Rauschenbusch was a severe critic of modern culture and attacked it with a moral passion seldom equaled. This was particularly true in the area of economic organization, business, and labor relations. Yet, with regard to the democratic element in American life Rauschenbusch saw a profound harmony between the values of Christ and the values of culture. Indeed, many of the faults which he found in American business could be overcome, he felt, if democratic principles were applied to the economic realm. Thus, at least with reference to democracy it can be said that Rauschenbusch is one of those men who, in the words of H. Richard Niebuhr, "hail Jesus as the Messiah of their society, the fulfiller of its hopes and aspirations, the perfecter of its true faith, the source of its holiest spirit."[46] The Jesus Rauschenbusch knows is fundamentally a "Christ of culture."[47]

Christianity, then, according to Rauschenbusch, began with a democratic view of God, but soon monarchical and autocratic ideas triumphed. The social gospel is God's predestined agent to complete the process of redemocratizing the idea of God. The God of the social gospel seeks the redemption of all mankind and the union of all men in a world-wide brotherhood. Theology must revise its doctrine of God, he contends, in the light of this kingdom ideal.[48]

3. THE PRINCIPLE OF IMMANENCE

The democratic view of God which Rauschenbusch holds to be normative for Christianity requires a doctrine of immanence. A transcendent view of God as a being who dwells on high and distinct from human life, he remarks, was the natural basis for autocratic ideas. If God is transcendent, he needs popes, vicegerents, and kings all established by divine right to rule for him. On the other hand, he continues, if God lives and moves in the life of mankind, he can act on the multitudes of men directly. A democratic God is one who is among men striving within their striving, flooding their minds with moral ambition and energy, and urging them onward toward greater achievements.[49] The element of transcendence is sharply subordinated in Rauschenbusch's writings, although it is not totally lacking.[50] Rauschenbusch seems to view God as an infinite, eternal, all-pervasive fund of spiritual energy who is the ground of all life and the source of all goodness. The element of personality in God tends to be subdued by this emphasis. Men and God do not encounter each other so much as they interpenetrate each other. Likewise, God does not appear to men in a revelation from without so much as he simply wells up from within in the moral strivings and spiritual aspirations of men. The mystical strain in this conception of God is unmistakable. This mystical element in connection with a strong doctrine of immanence tends to reduce the importance of a historical revelation in Christ, although Rauschenbusch does insist on the normative character of this revelation.

The extent to which the doctrine of immanence is carried gives strong weight to the charge of Visser 't Hooft that Rauschenbusch is a pantheist,[51] despite the strenuous protests of some interpreters.[52] Rauschenbusch had little interest in metaphysics or cosmology, and he leaves many questions unanswered. However, it is very clear that Rauschenbusch does not intend to affirm an impersonal pantheism, although many of his statements taken alone would tend to indicate this. The optimism of Rauschenbusch about man· and his mystical tendencies perhaps further incline him toward the use of language which stresses the union of God and man rather than their separation and moral distance. Yet, it is quite evident that in Rauschenbusch's thought the being of God transcends the human consciousness. God is in some sense over against men as well as present in them. Evidence can be adduced which indicates a more dynamic and personal view of God than that presented in some extreme passages. His conception of personal religion as fellowship with the living God, his rejection of quietistic mysticism, his strong emphasis on the religion of the prophets, his interpretation of God as personal moral will, and supremely his own personal religious life[53]—all of these things certainly seem to put Rauschenbusch in the tradition of personalistic Christian theism. Any accurate labeling of Rauschenbusch, then, as a pantheist is therefore ruled out. Nevertheless, it remains true that when Rauschenbusch speaks of God, it is usually in terms of immanence.

4. SUMMARY

Rauschenbusch sets forth a doctrine of God strictly from a practical point of view. His intense interest in social reform discouraged his concern with the technical problems associated with the doctrine of God. He does not deal with the proofs for the existence of God, the doctrine of creation, the nature of God's internal being,[54] and other traditional problems. As God is for Fosdick primarily the source and ground of moral values, so for Rauschenbusch he is viewed as the immanent power and spirit undergirding the movement for social redemption. God is a democrat in that he believes in liberty and equality for all men and has the utmost respect for the rights of every individual. He is a kindly Christlike Father who plays no favorites among men but rather seeks the full redemption of them all. Therefore, arbitrary decrees of election and reprobation, special revelations, favoritism expressed in miracles, or any other actions on the part of God which would override human freedom, insult the dignity of man, or be contrary to the highest human values have no place in his thinking. In stressing the immanence of God, Rauschenbusch veers dangerously toward pantheism, and in insisting on the necessity of a democratic view of God, he allows the relativities of a particular culture to influence his interpretation of the Biblical view of God. Nevertheless, his interpretation of God as primarily a moral being and his intense moral passion are both so intimately connected with the Old Testament prophets and Jesus that it would be grossly unfair in the largest sense to say that his view of God was un-Biblical, however much he may have been misled at some points. It is probably true to say, however, that his own personal Christianity is more firmly rooted in the Biblical tradition than his intellectual credo.[55]

C. *The Doctrine of Man*

1. THE DOCTRINE OF MAN AND THE PRINCIPLE OF IMMANENCE

Rauschenbusch nowhere develops a systematic doctrine of man in the technical sense. However, there does appear in his writings a set of convictions about man which are distinctly liberal. Many interpreters point to faith in man as the central conviction of liberalism.[56] It is certainly true of Rauschenbusch that he holds a very high view of man and his possibilities. The background for this estimate of humanity is his doctrine of the immanence of God. God is in man, and man is in God. It is in and through man that God works out his purposes. The moral distance between man and God has been extremely narrowed in Rauschenbusch's thought and almost done away with altogether. He affirms that Jesus both raised the value of the human soul and its life and brought God down close to man as Father.[57] The immanence of God in man and the participation of man in the life of God are the bases for holding that the soul is of such precious value. The Fatherhood of God, the brotherhood of man, and the infinite worth of the human soul are all implied in the revelation of God in Christ, according to Rauschenbusch. All three doctrines rest on a doctrine of immanence.

2. THE DOCTRINE OF SIN

Most of what Rauschenbusch has to say about man is found in his teachings about sin and salvation.[58] In describing the nature of sin, Rauschenbusch follows the familiar pattern already observed in Brown and Fosdick. The background which Rauschenbusch presupposes is the struggle in man between his spiritual aspirations and his natural impulses. Sin arises, he contends, out of the conflict within man between the passionate nature, with its impulses and appetites, and the conscience, with its ideals and sense of obligation. Ignorance and inertia also contribute to wrongdoing. Here again sin does not seem to touch the center of personality. It arises out of the weakness of the spirit, not in its self-willed corruption. Sin is not a deliberate usurpation of the prerogatives of God on the part of the self but a failure to attain the higher moral possibilities defined by the ideals of the conscience. Rauschenbusch means, however, to take sin seriously. He has a poignant sense of the tragedy, frustration, suffering, and destruction of life which result from the victory of selfish impulse over moral ideals. We are, he says, "involved in objective wrong; we frustrate our possibilities; we injure others; we disturb the divine harmonies. We are unfree, unhappy, conscious of a burden which we are unable to lift or escape."[59]

Two further emphases of Rauschenbusch serve to point out the difference between liberalism, on the one hand, and orthodoxy and neo-orthodoxy, on the other hand. Rauschenbusch insists in familiar liberal fashion that guilt in the full sense enters only when intelligence and will come to play a part in the sinful acts of the self. Will here seems to refer to the capitulation of the higher self to the temptation of the passionate self, by which the spirit gives consent to nature. By contrast orthodox and neo-orthodox thinkers stress the fact that the will itself, not natural impulse, is the originator in some mysterious way of the sinful act. Again, Rauschenbusch sets himself over against the view that the essence of sin is prideful rebellion against the sovereignty of God and insists that sin is essentially selfishness. The theologies which view sin primarily against God are based on the social model of monarchical institutions, Rauschenbusch claims, and are therefore in conflict with the democratic pattern, which he takes to be normative. Sin is not a private transaction between the sinner and God. Humanity is always involved.[60] However, since God is immanent in humanity and even "identified with it,"[61] sin against the neighbor is sin against God. Thus, sin against man is not just symbolically or indirectly sin against God but literally and immediately.

A theme constantly recurring in Rauschenbusch is the solidarity of man, i.e., the continuity between the individual and society. It is from the standpoint of his convictions regarding the solidarity of man in society that he deals with the problem of original sin. Liberals in general dismissed the ideas having to do with the fall of Adam. This was, they felt, an outmoded, prescientific way of dealing with the origin of sin. For the orthodox scheme liberal thinkers substituted the Darwinian notion of the origin of the human race and viewed man's history as a long, difficult struggle upward from the level of the beasts toward the attainment of moral personality. When they retained the idea of original sin at all, they dealt with it only in passing. About the only meaning they could give the doctrine was to see in it an awkward and obsolete way of pointing to the social transmission of sinful influences from one generation to another and from society to the individual. Brown and Fosdick view the problem of original sin in this light. Rauschenbusch, too, views the doctrine of original sin as a way of pointing to the solidarity of men in sin. However, he makes a great deal more of this point and develops it in much greater detail than did any other liberal thinker. It is the importance which he attributed to the social factors in the transmission of sin and his profound insight into the nature of the kingdom of evil which constitute the contribution of Rauschenbusch to the liberal interpretation of sin. One interpreter, in fact, has been led to speak of Rauschenbusch's revival of the doctrine of original sin.[62] Rauschenbusch states that he wishes to defend this doctrine because it represents the only attempt of orthodoxy to get a solidaristic view of man.

While he recognizes much truth in the doctrine of the biological inheritance of evil,[63] Rauschenbusch contends that the social inheritance of sin is far more important. This refers not only to the force of evil example but also to the authority of society over the individual. Social groups, he points out, are organisms which influence and even control individual behavior. They also exert pressure on other social groups and affect society as a whole. These social organisms manage to idealize evil practices and make them seem harmless or even necessary and good. These evil practices are institutionalized and become part of the established social order. These patterns are then passed on to the next generation. In short, there are superpersonal forces of evil.[64] Just as the new growth of vegetation in a swampy forest springs out of, and adds to, the rank mass of life already present, so the life of humanity is infinitely interwoven in such a way that the evils of one generation are caused by the generation that preceded it and will condition the life of the generation to follow.[65] This concept of the solidarity of men which gives superpersonal force to sin is the modern substitute, says Rauschenbusch, for the older view of Satan and his demons. These superpersonal influences give rise to the kingdom of evil. This concept refers to the compounding of social evil into a vast and powerful network of sin which persists from one generation to another. At this point, remarks John Bennett, Rauschenbusch "pushed theological thought forward."[66]

3. THE DOCTRINE OF SALVATION

While any balanced theology will include both the religious and ethical aspects of the doctrines of sin and salvation, there is a tendency among theologians to focus attention primarily on one or the other. On the one hand, Reformation thinkers and recent theologians who have revived Reformation patterns of thought—such as Reinhold Niebuhr, Karl Barth, and Emil Brunner—interpret salvation primarily as justification—the reconciliation of God and man.[67] On the other hand, liberals view salvation primarily as sanctification—growth toward moral perfection. There is doubtless an oversimplification involved in treating both Reformation and liberal thinkers in such neat fashion. Nevertheless, as a general orientation this pattern holds true. The stress on the ethical side of salvation is certainly evident in Rauschenbusch. Salvation is the moral transformation of individuals and of society, and in both cases it consists in coming under the law of Christ.

Rauschenbusch deals with both personal and social salvation. Adherents of the social gospel are sometimes accused of concentrating so intently on the redemption of society that personal salvation and the role of the individual in the remaking of society are neglected. Now it is certainly true that Rauschenbusch devoted his primary attention to the salvation of society, but he does not intend to leave the individual out. Rather, he insists that "the salvation of the individual

. . . is an essential part of salvation."[68] Rauschenbusch took for granted an interest in individual salvation on the part of his generation. His purpose was to begin at this point and expand the conception of salvation so that it would also apply to groups. "The social gospel is the old message of salvation, but enlarged and intensified."[69] The social gospel creates a new type of personal religion because it includes some insight into the social nature of redemption. Salvation in the individual means a thorough transformation of selfishness into love and co-operative service in every realm of life. This means that the salvation must include a conversion of the individual's social attitudes and behavior.[70] This transformation of the individual is never perfect in this life but "in some germinal and rudimentary form salvation must turn us from a life centred in ourselves to a life going out toward God and men."[71] While it begins with the individual, the social gospel, Rauschenbusch points out, is pre-eminently concerned with the transformation of the superpersonal forces of evil. The salvation of these composite personalities consists in substituting social service for selfishness as the motive and rule of action.[72]

The concern of Rauchenbusch for the individual can be seen even more clearly when he comes to speak of the process by which social salvation can be obtained.[73] The accomplishment of this goal involves a process which begins simultaneously with social groups and with the individual. Society must be redeemed in order to create an environment which is propitious to the renewal of the individual, and the individual must be converted in order to remake society. However, as a matter of actual strategy "the most immediate and constant need in Christianizing the social order is for more religious individuals."[74] Social salvation must begin with individual repentance and renewal.[75] Since society is a close-knit organism, as individuals change and begin to live according to the law of love, their influence will spread throughout the whole social body. Rauschenbusch had great faith in the social power of a life transformed by the spirit of Christ and infused with his God-consciousness. "I believe in the miraculous power of the human personality. A mind set free by God and energized by a great purpose is an incomputable force."[76] "Create a ganglion chain of redeemed personalities in a commonwealth and all things become possible."[77] Once this process is set in motion by a few transformed individuals, there is no limit to what can be accomplished.[78]

4. SOCIAL PERFECTION

A common charge against liberalism is that it suffered from utopian delusions. Examples of extreme optimism can certainly be found among liberal thinkers.[79] It is true, moreover, that in the light of present realities even the more cautious hopes of Brown and Fosdick thus far surveyed seem overconfident, as Fosdick himself admits. But nobody can call either of these men fatuous utopians or naïve optimists. Neither would these designations hold true of Rauschenbusch. Rauschenbusch was very optimistic about the ultimate triumph of the kingdom of God on earth, but he was not blind to the sinful realities of his own day. His own experience and attempts at reform were enough to convince him of the depth and power of social evils. He was aware that vested interests held tenaciously to their privileges and would stoop even to violence and totalitarian efforts to preserve them.[80] He warned that "any effort at social regeneration is dogged by perpetual relapses and doomed forever to fall short of its aim."[81]

Thus, Rauschenbusch maintains that complete moral and social perfection on earth is not within the realm of possibility, but progress toward social perfection is possible. The practical goal which Rauschenbusch sets for society is not perfection but the Christianizing of the social order.[82] This is a realizable end. In fact, in 1912 Rauschenbusch contended that the largest and hardest part of the task of Christianizing society had already been done. The family, the church, education, and the state have passed through certain progressive stages which have made them suitable organs through which the spirit of Christ may operate.[83] The greatest section of the social order still governed by the law of selfishness and mammon rather than the law of love and service, he felt, was the economic life of the nation. However, Rauschenbusch's hope was that it too could be redeemed. Thus, said Rauschenbusch, "within the limitations of human nature I believe that the constitutional structure of the social order can be squared with the demands of Christian morality."[84] Moreover, the rate of progress is increasing.[85]

However, he stresses the point that Christianizing the social order does not mean moral and social perfection. Every child is born an egotist and has to learn for himself how to adapt his life to the growing order of love in society. Moreover, since society is dynamic, new adjustments are continually needed as sinful powers continue to emerge to corrupt every attained good.[56] At best there is but an approximation of the social ideal. The kingdom of God is always but coming.[87]

5. RAUSCHENBUSCH AND NIEBUHR

It will be instructive to compare Rauschenbusch with Reinhold Niebuhr at this point, since these two are respectively the outstanding American representatives of the liberal and the neo-orthodox versions of social Christianity. While it is true generally to say that Rauschenbusch is more optimistic than Niebuhr, their ultimate outlooks with regard to social progress show some similarities.[88] Both believe that no prior limits can be placed on the degree to which Christian social patterns may be achieved, and yet both insist that perfection is not an attainable goal within history.[89] Rauschenbusch, however, put his emphasis on the possibilities of progressive achievement, while Niebuhr has stressed the limitations of progress and the inevitability of corruption at every new level of achieved good. The contrasts between them are grounded ultimately in differences in the social experience and the theological theory of the two men. The rapid succession of world catastrophes since 1914 has chastened for Niebuhr the more sanguine hopes which Rauschenbusch shared with his less turbulent generation. The theological differences which are of most importance in this regard have to do with their analyses of the nature of sin, of the Christian life, and of love.

For Rauschenbusch the locus of sin is in the natural impulses of the self. Hence, sin does not vitally affect the essential self (mind, will, or spirit). For Niebuhr, on the other hand, the locus of sin is in the self-willed corruption of the very center of personality, which consists in man's capacity for reason, memory, and self-transcendence.[90] In other words, Rauschenbusch tends to identify freedom with virtue and to see the origin of sin in the weakness of this virtuous freedom in its struggle with the natural impulses of the animal self. In contrast, Niebuhr sees that the lack of virtue is due to the inevitable corruption of freedom which causes the self to defy the moral norms which it may even acknowledge as the true law of its existence.

Similarly, with regard to the Christian life Rauschenbusch views the life of faith as a process of continuous growth in moral achievement as a result of the influx of spiritual power mediated through Christ. Niebuhr, on the contrary, tends to employ an existentialist view of time and to see the Christian life as a series of discontinuous moments in which the decision for or against God and the good has to be perpetually renewed.[91] Grace is primarily pardon and only secondarily power. Niebuhr does not deny growth in grace or that permanent moral gains can be made, but he does insist repeatedly that no new level of achievement can be regarded as a secure possession, since it may be corrupted by the next decision the self makes.

Finally, while they agree that love is the supreme Christian virtue and the norm of the Christian life, they disagree with regard to its relationship to the empirical and historical life of men. For Rauschenbusch love, though it is the highest virtue, is directly continuous with the virtues and the spirit of brotherhood, social service, good will, democracy, unselfishness, etc. In short, love is immanentized. In this view, the kingdom of God is identified with the perfection of the human social order, and thus progressive achievement of this ideal is a real historical possibility.[92] Niebuhr, on the other hand, interprets love in an absolute and perfectionist sense. Love is transcendent to the empirical life of men and touches history only at its edge, although it is related dialectically to life and history. Love is discontinuous with the lesser ideals of justice, equality, and freedom, although it is the ground and ultimate criterion of all moral norms.[93] Thus, Niebuhr can speak of the relevance of an impossible ideal. In this view, the kingdom of God ceases to be an attainable good in this world. Rather, it is a transcendent ideal which can never be identified with any human kingdom no matter how advanced.

6. ESCHATOLOGY

The most important item, of course, in the eschatology of Rauschenbusch is his concept of a gradual, evolutionary development of the kingdom of God on earth. But there is a consummation of God's purposes for man beyond this life. For the individual there is a destiny beyond death in which the moral progress he has made—or failed to make—will be the starting point for the life beyond. There will be continuous growth and development for all, the good and the bad alike, and none will ultimately be left unredeemed. Thus, life in the kingdom of God beyond history stands in direct continuity with the upward movement of the kingdom within history.[94] Here again the liberal principles of continuity and dynamism have overcome the radical dualism which the older theology posited between the saved and the lost and between the present age and the coming age, to be introduced by a sudden, catastrophic end to world history at the second coming of Jesus.

D. *The Meaning of Jesus Christ*

1. THE PERSON OF CHRIST

Two basic features of modern thinking about Christ are clearly in evidence in the thought of Rauschenbusch. First of all, there has been a tendency to shift from the use of the static, impersonal, metaphysical categories to dynamic, personal, ethical categories. Since Kant personal existence has been construed less as some impersonal essence and viewed more concretely in terms of responsible moral decision.[95] The shift to this sort of analysis has had widespread results in modern thought regarding the person of Christ. Thus, Schleiermacher understands the divinity of Christ in terms of the perfection of his God-consciousness. Ritschl concludes that Christ is the perfect moral personality who has the value of God for those whom he initiates into the kingdom of God. Rauschenbusch, under the influence of both, remarks that the social gospel has "more interest in basing the divine quality of his personality on free and ethical acts of his will than in dwelling on the passive inheritance of a divine essence."[96]

A second characteristic of liberal Christology, particularly in its ethical-social varieties, has been a loss of interest in the metaphysical problems associated with Christology and a focusing of attention on the practical side of the issues. This tendency is due to a large extent to the influence of Ritschl, who demanded that theology abandon metaphysics and base its formulations on the revelation of God in the historical Jesus. For Ritschl religion was a practical matter of attaining divine aid to overcome the threat of nature to the development of moral personality. Ritschl, of course, himself had been profoundly influenced by Kant.[97] This feature of liberal Protestantism is also taken up by Rauschenbusch. The real Christological problem, he says, is not how the divine and human natures can both be present in the person of Christ but how the divine life of Christ can get control of society. The social gospel is concerned with a progressive incarnation of God in history as the spirit of Christ comes to reign in human affairs.[98]

The divinity of Christ consists in his unique God-consciousness.[99]

Jesus is "a perfect religious personality, a spiritual life completely filled by the realization of a God who is love."[100] However, once having established the uniqueness of Jesus, Rauschenbusch proceeds immediately to assert the continuity of Jesus with other men. There is no unbridgeable gulf between the moral and spiritual attainment of Jesus and the potentialities of ordinary men. While Jesus is the "crowning summit" of the development of the race thus far, he is "a prophecy of the future glory of humanity, the type of Man as he is to be."[101] Thus, the principles of continuity and dynamism have combined to lead Rauschenbusch to predict that all men are moving toward the achievement of the moral perfection exemplified in Jesus.

2. THE WORK OF CHRIST

The strong influence of Schleiermacher can be seen throughout Rauschenbusch's discussion of Christology. Both of them interpret the person of Christ in terms of the perfection of his spiritual life—his God-consciousness. Now, like Schleiermacher, Rauschenbusch views the work of Christ in terms of the perpetuation of the spirit of Christ in other men through the communication of his God-consciousness.[102] However, the mystical tendencies emanating from Schleiermacher are balanced in Rauschenbusch by the ethical-social tendencies deriving from Ritschl. The effect of the life and death of Jesus was the establishment of a divine community of love and brotherhood which reaches out to embrace all men—the kingdom of God. Men are saved, then, as they are drawn into the influence of Jesus and are led to share his spiritual life within the growing community of those who are striving to organize humanity according to the will of God.

In *A Theology for the Social Gospel* Rauschenbusch devotes a long section to a discussion of the atonement. Like William Adams Brown, Rauschenbusch attempts to maintain a connection with the older theology at this point. He raises three questions which are prominent in the traditional formulation of the doctrine of the atonement and answers them in the light of the insights of the social gospel. (1) Jesus innocently bears the sins of men in the sense that it was racial sin organized as the kingdom of evil that killed Jesus. The solidarity of men involves every man in Jesus' death, since the same sins that killed Jesus are universally prevalent.[103] (2) The death of Jesus affects God in that he is immanent in the life of humanity and in Jesus in such a way that the suffering of Jesus was of significance for God. Moreover, the saving impact of Jesus' death changed the objective status of men before God. (3) The death of Jesus affects men in that it reveals the power of sin in the human life, shows forth the love of God, and has powerfully reinforced ethical, prophetic religion.

E. *The Church*

Given his passion for the social gospel, it is no surprise that Rauschenbusch further magnifies the common liberal tendency to subordinate the church to the kingdom of God. The church exists, he says, not for its own sake but for the sake of the kingdom. "Like all the rest of us, the Church will get salvation by finding the purpose of its existence outside of itself, in the Kingdom of God, the perfect life of the race."[104]

The church, which Rauschenbusch defines as "the social factor in salvation,"[105] has powerful resources which can be employed in the interests of social redemption. Ideally, it would bring its manpower, its composite personality, its collective memory of sacred Scriptures, hymns, and prayers, its disciplined membership, its trained moral and aesthetic feelings, and its morale to bear on the power of evil. It is a superpersonal force for good set against the superpersonal forces of evil. It is organized around the spirit, the purposes, and the teachings of Jesus, and it continues the work which he began to do in his own ministry.

Needless to say, the churches generally are not what they ought to be according to the ideals of the social gospel. In *Christianizing the Social Order* Rauschenbusch lists a number of ways in which the church needs to change. First of all, the churches must abandon their concern with issues which have no practical meaning today. Secondly, the churches must forget ancient quarrels and join together in the common task of Christianizing the social order. Thirdly, to become fully Christian, the church must come out of its spiritual isolation and join in the social battle for a better world. Finally, the church must further emancipate itself from the dominating forces of the present age and refuse to compromise its message of social justice for opulent financial support. In short, the church needs to re-evaluate all of its activities in the light of the kingdom ideal and reorient its total resources to the practical task of organizing humanity according to the will of God.[106]

F. *Conclusion*

If William Adams Brown was liberalism's most eminent teacher, and Harry Emerson Fosdick its foremost preacher, then Walter Rauschenbusch was liberalism's greatest prophet. It is a tribute to the strength and importance of ethical-social liberalism that all three of these towering figures were to be found in this wing of the liberal movement. The ethical-social, as contrasted to the theoretical-metaphysical, interest is perhaps stronger in Rauschenbusch than in either Brown or Fosdick. His writings have all of the marks of a passionate crusader and few of the disinterested thinker. The theoretical formulation of religious doctrines was a decidedly secondary interest with Rauschenbusch, ranking far behind his concern for the practical reorganization of society according to the ideals of Christ. There were others, however, who were evangelical rather than modernistic in their orientation but who nevertheless believed that theology must be theoretically grounded as well as practically motivated. This perspective must now be examined.

CHAPTER 6

THEOLOGICAL PERSONALISM:
A. C. KNUDSON

The next two men to be considered—A. C. Knudson and E. W. Lyman—view the content of Christian doctrine in much the same way as the theologians already discussed. They have a sense of continuing the main stream of Christian thought, although they recognize that they are reinterpreting Protestant theology in the light of developments in modern thought and culture. But they understand this procedure simply as a means of making Christianity relevant to the needs of twentieth-century man and not as an abandonment of essential Christian principles. However, there is a distinct difference in the way they approach the task and method of Christian theology. They share with all liberals an interest in the practical side of religion, but they insist on the necessity of incorporating Christian belief within an overall view of the nature of things. In short, Knudson and Lyman are metaphysical liberals, who manifest an interest in the theoretical aspects of theology which is generally lacking in the thinkers previously considered.

Albert Cornelius Knudson (1873–1953), the first man to be considered who was not a native of New York, was born in Grandmeadow, Minnesota, the son of a Methodist preacher. He attended the University of Minnesota and afterward went to the Boston University School of Theology for his theological education. After his graduation from the seminary in 1896 he remained an additional year at Boston for study in philosophy with Borden P. Bowne. Following this he went to Germany for a year of study in the field of New

Testament. After teaching for eight years at three different institutions, he returned to Boston University in 1906 as a professor in the field of Old Testament and later became Professor of Systematic Theology and Dean of the School of Theology. He became Dean Emeritus in 1938.

Like most of the other liberal thinkers under consideration here, Knudson grew up in a home in which a warm evangelical piety flourished. He remarks that religious experience was emphasized in his family. The religious life was thought to begin with a unique emotional experience at conversion and to be followed by a life of trust and obedience afterward. These early influences no doubt had a great deal to do with his later emphasis on the grounding of religion in experience, and this was undoubtedly true of other liberals who had a similar background. During his college and seminary years he went through a period of doubt and questioning having to do with the conflict between the beliefs associated with the simple piety of his childhood and the demands of common sense, science, and philosophy. His intellectual conflicts were resolved under the influence of Borden P. Bowne, who convinced him of the truth of personalism and helped him to discover a metaphysical foundation for theology which could preserve the essential truths of the Christian revelation.[1]

Knudson was convinced that theology should be a full-orbed theistic and Christian philosophy, able to defend itself on rational grounds, and personalism showed him how such a theology could be constructed.[2] Personalism, a form of metaphysical idealism, interprets the real in terms of persons and their experiences.[3] There is a society of free and active finite persons, capable of realizing values, who live in a natural environment which has phenomenal reality only.[4] There is also a Supreme Person who is the ground of the realm of finite persons and the realm of nature. Knudson found in this outlook a metaphysical scheme which fully satisfied his demands for a Christian philosophy, and was convinced that "the great theological task of the present is to reinterpret Christian doctrine in the light of the personalistic type of thought."[5] He devoted his own professional life to the carrying out of this task.[6]

Knudson's theological system appeared in two volumes: *The Doctrine of God,* published in 1930, and *The Doctrine of Redemption,* published in 1933.[7] He sets forth a system thoroughly permeated with liberal presuppositions and one which reveals an Arminian and Methodist background. These volumes have never had the wide use which Brown's work had, partly because by the time they appeared, neo-orthodoxy was making deep inroads into the liberal movement. This development attracted theological attention in other directions. Also, Knudson's work seems to have been restricted by its denominational and philosophical connections more than Brown's volume. Knudson has had most influence among Methodists and among those inclined to personalism. Since the influence of idealism has declined in recent years, this too has tended to limit the appeal of Knudson's system. Boston University is still the stronghold of theological liberalism of the personalistic type.

A. *Religion, Christianity, and Theology*

1. RELIGION

It is characterirstic of liberal thinkers that they preface their discussion of Christianity and theology with an analysis of religion in general. This tendency is not unrelated to the pervasive principle of continuity. The Christian religion is not *sui generis* but is one version of a universal phenomenon. Simply as religion, Christianity has traits in common with all other world faiths. Moreover, it was the conviction of liberal thinkers that religion or personal experience is prior to theology, thus connecting this tendency also with the principle of autonomy. Theology is not so much a description of God's redemptive activity as it is an elaboration of man's experience of God. The same tendency is seen in the fact that Knudson claims finality for Christianity rather than for Christ. Liberalism characteristically put the emphasis upon religion rather than upon God. Thus, Knudson begins by defining the essential nature of religion as such. Religion, he says, is a personal attitude toward an objective realm of values. It consists of three elements: trustful dependence on a higher power, a longing for redemption, and a sense of obligation toward God and man. These subjective attitudes have an objective reference and imply belief in a superworld. However, only those who respond in faith, hope, and love can apprehend this transcendent world of spiritual reality.

2. CHRISTIANITY

Evangelical liberals were convinced that Christianity was the final form of religion. Nevertheless, they felt that the difference between

Christianity and other religions is a matter of degree and not of kind. Christianity is the absolute religion because it represents the highest form of religion yet reached in the evolutionary historical process. It is the climax of religious development and the fulfillment of all earlier forms of religion. This is precisely Knudson's position.[8] Absoluteness applied to Christianity means that in Christ there is a revelation of the absolute and that this revelation is the highest known to man. While he admits that any judgment that one religion is superior to another ultimately involves subjective factors which are not subject to rational control, Knudson contends that there are objective standards which can be employed to show that Christianity is superior in its theological outlook, its ethical content, and in its power to satisfy the deepest needs of the soul.

However, he adds that it is only the essence of Christianity which is absolute and not any particular version of it. This essence cannot be defined in a completely objective manner, since subjective judgments always enter in. Christianity cannot be reduced to a formula or to any set of specifiable principles. Yet, there is a continuity in the Christian tradition which identifies it from age to age and which can be determined by a study of the Bible and church history. Knudson never really says what the essence of Christianity is that continues from age to age, although it is safe to surmise that he would locate it in one way or another in the revelation of God in Christ. He quotes with apparent approval the Christocentric definition of Christianity given by Schleiermacher and Ritschl.[9]

3. THE RELATION OF SCIENCE, PHILOSOPHY, AND THEOLOGY

Knudson expounds the positivistic view of science common among personalists. Science deals only with the phenomenal world and is purely descriptive. Its task is simply to discover and correlate the laws of phenomena.[10] Philosophy deals with the metaphysical realm underlying the observable world and investigates the world of power, cause, and purpose. An adequate philosophy should include the approach to reality based on moral experience, but it needs to be supplemented by the objective and rational support of an intellectually-grounded metaphysics of a theistic type.[11] In short, Knudson believes that personalism offers the type of philosophy which reason demands and that it is the most satisfactory metaphysical foundation for Christianity.

On this basis Knudson now differentiates theology from philosophy and philosophy of religion.[12] While theology and philosophy alike deal with metaphysics, theology differs from philosophy in that the former concentrates on the subject of religion; that is, theology has a more restricted field of experience. In this regard theology is closely akin to philosophy of religion. Indeed, they have the same basis and employ the same methods of validation. All truth is judged by the same standards. Theology appeals to no external, arbitrary standards outside the mind itself. Knudson, then, is willing to abandon the traditional distinction between natural theology and revealed theology in so far as the latter refers to a body of truths which are imposed upon reason from without. The influence of the principle of continuity in this connection is obvious. Theology differs from philosophy of religion in being conditioned by its relation to the church. Theology has its own special province and its own distinctive sources. It concentrates attention upon the Bible and seeks to commend Christian beliefs to the modern mind in a way that philosophy of religion does not. Theology, in short, is the servant of the church, and it is distinguished by this ecclesiastical function.

4. THEOLOGICAL METHOD

Evangelical liberals were united in affirming that the Bible is the primary source of theology. This was one point at which they maintained a connection with Protestant orthodoxy. However, their interpretation of the Bible as a shifting framework of categories which gives expression to the human experience of God, rather than as an infallible source of dogma, set them apart from the orthodox divines. Knudson is clearly an evangelical liberal in his understanding of the Scriptures in both respects. On the one hand, he affirms that the Bible is the most trustworthy record of the unique revelation of God which was mediated to the world through Christ.[13] On the other hand, Knudson rejects what he calls the "dogmatic method" of orthodoxy, which implies that there is an authoritative standard of belief external to reason and experience. Instead, he adheres to a "critical method," which takes into account the subjective factors which enter into religious knowledge. This method begins with man and his faith and moves toward God. It also includes a combination of the empirical and the speculative approaches to religious truth. Finally, the "critical method" takes into account the practical needs of the church as it develops its doctrines.[14]

5. FAITH AND REASON

The problem of faith and reason is solved by Knudson along typical liberal lines. The distinction between revelation and reason is reduced by a combination of the principles of continuity and autonomy. The highest insights of the mind, he urges, are themselves to be regarded as divine revelations. Moreover, nothing that purports to be revelation is to be accepted that is not in harmony with what is reasonable.[15] Knowledge, he concludes, is not a biarchy in which reason and faith hold rule over separate and unconnected provinces but a monarchy governed by rational faith or believing reason. This is to say that all faith involves reasoning, and all reasoning involves an element of belief beyond absolute certainty.[16] A number of elements enter into this conception of knowledge as a jointly-ruled monarchy. Knudson is an idealist and thus has an organic conception of truth. All truth is part of one continuous whole, so that no radical gap can exist between reason and revelation. Moreover, as an idealist and a liberal he holds to a doctrine of the immanence of God, which means that God reveals himself in the whole range of experience and not simply in some special, miraculous way to a few inspired ancient writers.

B. *The Doctrine of God*

1. THE EXISTENCE AND NATURE OF GOD

It is understandable that Knudson should feel that personalism is a Christian philosophy. Personalist thinkers speak of a supreme, intelligent, purposive Person who is the causal ground of the world and the creator of other persons, and this philosophical absolute seems to Knudson to be identical with the God of religion. Belief in the existence of this Supreme Person follows from three types of rational considerations: man's religious experience, his sense of moral obligation, and the traditional theoretical arguments.[17] The theoretical arguments, he says, do not prove the existence of God, but they do demonstrate that "the theistic world-view is 'the line of least resistance' for the intellect as it is also for the moral and religious nature."[18]

Knudson proceeds to give a complex and detailed account of the being and attributes of God which need not be summarized here. However, it should be noted that his careful philosophical delineation of omnipotence, omnipresence, eternity, etc., serve to point out the essential difference between him and the ethical-social liberals. Knudson has a confidence in the power of reason to make such an analysis and a belief in the theological necessity of doing so which distinguish him from Brown, Rauschenbusch, and Fosdick.[19] One point, however, deserves further consideration. Knudson, as a personalist, puts great stress on the personality of God. He recognizes that the view of God as *a* Person is a relatively modern development and makes reference to C. C. J. Webb's contention that traditionally the emphasis of the church has been on personality *in* God and not on the personality *of* God.[20] Knudson attributes this change in thought to modern personalism, to the demands of science for a unitary world ground, and to the opposition of theology to the materialistic and pantheistic tendencies in modern philosophy. It might be added that this emphasis is related also to liberalism's faith in man as the clue to God.[21] Since man is characteristically defined as a moral personality, it follows easily that God must also be a Person.

Personality, according to Knudson, means basically spiritual or psychical existence. However, God is unlike human persons in that he does not need to struggle constantly to adjust to his environment, but rather his spirituality is "to be found in the firmness and faithfulness with which he adheres to his saving purpose, in the unchangeable steadiness of his holy will."[22] God thinks, feels, and wills, but these activities are not limited as they are in humans. "Personality in its essence means 'self-hood, self-knowledge and self-direction,' and in these respects it may be either finite or infinite."[23] Moreover, personality, far from implying isolation and exclusiveness, involves social relations as well as distinct individuality. Fellowship between man and God is not only essential to the religious view of God but is also necessary for God's full expression and realization of himself. To speak of God as being related to finite persons does not compromise the absoluteness of God, he argues, if absoluteness is defined in causal terms, i.e., if God is viewed as the self-existent Person who is the ground of the world.

In short, Knudson thinks of God as a Person who is metaphysically absolute and ethically perfect. The doctrine of the goodness of God is derived from the Biblical revelation of the holiness and love of God and is corroborated by philosophical analysis. Evidence based on the analogy between free intelligence and moral responsibility, on the moral structure of human nature, and on the consciousness of moral obligation lead to the postulation of a supremely good Being, who is identical in Knudson's thought with the Father of Jesus Christ. Knudson solves the problem of theodicy, which might seem to be a threat to the goodness of God, by an appeal to ignorance. He holds that "if we knew all, as God does, the unideal aspects of the world would not seem so entirely out of harmony with an absolute and holy love as they now do."[24]

2. THE TRINITY

Knudson is typical of a large number of liberals who want to preserve certain values inherent in the classical views of the Trinity without affirming the doctrine itself. Thus, while Knudson points out the advantages which Trinitarianism has over all forms of monarchianism and unitarianism, he sees insuperable difficulties in the orthodox pattern of thought. If the three are considered as individual persons, there is the danger of tritheism and the dubiety of the need for more than two persons. If the three are less than persons, there is the difficulty of conceiving of a person as something midway between a substance and an attribute and the loss of the religious value of the idea of a divine society. Moreover, the traditional dependence on Platonic realism, which subordinates personality to essence, has been outmoded by the shift to personalistic modes of thought, while modern conceptions of incarnation and salvation no longer call for a metaphysical union of the divine and the human. The best way to preserve the value of the classical doctrine, Knudson feels, is to assert the Christlikeness of God. This approach focuses on the most fundamental contribution of Christianity—a new ethical conception of God. Moreover, it associates our knowledge of God with the historical revelation in Christ. Finally, it directs attention to God's unity. God is fundamentally *a* Person, not a complex unity of three Persons. In God, he says, there may be three eternal and necessary distinctions, but it is not at all certain that the absoluteness of his love is dependent on his triune nature. One may reasonably conclude that for Knudson the doctrine of the Trinity is not really essential to the Christian view of God.[25]

3. GOD AND THE WORLD

A distinction of some validity can be made between certain Christian thinkers who orient themselves in terms of the doctrine of creation and others who base their thought on the doctrine of redemption.

The former orientation gives rise to an optimistic type of thought which centers on the goodness of the world and man, while the latter concentrates on the evil in the world and the sinful state from which man must be extricated. Certain types of Protestant orthodoxy and Barth's theology are examples of the latter type of thought, while liberalism is more akin to the former.[26] Of course, this is a relative distinction, but, employed cautiously, it casts light on basic tendencies which affect the temper and mood of a theological system. Knudson employs this distinction and makes it clear that he prefers the monistic, optimistic outlook inherent in the doctrine of creation.[27] The world is fundamentally good, although it stands in need of redemption. Redemption is necessary, however, not because the world is intrinsically evil but because "of the transitory and instrumental nature of the world" together with "its bewildering complexity and apparent indifference to human ends."[28]

Knudson maintains that the essential elements of the Christian view of the world are (1) that the natural order is dependent on God and (2) that it is adaptable to the ends which he has in view. Speculative questions, such as whether this is the best of all possible worlds, and questions having to do with the origin of the world, its history, its inner structure, etc., may be legitimately dismissed as being of no essential concern to faith. Knudson, therefore, is able to accept the views of modern science without hesitation. It is, however, a present task of theology, he feels, to incorporate the newer findings into the creeds and liturgy of the church. Knudson, of course, affirms the free creation of the world in preference to a necessitarian view, but he admits to being able to make no decision in regard to the question of eternal or temporal creation. As a personalist Knudson believes that the physical world has phenomenal reality only, being the immediate product of God's mind. He does not, of course, insist that this idealistic position is necessary to a Christian view.

The problem of miracle is recognized by Knudson as the most recent and most complicated of the controversies which have arisen regarding the physical world. Liberals in general played down the role of miracle both on grounds of historical criticism and on the basis of the principle of immanence. God, it is said, is to be found active everywhere and in everything, not simply or primarily in isolated cases of supernatural intervention. Knudson is an example of this tendency. Knudson makes a distinction between the principle of *miracle* and the fact of *miracles*. One may believe that God stands in a free and living relationship to the world (miracle) without believing in the actuality of physical wonders as are described in the Bible (miracles). Knudson thinks that the former is necessary to distinguish the Christian view of the world from a mechanistic philosophy, but he does not insist that God ever violates the established phenomenal order. However, he apparently accepts in principle the historicity of the healing miracles of the Gospels, since many of them are "scientifically explicable," but he has grave doubts about the nature miracles, such as the virgin birth and the bodily resurrection. He does not rule out this latter group absolutely, but he insists that belief in them is not essential to faith.

C. *The Doctrine of Man*

1. THE NATURE OF MAN

Knudson, as a metaphysical liberal, is very interested in the contribution which philosophy has made to the theory of man. The tradition which he finds most appealing from the Christian point of view is that represented by Plato, Descartes, Leibniz, Berkeley, Kant, and Lotze. At the highest stage of this philosophical development the idea emerges that the self or soul is a mental agent, "a being whose very existence is constituted by its self-consciousness and self-direction."[30] This, of course, is the personalistic view of man, and Knudson finds it to be rationally cogent and Biblically sound. Again, reason and faith point in the same direction. With regard to further problems Knudson decides in favor of creationism over traducianism, affirms that man is a dichotomy of body[31] and spirit and not a trichotomy, affirms the reality of metaphysical freedom (power of contrary choice), and contends that the difference between men and animals is one of degree rather than of kind. In every case his decision is based as much on philosophical and scientific grounds as on Biblical evidence. He maintains explicitly that the views of the Biblical writers on traducianism "would not be decisive for us."[32] Needless to say, this is a wide departure from the method of Protestant orthodoxy. On the essential issues, of course, he is confident that no real contradictions exist between Biblical religion and modern science and philosophy, but he has departed from a proof-text method of settling controversial theological questions.

Knudson affirms a belief in immortality, which means the continued personal and conscious existence of the self beyond death characterized by moral growth and the continuous enjoyment of an ever-present good. While various types of moral and theoretical arguments can make immortality seem reasonable, the real ground of hope lies in the religious conception of the nature of God revealed in Christ. This resting of ultimate hope on Christ is an instance of the Christocentrism of evangelical liberalism. Since immortality is a gift of God and not a natural endowment, there is reason to think that some may not attain it. This eventuality seems to be implicit in the fact of man's freedom, and Knudson seems attracted to it. This willingness to entertain the possibility that some souls may be annihilated stands in contrast to the general liberal tendency to affirm a doctrine of final universal salvation.

Much recent theology has pointed to the resurrection of the body as an essential ingredient of Biblical eschatology.[33] The differences between this view and the Greek idea of the natural immortality of the soul have been pointed out. The tendency in liberalism, however, is to merge these two conceptions. It is often pointed out by liberals that the idea of a bodily resurrection is a crude and outmoded phrasing of hope. While Knudson shares this general outlook, he does point out that the idea of the resurrection of the body "symbolizes a richer and more definite mode of being than that suggested by a bodyless soul."[34]

2. THE DOCTRINE OF SIN

Knudson's doctrine of sin incorporates many of the characteristic liberal ideas which have already appeared in Brown, Fosdick, and Rauschenbusch. Liberals shied away from an idea of sin which necessarily involved all men in guilt. They insisted that there can be no guilt where there is no responsibility. Knudson makes a great deal of this point. Sin presupposes the power of contrary choice. Accountability is of the essence of sin and defines its formal nature. This means that the standard by which sin is measured is not fixed but varies with the total set of circumstances which affect each individual at each stage of his life. This tendency to measure sin by human ability rather than by the absolute will of God stands in sharp contrast to orthodoxy and to recent revivals of Augustinian and Calvinistic views of sin. Knudson's strict insistence on accountability is another aspect of the principle of autonomy at work in liberalism.

Knudson's views regarding the origin of sin also embody with unusual clarity tendencies which are present in all liberal thinking. Knudson explicitly and emphatically rejects all necessitarian theories and all ideas which conceive of sin as independent of the individual will. This rules out all doctrines of original sin and any attempt to explain the origin of sin by reference to Satan.[35] The only essential factors which enter into the beginnings of sin are "the raw material of our emotional and conative nature, the power of self-direction, and a difficult goal to be attained."[36] Stated here with precision is the basic liberal conviction that sin arises out of the inability of the spirit to master the non-moral impulses of the body. Sin is a kind of weakness by which the will is overpowered and its consent given to the surging passions of the animal nature.

Given such a situation, it is probable that all have sinned, but this cannot be proven. In fact, in order to be consistent to his volitional view of sin, Knudson must leave the possibility open that men can come to maturity without sinning. Nevertheless, Knudson can speak of the "practical universality" of sin and attribute it not "to a native tendency to evil, due to a temporal or extratemporal fall, but to the enormous difficulty involved in the task of moralizing the non-moral impulses, desires, and interests with which we are endowed by birth."[37] Thus, the mystery of sin is removed by attributing it to the almost inevitable victory of nature over spirit. But nowhere is there any suggestion of any basic corruption in man's spirit as such. Reason and freedom are basically on the side of virtue.

A critic could point out that Knudson is still involved in a dilemma. If the choice of sin is genuinely a free act, then freedom itself must be corrupt, or the self would always choose the highest good. In this case Knudson would have to add this consideration to his doctrine. Or, if the self cannot resist temptation, then freedom disappears, in which case non-volitional factors would have to be cited not only as the occasion but also as the cause of sin. Knudson does not admit to this dilemma in his formulation of the problem, but it is real nonetheless. However, there are three other factors which Knudson mentions which do not eliminate this dilemma altogether, but which at least reduce the distance between the two alternatives. First of all, he insists that sin does not arise out of conscious hostility to God, except in extreme cases. Secondly, sin is never a deliberate choice of pure evil but a choice of a lesser good in the presence of a higher good. Thirdly, ignorance is usually involved as one factor. Thus, at the beginning of sin there is little consciousness of wrongdoing.

The entrance into sin, then, is a gradual, imperceptible, almost unconscious process. The self does not deliberately plunge into sin but eases into wrongdoing and acquires guilt by gradual stages.[38] This continuity between the stage of innocence and the feeble beginnings of sin and between freedom and inevitability enables Knudson to reduce the factor of deliberate choice to the extent that freedom does not appear to be basically corrupt. At the same time, it enables him to retain the idea of freedom sufficiently to speak of accountable guilt. Hence, he is not even conscious of a dilemma because he has overcome it by practically merging the alternatives on the basis of a skillful use of the all-pervading principle of continuity.

Liberals were very anxious to relieve God of the responsibility for sin. Knudson, for example, affirms that God is responsible for sin, not in causing it, but only in creating the possibilities under which it could (and almost certainly would) arise. God probably foresaw sin but yet permitted it in view of his "faith in the power of his own redemptive agency."[39] That complete avoidance of sin is practically impossible is no indication that God purposed its existence as part of his divine plan. "Rather it is an evidence of the divine faith in man, in his spiritual independence, in his high destiny, and in his ability to avail himself of the resources of divine grace."[40] That God himself is thought to share liberalism's faith in man is evidence of the assurance with which this conviction was held.

3. THE DOCTRINE OF SALVATION

The principle of continuity dominates the liberal conception of salvation, as it does every other doctrine. Thus, Knudson teaches that salvation is both religious and ethical, individual and social, present and future. The terms of each of these pairs are bound up with each other and are harmoniously related to each other. The significance of the principle of continuity may be clearly seen by contrasting Knudson's doctrine of salvation with that of Reinhold Niebuhr. Niebuhr is a dialectical thinker who develops his thought by setting over against one statement a contrary statement which stands in balanced tension with the first. He contends that to dissolve this tension in the interests of logical clarity runs the risk of obscuring essential factors which enter into the total situation. Following this procedure, Niebuhr speaks of the tension between being redeemed in principle and being redeemed in fact, of moral man and immoral society, and of the contrast between redemption in history and redemption beyond history.[41] Thus, where Knudson sees harmony and continuity, Niebuhr sees paradox and discontinuity.

Salvation has both a Godward (religious) and a manward (ethical) aspect. With reference to God salvation involves repentance and faith. The redeemed life begins in conversion and continues as a process of growth in grace. Justification, sanctification, regeneration, and election are metaphors which point to the religious aspect of salvation. On the ethical side the Christian life is characterized by an outgoing, positive attitude toward the goodne s of the world and the physical life. The dynamic of the moral life is the ideal embodied in Jesus, whose impact on human personality today awakens in men a response which makes love the controlling motive of their lives.

Knudson contends that Christianity adds its greatest impetus to ethics by setting the moral life within the context of the Christian world view with its conception of God and its high estimate of the worth of man. The moral ideal of Christianity centers in the idea of sacrificial love. Underlying this ideal is the presupposition that the way to personal self-realization is through the sacrificial service of others. The Christian ideal can thus be defined as "the perfect and harmonious union of self-love with the love of others."[42] In *The Principles of Christian Ethics* Knudson further develops his concept of Christian love. He accepts the Augustinian synthesis of *agape* and *eros,* contending that there is no conflict between them. Here again the principle of continuity is determinative.

This characteristic liberal view stands in sharp contrast to the discontinuities which some recent Christian ethicists find in the concept of love. Paul Ramsey insists that self-love cannot be allowed under any circumstances on the ground floor of Christian ethics; Anders Nygren sees an irreconcilable conflict between *agape* and *eros;* and Reinhold Niebuhr makes a paradoxical distinction between sacrificial love and mutual love.[43] In Ramsey's inverted self-love, in Nygren's *agape,* and in Niebuhr's sacrificial love, the good of the self is practically excluded from consideration as a legitimate motive in Christian moral action.

4. SOCIAL SALVATION

Individual salvation and social salvation are closely related in the thought of Knudson, although he gives relatively less attention to the social gospel than do Brown, Fosdick, and Rauschenbusch. Moreover, the element of other-worldliness is slightly more prominent in Knudson than in the preceding thinkers. The Christian ideal for society is the kingdom of God. Knudson recognizes, however, that this is not exactly the sense in which Jesus originally used the term. Knudson is writing after Weiss, Schweitzer, and others had re-established the apocalyptical interpretation of the kingdom. Nevertheless, Knudson feels that the modern practice of interpreting the kingdom as an ideal human society is legitimate, and he follows this trend. The modern conception of the kingdom, he says, owes its rise to the belief in social progress and the influence of the doctrine of divine immanence. The kingdom of God is now defined as "the progressive amelioration of human life" and this is "commonly regarded as an end to be achieved through the steadily increasing co-operation of the human with the divine will."[44]

But while the social hope is necessary and valid, the main emphasis of religion, Knudson feels, should be on man's eternal hope. Furthermore, while real social progress can be expected, the social ideal can never be fully reached in human history. As soon as one problem is solved, another rises to take its place. Knudson affirms that fundamentally the kingdom of God is within. This does not mean that the social struggle is futile or that it yields no real or permanent value. It does mean that "the human spirit is too large for its earthly environment, that man is 'overendowed with qualities and powers for which the world finds no worthy place.' "[45] Whatever else one may say about Knudson's theology, he cannot legitimately say that he dissolved the Gospel into a message of social idealism or that he is utopian with regard to the prospects for the future of man on earth.

D. *The Person and Work of Christ*

1. THE PERSON OF CHRIST

No part of Knudson's theology is more typically liberal than his Christology.[46] He rejects the static, dualistic, and impersonal elements in the orthodox view of Christ based on the older doctrine of the transcendence of God and Greek philosophy. He substitutes for this a dynamic, monistic, ethical concept of the person of Christ based on a doctrine of immanence and personalistic idealism. As a result of the complete dependence of Jesus upon the will of God and his unequaled interaction with the divine Spirit, there was produced in him a "unique God-consciousness, in which God was actually present and which made Jesus both the ideal man and the perfect organ of the divine revelation."[47] Knudson maintains that this view of Christ, which he calls the "consciousness and dependence theory," is more theistic and more personalistic than the orthodox view in that it preserves both the unique, ultimate, and underivable character of personal unity and the distinct individuality of God and man.

Knudson contends that three specific changes are called for in the new doctrine of Christ's person. First of all, complete humanity must be attributed to Jesus, including the idea that his personal center, his ego, was like that of other men. Secondly, the uniqueness of Jesus is not due to the presence of two natures within him but to his unique dependence upon the divine will and to his unique endowment with the Spirit. Thirdly, divinity must be ascribed to Jesus, not because of his possession of omnipotence or omniscience, but because of his unique consciousness of oneness with God and because of his function in founding the kingdom of God. What makes this sort of Christology possible, of course, is the presupposition of the doctrine of immanence. Knudson insists, however, that his doctrine of immanence achieves the same religious result as the older doctrine of incarnation. The purpose of both doctrines, he says, is to bring God near to man. The doctrine of incarnation presupposes a metaphysical and ethical dualism between God and man and finds the presence of God supremely in one unique event, whereas the doctrine of immanence finds God everywhere. However, there are degrees of immanence, the supreme degree of immanence being found in Christ. Hence, God is present in a unique way in Christ, and this, in a sense, amounts to incarnation. There is continuity between the doctrine of incarnation and the doctrine of immanence, and in Christ the two merge. There is continuity also between Christ and other men. "The incarnation in Christ . . . needs to be supplemented by the idea of an incarnation in mankind as a whole and also in nature."[48] At no point, then, is a radical break or gulf to be found in this scheme. Nature, ordinary men, Christ, and God are all part of one organic whole. Knudson differs from absolute idealism in that he insists on the distinct individuality of human persons and of the personality of God, but the monistic tendencies are strong even in personalism.

2. THE WORK OF CHRIST

Doctrines of atonement can be conveniently classified as objective and subjective. Theories of the former type insist that reconciliation is conditioned upon a change within God or in the objective situation in which man exists. Either God's justice must be satisfied, or evil powers which enslave man must be conquered. The latter theories dismiss these objective factors and insist that only man's attitude and orientation to God need to be changed. These two ways of viewing atonement are not mutually exclusive, but thinkers characteristically tend to emphasize one aspect more than the other. Orthodox thinkers tend toward the objective theories. Liberals as a group were found in the subjective camp. Knudson, for example, rejects outright every major objective theory which has been developed in Christian history. All of them, he says, represent God as being hampered or controlled in his relation to men by non-personal factors. Even more objectionable, says Knudson, from a personalistic viewpoint is the abstract way in which merit, guilt, and punishment are dealt with in these theories. Moral and personal realities are treated as though they could be abstracted from personality and transferred from one account to another.

Knudson proposes in place of these objective theories a subjective theory, which he calls the moral or personal theory.[49] The moral theory, which was first stated explicitly by Abelard, differs from the other doctrines, he says, in concentrating on the manward side rather than on the devilward side (the ransom theory) or on the Godward side (the satisfaction, penal, and governmental theories). The real question is not how God can be appeased or reconciled but how man can be redeemed. The obstacle to salvation is not in God, for God is love and ever willing to forgive. The obstacle is in man's waywardness, selfishness, and indifference. It is from this standpoint alone that the death of Christ should be interpreted. The problem should be approached, he maintains, purely in the light of moral and spiritual dynamics. In the death of Christ are to be found two great sources of redemptive power, the revelation of divine love and perfect example of devotion to duty. In sacrificing his life for the kingdom of God, Jesus revealed his own personal holiness and unveiled the character of God. The significance of the Cross, then, is its revelational value, and it has this because of the incarnation.

In the background of this moral influence theory is a doctrine of God in which the element of wrath or holiness has been absorbed into divine love. This continuity between holiness and love makes an objective atonement unnecessary. The suppression of holiness is in turn connected with the tendency to view sin as weakness of spirit rather than as a deliberate usurpation of the divine prerogatives on the part of a rebellious self. Thus, the abandonment of the serious view of sin held by orthodoxy makes possible the easy harmonization of the divine holiness and love. In short, liberalism lessens the stress on the divine judgment against man and the need for an objective reconciliation within the divine life, by which wrath is neutralized, and emphasizes the human need of being morally empowered in order to overcome the drag of nature on a free and virtuous but weak spirit.

E. *The Doctrine of the Church*

Two convictions concerning the church basic in all liberalism appear clearly in Knudson: the instrumental nature of the church and the priority of present Christian experience over tradition. The first conviction means that the church is not an end in itself but only an instrument for realizing the kingdom of God. The second means that the church is not dependent on, or bound to, the patterns of the past. Rather, it is free to organize itself in such a way as best to realize its purposes in the contemporary world. Its divinity does not depend on any special supernatural origin but only on the fact that its spirit is akin to the spirit of Christ. The church, then, according to Knudson is a purely moral and spiritual community which arose under the impact of the personality and teachings of Jesus. However, since the church arose as a fellowship of the Spirit, the Holy Spirit may also be said to be the author of the church. It does not depend for its validity upon the continuity of a particular institution, upon a particular form of the ministry, or upon any kind of historical guarantees.

The ministry is divine, but this fact is not based upon a divine command, nor is its authority dependent upon apostolic succession. "It is divine because it arose in harmony with the divine will and does a divine work." This conception is based on the doctrine of divine immanence and on a doctrine of a divine "call" to the ministry to certain persons. The means of grace are the Word and the sacraments. The Word is primary, but the sacraments are also important for the reason that "the unseen may be symbolized by the seen and that divine truth and grace may in this way be communicated more effectively to the human mind and heart than by the spoken word."[51] Baptism and the Lord's Supper "symbolize and mediate the spiritual influence exercised by Christian society upon the individual. In this sense they may be said to represent an objective or superindividual reality, but it is only in this sense that they do so."[52]

F. *Conclusion*

If the primary aim of the ethical-social liberals was to show that Christianity was practically relevant, Knudson's life purpose was to demonstrate that Christianity was rationally convincing as well. He agreed with the earlier Platonic conception of theology as the philosophy of the Christian religion, and he was firmly convinced that personalism provided the clue both to philosophical and theological truth. Another prominent thinker who accepted Knudson's view of the necessity of exploring theoretical foundations of theology but who found philosophical truth elsewhere than in metaphysical idealism was Eugene W. Lyman, whose outlook will be examined next.

CHAPTER 7

EVOLUTIONARY THEISM:
EUGENE W. LYMAN

Eugene William Lyman (1872–1948) was born in Cummington, Massachusetts. He was reared in a Congregationalist home in which a "liberal orthodoxy" of the type represented by Horace Bushnell prevailed. He attended Amherst College and later went to Yale Divinity School for his training in theology. Like many other students of his generation he went to Germany for further preparation after he had completed his work in America. During his two years there he studied with Reischle, Kaftan, Hermann, and Harnack. He returned to America and in 1901 began teaching Philosophy and Psychology at Carleton College in Minnesota. After three years at Carleton and one year in Montreal, Lyman took a position at Bangor Seminary in Maine, teaching Theology there for eight years. Shortly before World War I he returned to Europe for more study, this time taking work with Bergson, Eucken, and Troeltsch. In 1913 Lyman moved to Oberlin School of Theology, where he occupied the chair of Christian Ethics and Philosophy of Religion. In 1918 he became Marcellus Hartley Professor of Philosophy of Religion at Union Theological Seminary in New York, a position which he held until his retirement in 1940.[1]

Lyman was an evangelical liberal in that he found in Christ a permanent and irreplaceable norm for the religious life and theology.[2] He was a metaphysical liberal because, like Knudson, he thought it imperative for theology to correlate Christian convictions with some appropriate world view. He was primarily a philosopher of religion and devoted relatively little attention to many of those problems which

127

fall within the more narrow province of systematic theology. Only one article in a long list of his writings is concerned with the Bible. He practically ignored the doctrine of the church and the Trinity, although he dealt in some detail with Christology. Lyman concentrated on those issues which have a more philosophical bearing, such as epistemology, metaphysics, and the doctrines of God, man, immortality, etc. As a Christian thinker he was concerned to incorporate a Christocentric religion into a defensible, modern philosophical outlook.

Lyman's thought kept growing and changing throughout his career. Early in his theological pilgrimage he accepted the Ritschlian theology with its emphasis on the historical Jesus and its ethical interest centered around the kingdom of God. His reading of Kant and Schleiermacher convinced him of the autonomy of ethics and religion and that these two areas of experience have their own reports to make of reality which are as valid as the findings of natural science and philosophy. However, he was dissatisfied with the metaphysical agnosticism inherent in Kant and Ritschl, and he continued to search for a basis for religion in some reasoned theory of the nature of things. It was pragmatism which provided for him the kind of foundation which he believed to be essential. In his first book, *Theology and Human Problems,* published in 1910, he tried to show that pragmatism provided a way of developing a dynamic, empirical, ethical, theistic metaphysics which is congenial to Christian belief. But this was only the beginning. A reading of Troeltsch, Rauschenbusch, and the creative evolutionists added other ingredients to this thinking. After World War I Lyman's thought moved generally in those directions marked out by the rising tide of neo-orthodoxy. His greatest work, *The Meaning and Truth of Religion,* published in 1933, reflects new emphases drawn from twentieth-century social catastrophes, the new science, the realistic movement in epistemology, process philosophy, and the newer currents in theology.[3] It is, however, fundamentally a liberal volume. In the years following he moved slightly more in the direction of neo-orthodoxy. In short, at the end of his career it may be said that Lyman was a chastened liberal but a liberal nonetheless.[4]

A. *Theology and Philosophy of Religion*

1. THEOLOGY

Lyman gives a thoroughly liberal presentation of the function of theology. The role of theology, he says, must be determined in relation to the assured results of modern theology, by which he means, of course, nineteenth-century liberal theology. These established conclusions include the conviction that theology is distinct from religion and subordinate to it (Schleiermacher), that the historical method must be used to investigate Christianity and other religions (Hegel and Ritschl), and that morality and religion are inseparable.[5] It is interesting to notice at this point that the three convictions which Lyman mentions here involve, in turn, aspects of the principle of autonomy, the principle of dynamism, and the principle of continuity. He concludes that "the special function of the Christian theologian is by the methods of the philosophy of religion to discover and interpret the essential nature of Christianity, thereby aiding in its further development and that of life as a whole."[6] A persistent conviction of Lyman, and one basic to liberalism, is that theology is fundamentally a practical enterprise. "Theologies are judged, in the long run, not by their symmetry or elaborateness, but by their contribution to the solution of human problems."[7] Two theological methods, he says, may be distinguished, that of the cloister and that of the clinic. The first protects religion on the basis of existing philosophies and employs an *a priori* method. The latter aims to develop religion by discovering its essential nature and employs the method of experience. Lyman makes it perfectly clear that he prefers the clinic to the cloister.

2. PHILOSOPHY OF RELIGION

a. *Pragmatism*

In his earliest period Lyman was convinced that pragmatism offered the most fruitful way of making religion intellectually sound and practically relevant. Pragmatism makes will prior to intellect and tests truth by its practical consequences in experience. It is able, he felt, to preserve the values offered by absolute idealism (the idea of immanence) and of Ritschlianism (the emphasis on moral faith and historical revelation) without falling into its errors.[8]

In an article in this early period entitled "Must Dogmatics Forego Ontology?"[9] Lyman concludes that Ritschl performed a great service to theology by foregoing ontology in the interest of ethical religion in his fight against the use of ontology by absolute idealism and by orthodoxy. However, he contends that ethical religion itself needs an empirical ontology (1) to defend the reality of religious experience,

(2) to support the ethical interpretation of the universe, and (3) to justify the faith that moral personality is a constructive factor in the universe.

In *Theology and Human Problems,* written in 1910, Lyman spells out a little further the direction which an empirical theology based on pragmatism must take. Pragmatism recognizes the primacy of faith and the value of experience but goes on to set the truth of Christianity into the larger framework of a comprehensive empirical metaphysics. The theory of religious knowledge which results synthesizes the historical revelation in Christ with immediate personal experience. Christ reveals through the excellence of his moral character the nature of the Infinite Moral Power who is at work in us as the Immanent Spirit creating and developing ethical personality. Thus, on the basis of the principle of continuity Lyman is able to unite the experiential and the revelational sides of his thought. There is no conflict between the experience of God in the present and the revelation of God in the past in Christ; the latter merely clarifies the former. Neither is there any gap between the knowledge of God derived from other sources and that found in Christ; the latter represents simply the highest degree of truth. This Christocentric way of joining experience to revelation is basic to evangelical liberalism and has already been seen clearly both in Brown and Fosdick and is implicit in Rauschenbusch and Knudson.

b. *Realism*

In the mature period of his thought Lyman moved from pragmatism to realism. This shift reflects the response of Lyman to a number of contemporary intellectual movements, and it involves a modification of some of the fundamental principles of this thinking. In particular, this change marks a break with subjectivism and relativism in epistemology, cosmology, ethics, and religion.[10] Moreover, the liberal principles of autonomy and continuity are qualified. Reality is now interpreted as a realm over against man with its own given structure and not as a system of phenomena which is patterned from within by a projection of the necessities of the theoretical and practical reason. Moral and religious experience are now not thought to be determinative of reality but as determined by reality. Moreover, a new element of transcendence now informs Lyman's doctrine of God, and the idea of revelation comes to play an indispensable role. Nevertheless, Lyman does not break with liberalism altogether, for experience is still foundational, and the continuity between transcendence and immanence is not abandoned. The results of this new orientation are worked out systematically in *The Meaning and Truth of Religion,* published in 1933. Here Lyman develops a realistic epistemology based on a synthesis of intuition, reason, and faith.[11] Intuition is a direct and immediate apprehension of an objective order of being and a realm of value which yields insights which are true and dependable in the areas of science, ethics, and religion.[12] Reason tests these intuitive insights in terms of their contribution to, and coherence with, some comprehensive understanding of the totality of things. Faith is trust in God as Cosmic Moral Will and adventurous commitment to discovered and tested values by which religious truth comes into its fullest realization.

c. *Conclusion*

Theology and philosophy of religion are closely related in Lyman's thought. There is no sharp distinction either between knowledge in general and religious knowledge or between religious knowledge and the Christian revelation. Lyman can easily connect the teachings of Jesus with similar intuitions which other men have. He can move smoothly from a discussion of religious truth as discerned according to the methods of the philosophy of religion to the truth known through Christ. The intuitions accepted in faith and tested by reason within the Christian community represent simply one systematic body of insights which are continuous with other religions and religious philosophies. Revelation, then, cannot possibly be conceived to stand in contradiction to reason or experience. Philosophy of religion and systematic theology tend to merge in liberalism, and this is but another manifestation of the principle of continuity.

B. *The Doctrine of God*

1. THE PERIOD OF PRAGMATISM

In his thought about God Lyman moved from a conception of God based on the pragmatism of James to a view developed in connection with the new cosmology of Whitehead and others. In each case his conclusions represent a synthesis of the Christian tradition, religious experience, and modern science. His earliest book, *Theology and Human Problems,* points out the contributions of pragmatism to the doctrine of God. In the first place, pragmatism recognizes that the interpretation of nature depends on the postulates of the mind, to which moral and religious experience can contribute. This offers a way of escape from scientific materialism and mechanism. Secondly, pragmatism contributes the idea of a growing universe which (1) accepts the reality of time and (2) recognizes the emergence of new levels of being which (3) enlarge and enrich the existing order of things. All of this seems to make it intellectually possible to believe in the Christian view of a dynamic moral being who acts to realize his purposes. This belief seems to Lyman to be validated by the continuous upward development of man's moral life. Rejecting James's pluralism and his finite God, Lyman arrives at a view which sees the universe as the manifestation of a creative Power, who by means of his immanent activity, progressively brings all things into harmony with one increasing divine purpose. Thus, at this point, Lyman confidently affirms the continuity between natural evolution and human progress and between the transcendent purposes of God and their gradual immanent realization in nature and history.

2. THE PERIOD OF TRANSITION

It was World War I which first shook the confidence of Lyman and his generation in the theory of certain progress. It was at the end of this conflict that Karl Barth issued his devastating attack on immanentism which marked the demise of liberalism in Europe. In America, however, the impact was not so immediately felt. It was not until men became disillusioned with the moral justification of World War I and until further tragedies struck, particularly the depression of 1929, that social progress was seriously called into question. Reinhold Niebuhr's *Moral Man and Immoral Society,* published in 1932, can be conveniently referred to as marking the end of progress thinking in America, as Barth's *Römerbrief* had done for Europe. But while belief in progress was not given up by liberals after 1918, the war did force renewed attention upon the problem of social evil. Writings after 1918 generally are more cautious than those which appeared before that time. Lyman's reaction to World War I was typical of the response of liberals in general.

In *The Experience of God in Modern Life,* published in 1918,

Lyman sees about him, as he had previously, a universe in the making in which God and man are co-operating to realize the tremendous potentialities of meaning and value inherent in the world process. He continues to find validation for the belief in progress in the actual moral advance of mankind and in the fact of emergent evolution. However, he reveals a greater consciousness of the depth and persistence of evil and points out that God works under certain limitations in his creative efforts to introduce universal harmony into nature and history. He manages to preserve his belief in the doctrine of immanence and in the goodness of God by referring evil either to the freedom of men or to the necessities of the cosmic process. Thus, while he does not break with progress thinking, he does give indications that his previous confidence has been shaken.[13]

3. THE PERIOD OF REALISM

A further shift in Lyman's thought becomes evident in *The Meaning and Truth of Religion*. The familiar pattern of seeking evidence for the reality and goodness of God in the evolutionary processes of nature and history appears again. Lyman now appeals to the newer developments in physics and biology and to the cosmology of Whitehead, all of which seem to him to corroborate belief in a creative, progress-making God. It is possible, however, to detect even greater concern than before with the problem of evil. Evil arises from the contingency, spontaneity, and freedom of finite centers of being and activity which introduce discord and conflict into the world. God is not immanent in these destructive processes as such, but he works within them to overcome disharmony and to transmute evil into good. This recognition of the power of evil, along with other factors, results in an increased emphasis on the transcendence of God. God is immanent in man and nature, but he works partly in opposition to them. The reality, individuality, and spontaneity of finite centers of being and the freedom of men result in natural and moral evils which are contrary to God's will. However, this does not mean that Lyman has any great sympathy with the Crisis Theology of Barth and Brunner. He accuses them of holding to an untenable dualism which breaks the connection between man and God, between faith and reason, between the historical Jesus and the divine Lord, and between the transcendence and immanence of God. Lyman is still fundamentally a liberal, and he still holds to the possibility and reality of moral and social progress as men respond to God's creative efforts and join with him in bringing into being the Beloved Community, which is the historical goal of the divine purpose.

4. SUMMARY

In short, Lyman has set forth a view of God which can be described as evolutionary, ethical theism. His interest in the doctrine of God was motivated primarily by a concern to discover cosmic support for the moral advance of man, and thus he always saw God fundamentally in relation to the creation and preservation of human values. He relied heavily upon the doctrine of emergent evolution and the reality of moral and social progress for evidence of the existence of a cosmic Power and Purpose. These elements remained constant throughout his career. Many features which are usually found in Christian treatments of the doctrine of God are missing. This is due in part to his primary interest in the philosophy of religion rather than in systematic theology, but, as has already been pointed out, these two disciplines tend to merge in liberalism. Missing also is any detailed concern with the internal being of God, either with reference to the Trinity or to the attributes of God. This may reflect a continuing influence of Ritschlian agnosticism and is surely connected also with the conviction that only those doctrines which have a clear practical relevance are worth dealing with.

C. *The Doctrine of Man*

1. THE NATURE OF MAN

Lyman develops his doctrine of man most fully in *The Meaning and Truth of Religion*.[14] The problems which most concern him are the reality of the self, the question of freedom, the conquest of evil, and the possibility of immortality. His thought is developed in the light of recent findings of biology, emergent evolution, and the new physics rather than in the light of the teachings of the Bible and the history of Christian thought. The absence of traditional terminology reflects his orientation as a philosopher of religion rather than as a theologian, but presumably he believes that his account of man is adequate from a Christian point of view without further contributions from the theologians. Implicit in the situation is the principle of continuity which makes it easy for Lyman to feel that what is really relevant from the Bible and from the history of Christian doctrine is also available from, or at least harmonious with, the findings of modern science and philosophy.

The study of evolution, Lyman feels, has demonstrated the reality of final causation in the universe. "Mind is a true emergent in the course of evolution and contributes guidance. And this is intelligible only if the emergent mind, in its mental character, is efficacious amidst physiological and psychical processes."[15] Moreover, the new cosmology, with its doctrines of panpsychism and indeterminacy, tends to bring human nature and physical nature into closer approximation. Lyman concludes that man belongs to nature, but his spiritual capacities and achievements illumine the nature from whence he has emerged. He sees man as a unity of body and mind, each of which interacts upon the other. This view requires the recognition of a genuine, unique center of selfhood possessing the capacities of self-consciousness, memory, anticipation, and freedom of choice. He makes use of the principle of dynamism to relate human freedom to divine sovereignty in that he affirms a process in which finite wills grow into oneness with the divine will as men become co-workers with God. This would seem to imply a doctrine of universal salvation, but he does not explicitly draw this conclusion in this connection. This conception of man leads to a belief in immortality, based on the premise that the self has a measure of genuine independence and a capacity for spiritual attainment such that the fate of the body cannot determine its final destiny.

2. THE PROBLEM OF EVIL

Mary Frances Thelen has spoken of the chronic neglect of the doctrine of sin among liberal thinkers.[16] Lyman may be fairly offered as an example of this tendency. While one ordinarily would not expect a philosopher of religion to deal in detail with the doctrine of sin as a special category, it can be said that he neglects the problem in the sense that in comparison with orthodox and neo-orthodox thinkers he underestimates the depths of moral evil in man. He agrees with the main line of Christian tradition in insisting that sin is man's most serious problem, but he does not follow this tradition in interpreting this seriousness in terms of a basic corruption of man's essential nature. Rather, he views sin in characteristic liberal fashion as a kind of weakness which may be progressively overcome as the spirit of man is strengthened by education and fellowship with God. The individual is also assisted by the fact of social progress. Moreover, he insists that all of these redemptive factors are undergirded by the upward trend in the cosmos itself. The result is a view of moral evil which stands in sharp contrast to most recent Christian analyses of the human plight. An example of Lyman's neglect of the power of evil in man is his statement in *The Meaning and Truth of Religion,* published in 1933, to the effect that Germany will not long tolerate a dictatorship, if she ever resorts to one at all, because of the high educational standards which prevail there.[17]

Lyman maintains that man is subject to three forms of evil: suffering, frustration, and sin. Suffering is physical evil which results from circumstances beyond human control. Frustration results from the defeat of human purposes. Sin is the gravest form of evil, "for this form of evil corrupts that which has intrinsic worth—personality— and is the chief source of the defeat of the highest good—a universal community of creative personalities."[18] Lyman defines sin as "moral evil seen as transgression against the total system of spiritual relationships to which man belongs or into which he may enter—against men as sons of God and against God as the Eternal Good Will."[19] While sin is most characteristically thought of in terms of those evil deeds which men do for which they are clearly and consciously responsible, Lyman affirms that sin also "denotes the rupture of moral and spiritual relationships even when it is largely unwitting."[20] Moreover, in sinning men choose consciously to forget.

In this view sin is continuous with other forms of evil. While human misuse of freedom plays a part, the seriousness of sin as deliberate wrongdoing is reduced in characteristic liberal fashion by relating it to inertia, atavism, ignorance, and social maladjustment. Lyman knows nothing about depraved sinners in the hands of an angry God, for both the notes of corrupt human nature and of wrathful divine judgment are missing. Men are basically sound in their essential nature because of their kinship to God. Their basic difficulty seems to be their immaturity, but nothing is really wrong that more rapid growth, enlightenment, and social reform cannot solve. Moral good will inspired through religion can lead men to join with God in the creation of the Beloved Community on earth. The principle of dynamism, interpreted here in terms of moral progress, then, offers a clue to the solution of the basic evils which afflict men. This, added to Lyman's belief in emergent evolution at the level of nature, is the basis for an optimistic outlook on life and on the future of mankind on this planet.

3. THE MEANING OF SALVATION

Lyman's doctrine of salvation is congruous both with his view of evil and with his whole metaphysical scheme. The world is a vast process of development toward higher stages and greater complexity. Evil is the conflict and disharmony which result from a failure on the part of persons to integrate themselves properly with the progressive tendencies in the total structure of the ongoing world process. It is lack of adaptation to the creative advance of the universe. In the light of this background Lyman defines salvation as wholeness or integrity of being. All religion, he says, is an "experience of securing spiritual integrity, whether arrived at by growth, maintained against disruptive forces, or regained by human faith and divine grace."[21] The kind of salvation that Christianity offers, he maintains, comes by way of transformation. Human nature is neither hopelessly bad nor perfectly good at the start, and the world is neither divine nor demonic. But a dynamic process may take place in which human beings are transformed by the creative processes in nature and in history in such a way that moral advance occurs as human actions are harmonized with the divine purpose for the world.

Lyman contended that real progress toward the overcoming of evil is possible and that history over the long run manifests a trend upward. However, in *The Meaning and Truth of Religion* he remarks that "our previous study of the new cosmology and of the new interpretations of evolution should not lead us to look for any automatic progress in history nor to conceive progress as something to be easily achieved."[22]

The hope which Lyman here expresses is somewhat less optimistic than his wartime lectures some fifteen years earlier. Yet, the belief in progress is still strong. Horton points out that in Lyman's writings after 1935, however, an even more drastic change in his ideas regarding the attainment of the kingdom of God on earth can be noted. It was the world depression, Horton remarks, together with the spread of nationalism and militarism, "which finally broke Lyman's faith in liberal progressivism, and opened his mind to neo-orthodox criticism."[23] In articles published in 1938 and 1940 Lyman was saying that the kingdom of God presents a goal which is relevant to history but transcendent to it as an end by which every historic movement must be judged. In his farewell address upon his retirement from Union in 1940, Lyman conceded that "the hope of 'a happy prosperous social environment,' trust in 'democratic political institutions,' or 'scientific culture' are but broken reeds today."[24] Only a hold on Eternal Reality is sufficient, he maintained. Nevertheless, even at this point Lyman never severed the transcendent goal of history from the possibility of realizing that goal on earth, although the distance between the goal and the attainment has been widened considerably. God was still seen to be immanent in the historic process bringing order out of chaos, and new realizations of the community of love, he believed, were still possible.

D. Christology

1. THE EARLY PERIOD

There are two primary sources for Lyman's Christology in the period under consideration. The first is his earliest book, *Theology and Human Problems*. The second is an article in *The Journal of Religion* in 1929, entitled "The Place of Christ in Modern Theology."

a. The Contribution of Jesus to Religion

In *Theology and Human Problems* Lyman deals with three issues which were always central to his thinking: (1) the direct apprehension of the immanent God in religious experience, (2) the importance of historical revelation, and (3) the development of moral personality as the goal of religion. Lyman concludes that the synthesis of all of these elements is to be found in Paul's conception of the Spirit. In Paul's thought and experience "two elements were perfectly blended —the fullest and richest moral activity and the consciousness of the indwelling presence of God."[25] Both of these were related to the historical revelation in Christ. It is just at this point and in this context that Lyman discovers the significance of Jesus. The abiding importance of Jesus for the religious life of the world consists in his transformation of ethical monotheism by effecting *"a synthesis between the religion of divine immanence and the religion of ethical personality,* thus protecting the latter from legalism and the former from vague mysticism, and giving to both an unparalleled depth and intensity."[26] Lyman, then, finds in the historical revelation in Jesus a union of the mystical experience of God with an active ethical endeavor which leads to the fulfillment of personality. Moreover, the unique perfection of Jesus' personality enables him to have such an impact on the lives of other men that he draws them into the religion of the Spirit which Paul had and in which mystical, historical, and ethical elements are harmoniously balanced.

b. *Historical Revelation and Religious Experience*

The type of Christology which Lyman espouses at this time may be called mystical Ritschlianism. It illustrates clearly the attempt which the evangelical liberals made to preserve the union of the historical revelation in Christ with the present apprehension of God in religious experience. The more the reality and value of the present experience of God is stressed the more the tendency is to neglect the importance of the revelation of God in Christ, particularly when the doctrine of immanence is assumed. The extreme example of a religion of experience alone is to be found in certain types of mysticism. The evangelical liberals believed that God is present everywhere both in nature and in man, and therefore he can be apprehended directly by all men here and now. Some, like Brown and Fosdick, stressed the moral element in religious experience, while others, like Rauschenbusch and Lyman, made more room for mysticism. Yet, all of them insisted that the believer's present experience of God is mediated through Christ. They saw continuity, of course, between moral values in general and the values of Christ and between the mystic's direct apprehension of God and Paul's historically grounded religion of the Spirit. But, regardless of whether they stressed the mystical or the moral aspects of religion, they all insisted that the unique revelation of God in Christ was indispensable for the believer's present religious life. The impact of the personality and the spirit of Jesus was thought to enter directly into the determination of the Christian's experience of God. These liberal thinkers, then, had no place for an unhistorical, unmediated apprehension of God characteristic of extreme mysticism. This description of the way in which the evangelical liberals preserved the union between the revelational and the experiential sides of Christianity also holds for Rufus Jones, who has been the most outstanding liberal exponent of mystical religion. It is true that the focus of his attention was on the direct and immediate apprehension of God in recurring states of mystical ecstasy. Nevertheless, in principle, Jones agreed with his fellow evangelicals.[27]

c. The Meaning of Atonement

Lyman also takes up the problem of atonement in his earliest book. Like Knudson, he insists that atonement is a completely moral term and must be disassociated from all commercial, penal, and governmental theories with which it has been connected in the past. Lyman means by atonement *"the process of recovering the sinful personality into a life with God, and of neutralizing the moral wrong done by man to man, through the power of self-sacrificing love."*[28] This means that both the taint which sin leaves in the wrongdoer and the injuries which are inflicted on others will have to be erased. The first is accomplished by the moral influence of Christ and of other superior personalities upon the sinner, which purifies the springs of moral action within him. The second is accomplished (1) by the healing effects of the natural forces in the universe which neutralize the effects of sin and (2) by efforts to remove the agencies which inflict injury. By this last item Lyman connects himself with the social gospel movement. The social causes of evil will have to be dealt with as well as the individual sinner.

It is worthwhile to notice the operation of the principle of continuity in this view of atonement. First of all, Lyman maintains that the death of Christ is not a unique act of redemption accomplished once and for all at Calvary. Rather, the work of Christ is continuous with the everlasting efforts of God to save men. He urges that "to limit atonement to a single event in history, however full of tragic sublimity we may know that event to be, is to narrow its power and to rob the faith in God's Fatherhood of its deepest meaning."[29] In the second place, Lyman insists on the connection between the atoning work of Jesus and that of other men. The principle of continuity, then, connects the work of Christ both with the eternal act of atonement in the divine life and with the works of reconciliation which the disciples of Jesus accomplish in history.

2. THE LATER PERIOD

Nearly twenty years later Lyman raised the question of Christology again, this time in an article in *The Journal of Religion*. The title of

the article, "The Place of Jesus Christ in Modern Theology," repro-
duced the name of the great book of Fairbairn written more than
three decades earlier. Lyman raises the question as to whether Fairbairn's estimate of Jesus as a unique creative personality can still be
sustained in the light of new knowledge and new problems which
have come to light since that time, and he gives an affirmative answer.
Jesus is still central for our understanding of man and God and for
our ideals and way of life. Moreover, Jesus is relevant for our own
religious lives because we learn from him a religion which combines
moral and religious creativeness, ethical endeavor, and mystical communion with God. Finally, Jesus is uniquely creative because "he was
the personal embodiment of truths which are permanently central for
the spiritual life of mankind."[30] Among these permanent truths are
man's sonship to God, the supremacy of love, the power of faith, the
human soul as having intrinsic worth, the conquest of evil by self-
giving, suffering love, the coming of a kingdom of God on earth, and
a God whose nature expresses these principles and with whom we
are related.

Horton feels that in this later period Lyman has gone beyond his
earlier Ritschlian emphasis on the ethical leadership and religious
excellence of Jesus and at least implicitly is affirming a metaphysical
doctrine of Christ's eternal sonship. He never worked this out on the
basis of his mature philosophy, but Horton thinks that on the basis
of principles enunciated in *The Meaning and Truth of Religion* the
task could be undertaken. Lyman "has no objection in principle, then,
to the Christological dogmas of the Greek Fathers, *in so far as they
represent a philosophical interpretation of the universal moral-religious
significance of the actual historical Jesus.*"[31] Horton goes on to say
that the reason that Lyman never attempted to reinterpret the historic
dogmas in the light of his own metaphysics is that the rise of the
Crisis Theology raised new problems which diverted the attention of
Lyman into other channels. What Lyman objects to in the theology
of Barth and Brunner is the discontinuity which they insist on between
the historical revelation in Christ and man's own highest ideas and
values.[32] Thus, whatever changes may have occurred in Lyman's
thought in the direction of traditional modes of thought, it is clear
that he still insists on the basic principles of liberal thinking about
Jesus. It is the historical Jesus who is still in the vital center of his
thought.

E. *The Doctrine of the Church*

Neglect of the doctrine of the church is typical of liberalism.[33] When the church is spoken of, it is often criticized as an institution which appears to be more interested in perpetuating ancient practices than in promoting the kingdom of God. When the church is spoken of positively, it simply takes its place as one among many institutions which can serve the interests of the good society and aid in the development and perfection of personality. Not much distinction is made between the church and the world, except to point out that the church is the religious community organized for worship and teaching and deriving its inspiration from the historical Jesus. As William Adams Brown points out, the focus of attention was on the coming of the kingdom through the inner changes in the spirits of individual men or on the radical transformation of society which would result from the application of Christian principles and not on the church. In his words, most liberals "had little use for the church."[34]

Lyman shares this liberal approach to the church. The kingdom of God, meaning an ideal society on earth, is clearly prior to the church in his mind, the latter being merely an instrument through which this social goal could be accomplished. In an article written in 1923, entitled "Religious Education for a New Democracy,"[35] Lyman clearly reveals these liberal assumptions. The great task before us, he says, is the creation of a truly democratic society. The creative energy of the churches rightly directed can do much to promote this social ideal. But the churches are hampered by premillenarianism and theological and social conservatism and are alienated from the major social movements of the day. The task of religious education, he concludes, is to re-educate the churches and to socialize their ideas and ideals in order to make religion relevant to social progress. Thus, Lyman in this period affirms the familiar theme of culture-Protestantism, which has already been seen in Brown, Rauschenbusch, Fosdick, and Knudson. The same basic thesis is set forth in an address delivered in 1917 and published as *The God of the New Age*. In this address he identified the kingdom of God with a "world-wide social democracy" and urged the churches to work for this ideal.[36]

Apart from this Lyman makes very little mention of the church. The word "church" does not appear in the index of any of his major books written before 1935, and a bibliography lists no article devoted entirely to the church. A few passing references are made here and there, but the focus of his attention is plainly elsewhere. It is not clear whether this silence should be taken as an indication that he does not consider this a problem with which a philosopher of religion would deal or whether it indicates a judgment with reference to the importance of the church. However, in the light of the importance given to the attaining of "the Beloved Community," "a world-wide community in which love and reason prevail,"[37] it might be expected that even a philosopher would give some attention to the smaller community of dedicated men who work for the attaining of this goal. It ought to be noted, finally, that the idea of the church as a distinctive community of faith in an alien world did begin to appear in some of his writings after 1935.[38] This is in keeping with the general movement of his thought toward the main stream of the Christian tradition in these later years.

F. Conclusion

This chapter brings to a close the consideration of the evangelical liberals. While each has his own special contribution to make and his distinctive emphases, all are agreed that there is abiding truth in the revelation of God in Christ which can be restated for modern man. Lyman makes his contribution to this group by trying to show how the facts of natural, historical, and moral evolution provide evidence for the existence of the sort of God called for by Christian theism and how the Christian religion unites historical, ethical, and experiential elements into a balanced synthesis. Lyman's belief in the normative nature of the historical revelation in Christ sets him and the other theologians dealt with thus far apart from the thinkers to be considered in the following section who elaborated an alternative way of dealing with the problem of relating the Christian tradition to modern modes of thought.

PART THREE

MODERNISTIC LIBERALISM

CHAPTER 8

SOCIAL CHRISTIANITY:
SHAILER MATHEWS

It is time now to turn from the evangelical liberals to the modernists represented by Shailer Mathews, D. C. Macintosh, and Henry Nelson Wieman. While there are significant differences between each of these men and the other two, they all share a common concern to develop a distinctly modern theological method which will free theology from any fundamental dependence on historical revelation. As a result each is led far from traditional Christianity, although neither breaks with the church as far as personal loyalty is concerned.

Shailer Mathews (1863–1941), a native of Portland, Maine, was born into a pious Baptist home in which an evangelical orthodoxy was professed. He was descended from a line of preachers and teachers on both sides of his family. Mathews attended Colby College and Newton Theological Institution. After teaching Rhetoric and Public Speaking at Colby and New Testament at Newton for a short while, he was transferred to the field of History and Political Economy at Colby, in preparation for which he spent two years at the University of Berlin. In 1894 he moved to the University of Chicago as Associate Professor of New Testament History. He was transferred in 1906 to the field of Theology in the Divinity School of the University of Chicago, at which he spent the remainder of his teaching career. He was Dean of the school from 1908 until his retirement. At his retirement in 1933 he was Dean of the Divinity School, Chairman of the Department of Christian Theology and Ethics, and Professor of Historical Theology.[1]

Mathews is a member of what can be called the Chicago school of theology. It is representative of the extreme left wing of the liberal movement and is characterized by an empirical and pragmatic approach to religion. Its chief members were associated with the University of Chicago. The strong influence of John Dewey can be seen in most members of this group. Its more extreme representatives not only gave up all real connection with the Christian tradition but also abandoned theism itself. Eustace Haydon and E. S. Ames are examples of men in the Chicago school who embraced a naturalistic world view and a humanistic religion. Others like G. B. Smith veered dangerously near this extreme. G. B. Foster agonized over the problem of the finality of Christianity. Henry Nelson Wieman also belonged to this group, but he developed his own distinctive outlook, which will be described in a subsequent chapter. Shirley Jackson Case, like Mathews, emphasized the socio-historical approach to Christianity. Mathews was one of the more moderate thinkers in the Chicago school in his earlier days, but in the end he moved far to the left. This group, then, included a wide variety of perspectives. Some stressed the empirical and pragmatic approach, while others emphasized the socio-historical method. All of them, however, agreed with the modernistic premise that the Christian tradition had to be radically rethought from the standpoint of modern culture if it were to survive in the twentieth century.

Early in his career Mathews became convinced that Christianity is not a body of truth but a religious social movement. It began to appear to him that the task of theology is to discover the functional significance of Biblical doctrines and then to translate them into a modern equivalent. This was the point of view which informed The Gospel and Modern Man, published in 1910. At this point Mathews is best described as an evangelical liberal, since he took the faith which appears in the New Testament to be in some sense normative, although it needed to be reinterpreted into modern thought forms.

Gradually Mathews moved to the left in his theological outlook. He came to see more clearly that theological beliefs are the product of the dominant social mind of a period and that they change when the social structure changes. This is the point of view expressed in a long article in *The Biblical World,* published in 1915, entitled "Theology and the Social Mind." The truth value of religious affirmations now became a central problem for him. How can the content of religious doctrines be separated from their form? And how can the truth of this content be determined? From this point onward Mathews is best described as a modernistic liberal. He no longer found the norm of religious truth in the Christian tradition itself. Rather, he sought for a new method by which he could evaluate the teachings of historic Christianity. He found in the methods and conclusions of modern science the clue to a new way of discovering and testing religious truth. This new point of view finds expression in *The Faith of Modernism,* published in 1924, and especially in *Atonement and the Social Process* and *The Growth of the Idea of God,* published in 1930 and 1931. He concludes in the last two books mentioned that religious doctrines are functional formulas which attempt to relate persons positively to the personality-producing factors in the world process. Fulfillment of life is attained when the self is properly adjusted to those forces which aid in the development of moral personality. Christianity is illustrative of the right way of adjustment to the cosmic environment, but it has no permanent, universal norm in its own nature which is accepted on the basis of its own intrinsic authority.

Mathews' concern for a methodology which could be employed to evaluate past theologies and to discover abiding religious truth is a mark of modernistic liberalism. Moreover, his adoption of modern science as the basis of adequate religious thinking is typical of this point of view. His employment of scientific methodology and terminology in the latter period of his career links him with the empirical modernists, but other considerations make it more accurate to list him in the ethical-social group. He had relatively little interest in connecting his conclusions with some metaphysical outlook. Basically he believed that theologies have a practical rather than a theoretical significance, and he looked to the natural and social sciences rather than to philosophy for insight into the meaning of religious doctrines. He rests the truth content of his conclusions upon the findings of empirical science and makes no effort to integrate his system into some explicitly held metaphysics. Furthermore, he does not manifest the kind of technical interest which Macintosh and Wieman have in epistemology. Finally, Mathews' intense concern with, and leadership in, the social gospel movement are also indicative of the fact that his approach to religion is basically from the practical rather than the theoretical side.

A. *Methodology*

1. CHRISTIANITY AS A WAY OF LIFE

Typical of liberalism is its insistence that Christianity is primarily a way of life rather than a way of believing, that it is grounded in experience and not in adherence to particular doctrinal propositions. Shailer Mathews expresses this liberal conviction in its most explicit form. Christianity, he says, is the religion of all those who have called themselves Christians, i.e., considered themselves loyal to Jesus Christ. This religion cannot be identified by reference to a static body of dogma but must be defined with reference to the continuing community of Christian people, who have expressed their convictions regarding Jesus Christ in a wide variety of intellectual patterns.[2] That this is a liberal definition of Christianity may be seen by comparing Mathews' point of view with the fundamentalist position represented by J. Gresham Machen in *Christianity and Liberalism.* Machen argues that

. . . if any one fact is clear, . . . it is that the Christian movement from its inception was not just a way of life in the modern sense, but a way of life founded upon a message. It was based, not upon mere feeling, not upon a mere program of work, but upon an account of facts. In other words it was based upon doctrine.[3]

This divergence of opinion regarding the essence of Christianity was at the heart of the fundamentalist-modernist controversy which was waged with such fervor during the second and third decades of this century by the two groups represented respectively by Machen and Mathews.

2. THEOLOGY AND THE SOCIAL MIND

The distinction between Christianity as a body of dogma and as a historical community loyal to Jesus Christ is basic for Mathews' thought, and it provides the clue to the theological methodology worked out by him. The problem which Mathews faced, and which was basic to the whole liberal movement, was the problem of how to make the ancient gospel available to modern men. Mathews made an attempt to deal with this issue in *The Gospel and Modern Man,* published in 1910, but it is in a long article published five years later in *The Biblical World* that the full implications of his developing point of view come to light. The fundamental thesis of this essay is that Christianity is a religious movement grounded in an experience of salvation centering in the life and work of Jesus Christ. The intellectual framework in which this experiment is expressed changes from age to age. This way of viewing the history of Christianity sounds so far very much like Fosdick's approach expressed in the phrase "abiding experiences and changing categories." The heart of Mathews' argument is that doctrines are the product of the dominant social mind at work in religion and that they must be understood in terms of the particular mind-set of the age. Social mind means "a more or less general community of conscious states, processes, ideas, interests, and ambitions which to a greater or less degree repeats itself in the experience of individuals belonging to the group characterized by this community of consciousness."[4] Mathews argues that the doctrinal expressions of Christianity have been influenced thus far by seven such successive social minds: the Semitic, the Graeco-Roman, the imperialistic, the feudal, the nationalistic, the bourgeois, and the modern or scientific-democratic. The doctrinal systems which were developed during each of these periods reflect the prevailing social mind.

This thesis, Mathews contends, has far-reaching implications for the understanding of the nature of Christianity and the theological enterprise. First of all, it means that Christianity is one phase of the general social history of Western civilization and that its doctrines are inextricably bound up with this larger cultural process.[5] Furthermore, theology is seen to be derived from social experience and not philosophy. Theologians are more akin to social analysts than to metaphysicians.[6] Doctrines reflect social patterns rather than purely metaphysical concepts. Finally, this thesis, as interpreted by Mathews, means that theology is functional and not normative, changeable and not permanent. Theologies must change in order to express and interpret religious experience in terms which are intelligible to the contemporary generation. Doctrines, then, are not eternal truths which need only to be repeated in every new generation but are reflections of changing social patterns. It is interesting to notice how these three implications cited by Mathews regarding his thesis involve respectively aspects of the principle of continuity, the principle of autonomy, and the principle of dynamism. There is continuity between Christianity and culture; doctrines are grounded in experience‡ rather than in revelation or metaphysics; and doctrines continually change.

3. SCIENCE AND THEOLOGICAL METHOD

What does this view of the relation between Christianity and culture mean for the contemporary theological enterprise? What is the meaning of Christianity for modern men? Mathews asserts that the prime task of contemporary theology is to discover a method by which the abiding truths of Christianity can be distinguished from its inherited framework and reinterpreted for modern men in terms which are meaningful.[8] In *The Faith of Modernism* Mathews sets forth the procedure which he feels is needed. He defines modernism as *"the use of the methods of modern science to find, state and use the permanent and central values of inherited orthodoxy in meeting the needs of a modern world."*[9]

Science, he maintains, presents a world of activity which is uniform throughout the ascertainable universe of fact. Mathews urges that while no cosmic purpose can be demonstrated, tendencies have appeared which are similar to what is called purpose in the human realm. One such tendency has resulted in the emergence of personality. Personality depends for its development on a proper adjustment between itself and the total environment in which it functions. Religion can be understood as a social hypothesis regarding the manner in which personality can avail itself of the help-giving aspects of the environment. Doctrines are ways in which a particular society states its convictions regarding the way personality can best be adjusted to whatever is conceived to be ultimate reality. They are stated in patterns taken from social experiences and applied analogously to the religious and cosmic realm.

In Christianity the mediating role between personality and the environmental process which has produced personality, according to Mathews, is played by the person and work of Jesus. The social patterns employed to interpret this function of Jesus have varied from culture to culture; yet the function of the doctrines remained the same. The task of theology is to discover the contemporary equivalent of these ancient patterns of atonement. In *The Atonement and the Social Process* Mathews explores the history of this doctrine in detail and offers his own modern version of it. A further problem has to do with the precise meaning and role of God in this process. In *The Growth of the Idea of God* Mathews takes up this problem historically and offers his own reinterpretation on the basis of the scientific methodology which has been described. Similarly, he feels, other Christian doctrines have to be reinterpreted to make them harmonize with the results of modern science.

Modernism, then, is primarily a method and not a system of dogma, according to Mathews. It is a method based on experience rather than on authority. The problem of faith and reason is resolved simply by reducing all belief to experimentally validated truths. The Bible in this framework cannot be employed as an authoritative or normative source of belief but is simply a trustworthy record of a developing religion. The object of the study of the Bible is to get beyond its doctrinal affirmations to the basic and abiding experiences which gave rise to the doctrines in order to discover how to reproduce the same faith in the modern age.[10] The theologian, he concludes, is neither a neutral investigator nor an apologist. He is simply the representative of a social and religious group who seeks to discover the perennially valid attitudes and convictions of the Scriptures and of tradition and to state these convictions in categories which are relevant to contemporary experience and which are in harmony with whatever else is known to be true.[11]

4. CONCLUSION

There are significant differences between the approach to theology spelled out by Mathews and that found in the evangelical liberals previously described. The basic difference, of course, has to do with the contrasting attitudes in the two perspectives with regard to the normative nature of the New Testament faith. The modernists feel less obligation to maintain a connection with traditional ways of thinking. The terminology employed by them is generally less recognizable as distinctly Christian language. There is also more consciousness among the modernists of having originated something new. One can also detect a greater sense of identification with modern culture. They seem to feel modern as well as to think in modernistic terms. Thus, the mood and temper of the modernists, as well as their basic convictions regarding the task of contemporary theology, set them apart from the evangelical liberals.

B. *The Doctrine of God*

1. THE PRINCIPLE OF IMMANENCE

One belief that unifies liberals of all varieties is the doctrine of the immanence of God. In *The Gospel and Modern Man* Mathews points out four basic differences which separate the modern world from previous generations: (1) the domination of the age by scientific thinking and a conception of world process, (2) a growing sense of social solidarity, (3) rejection of authoritarianism and deductive metaphysics, and (4) a doctrine of immanence. All of these principles enumerated by Mathews are basic to American theological liberalism, but the last named is without doubt the most important. In much previous theology, says Mathews, God has been not only transcendent to the world but also external to it, so that he interferes from time to time as he arbitrarily chooses. The modern world thinks of him as present continually in the cosmos as "the Universal Life and Will and Love."[12] God can no more be spatially absent from the world than a living man's consciousness can be absent from his body. "God must be either the personalized Whole, or, as I am forced rather to believe, the Person who, as over against our own personalities, expresses Himself in the Whole."[13] Miracle, in this scheme, loses its importance, and the God of love becomes a God of law who works, not merely occasionally and miraculously, but gradually and continually in a law-abiding process to achieve his goals.

Mathews develops this conception of God further in *The Faith of Modernism*. The predominant pattern of the past employed to interpret God, he affirms, has been that of monarchical sovereignty. The modern world seeks a democratic God with duties to the people as well as rights, and it finds him immanent in the whole world process. Thus, the modernist insists that "the divine personality is always operating, and that evolution is an ever increasing revelation of a Person immanent within the process itself."[14] Although God cannot, of course, be fully defined or conceptualized, modernism goes beyond the mere assertion that God is the God of cosmic law and process. "It trusts Him—the awful, mysterious God of abysmal space, of galaxies of stars, of ether, of evolution, of human liberty—as Father."[15] In Mathews' thought a familiar idea of God has emerged—the concept of a democratic, Christlike Being immanent in the evolutionary world process and working in a law-abiding way to develop personality.

This conception of God represents a combination of the Christian tradition with ideas derived from modern science and culture, and it is dominated by the principles of continuity and dynamism.

2. A CONCEPTUAL VIEW OF GOD

A significant development took place in Mathews' view of God between 1924, when *The Faith of Modernism* was published, and 1931, when *The Growth of the Idea of God* appeared. Mathews moves away from theism toward the humanism of Ames and the naturalism of Wieman. This is not surprising when one realizes that theism became more and more difficult to defend at the University of Chicago during those years. Mathews was confronted not only with Ames and Wieman but also with the strong influence of John Dewey and the actual presence of Eustace Haydon. In both of these latter thinkers humanism and naturalism were explicit and complete. Moreover, the methodology which Mathews had perfected seems more and more to control his positive affirmations. The view that theological concepts are social patterns leads to skepticism regarding the objective truth content of these patterns. Mathews had been able previously to speak of God as a person. But by 1931 he was able to say only that by analogy the reality symbolized by the idea of God can be called personal. The social meaning and the functional significance of the idea of God have come to overshadow its objective reality. A conceptual view of God has almost completely replaced a metaphysical view. Modern science, even more than before, rather than the Christian tradition furnishes the content of the idea of God.

To say it differently, Mathews moved in these later years toward a more extreme type of liberalism. The dynamic principle is strongly emphasized, and the principles of continuity and autonomy are applied more radically. His basic presupposition is that of a vast universe in process of development. The disjunction between God and this evolutionary world process is reduced still further and is almost dissolved completely. God is now defined more exclusively from a subjectivist standpoint.[16] He is thought of in terms of his value function for persons. There is a shift away from the interpretation of God as an independent, objective reality toward the concept of God, so that the objective content of the idea tends to be dissolved in subjective meaning.

An examination of *The Growth of the Idea of God* will help to clarify and interpret these tendencies. Underlying this book is Mathews' fundamental thesis that religious ideas are functional formulas which interpret the religious experience of a group and which change with the dominant mind-set of the group. The idea of God, he contends, arose in the religious quest for security and moral aid through personal relations with the cosmic environment. The meaning of the term is found by studying the history of its usage in religious behavior and not by making a metaphysical analysis. There is, moreover, no objective reality corresponding exactly to the changing ideas of God. In the light of these conclusions, what contemporary meaning can Mathews give to the idea and reality of God? He maintains that his analysis does not result in atheism. The social patterns in which the idea of God has appeared, he affirms, express relations between persons and their environment, and only realities can be in relation. The patterns point to something objectively real, even though the reality does not correspond exactly to the pattern. The basic problem, according to Mathews, is to discover a meaning for this objective reality which can be expressed in meaningful and verifiable terms.

Mathews' starting point for this reinterpretation is the world process described by modern science. In the universe there are organisms existing in relation to an environment which has produced them and which now sustains them. Among these organisms are human beings. Mathews believes that the only explanation for this fact is that there are personality-evolving activities in the cosmos. In short, there must be something akin to purpose in the world which gave rise to personality and which now sustains the conditions under which personality can develop. All of the social patterns which have been employed over the centuries to express the idea of God "stand for conceptions of the personality-evolving and personally responsive activities of the universe upon which human beings depend."[17] Mathews maintains that God cannot be thought of as a superindividual, and it is hardly accurate to speak of the metaphysical personality of God. However, God must be conceived of as personal and as responding in a personal way to the activities of men. Thus, in speaking of the personality-producing factors in the universe, it is legitimate to use analogies such as Father or Great Companion or even King and Almighty. Mathews suggests that the Christian will naturally think of God as Christlike.

Mathews concludes that the conceptual view of God has many practical advantages. It gives to men confidence that their struggle for a better life is aided by tendencies in the cosmos itself. Moreover, it provides an objective religious foundation for morality by virtue of the fact that the movement of "the total process in which men are involved is toward personal values, and that any antipersonal activity is devolution, contrary to the primordial activity with which men are inexplicably involved."[18] Finally, in this view religion becomes something more than conventional behavior. "It is a technique by which the human being gains more personal value from personal adjustment with responsive cosmic activities."[19]

3. SUBJECTIVISM AND OBJECTIVISM

The relations between the subjective and the objective in Mathews' doctrine of God are curious and complex. On the one hand, all ideas of God arise out of a kind of social subjectivism. They express in conceptual terms the religious experience of a group who reflect the dominant social mind. In this sense ideas of God have to do with the subjective meaning of God for persons. On the other hand, Mathews believes that there really is an Object out there which men encounter in religious experience. In his latest period he relies on the results of modern science to provide the objective content to which ideas of God refer. Presumably, science is describing the world as it really is. In this sense Mathews is objectivistic in his approach.

But now a curious problem arises as to whether this is really a genuine objectivism. Is the attempt of Mathews to give objective content to the idea of God by employing scientific categories simply another instance of social subjectivism, the expression of the contemporary social mind to be succeeded shortly by another social mind? Or has Mathews escaped from this relativism and subjectivism by means of science, so that now he has discovered precisely what it is out there that previous theologies have pointed to only vaguely through socially conditioned patterns of thought? Mathews' method would lead him to the former alternative, while his confidence in science as a reliable means of attaining objective knowledge about the world would seem to lead him to the latter alternative. It is clear that he does not believe that science has brought modern men any closer to an understanding of God in metaphysical terms, since he apparently does not believe human reason to be capable of such knowledge. Yet, he apparently thinks that science has at least discovered the empirical reality to which all ideas of God point. This would seem to be a step forward.

Moreover, it is clear that Mathews feels he has discovered the formal pattern into which all ideas of God fit. But the question still arises as to whether or not this formal pattern filled with the content furnished by modern empirical science amounts to a fund of objective knowledge which is any more permanent or reliable than previous ideas about God based on social patterns arising out of group experience. If so, Mathews would seem to have transcended his own historical method, but, if not, his own thought is just as subjective in a social sense as all previous theological systems. There appears to be a tension here between his socio-historical method and his empirical method, between a pragmatic subjectivism and a scientific objectivism.

4. SUMMARY

Beginning with the idea of a world process which has produced a personality with moral and spiritual capacities, Mathews erects what he chooses to call a conceptual theism. It may be legitimate to call Mathews' idea of God theistic in the sense that he believes that there are powers beyond men which are positively related to the furtherance of personal values, but it is not theism in the traditional sense. For God in this view is neither a personal Being, nor the creator of the world, nor sovereign over the world, nor in any real sense transcendent to the world—all of which have been generally assumed by previous Christian theists. It is difficult to know just what sort of reality can be ascribed to God. The term is simply a concept which is applied to whatever it is that produces and sustains personality. Beyond this the reality of God is left in a vague, nebulous state. It is not possible to know from whence these personality-evolving activities come or whither they go. All that can be known about them is that they are present to experience and cannot be avoided in the actual process of living.

Needless to say, one should not expect to find any discussion of the doctrine of creation, of God's internal nature and attributes, or any of the other related problems which have traditionally been associated with the Christian view of God. The doctrine of the Trinity, of course, has been completely abandoned. A comparison of the treatment accorded the doctrine of God by Mathews with that of Brown and Knudson gives some indication of how much further removed Mathews is from the main stream of historic Christianity. Mathews' only connection with Christian orthodoxy is his insistence that the patterns employed by these earlier thinkers were really crude ways of giving expression to the same realities which he has discovered by means of modern science.

C. *The Doctrine of Man*

1. THE NATURE OF SIN

Certain liberal thinkers employ with greater consistency and clarity than others principles which are fundamental in all liberal theology. This is certainly true of Shailer Mathews' doctrines of man, sin, and salvation. Concern for personality and its development is central to liberalism. With regard to this concern certain underlying themes appear repeatedly in the writings of liberal thinkers. Man is universally viewed as a being who has emerged out of nature through a process of evolution. Yet, man is superior to nature. His basic problem is how he can achieve the greatest possible development of his moral and spiritual capacities in light of the obstacles to this fulfillment which confront him by virtue of his connections with the world of nature. Salvation is viewed as the triumph of moral personality over the lower impulses of the body and the mechanisms of the physical environment. No liberal thinker investigated thus far has embodied these convictions more consistently or more explicitly than Mathews.

In *The Gospel and Modern Man* Mathews contends that man is confronted with three basic problems: natural evil, death, and sin. Natural evil arises out of the fact that man is subject to chemical, physical, and organic processes which cause pain and ultimately death, which is man's final problem. Man's basic problem is that he is a sinner. Mathews' concept of sin is consistent throughout all of his writings.[20] Sin is the victory of the passions of the body inherited from the animals over man's moral and spiritual ideals. It is the reversion to a previous stage of existence and the choice of outworn goods over present values. Sin, however, is not merely individual in Mathews' view; it has a social dimension as well. Society, too, is involved in the struggle against the backward pull of obsolete values. "Ideals and practices born of a simpler social order satisfy our moral needs no more than a nomad chieftain is a satisfactory substitute for the President of the United States."[21] The evil effects of sin become institutionalized and are transmitted from one generation to another and wield their sinister power over individual lives.

In the latest period of his thought Mathews' doctrine of man is based on an organism-environment scheme in which sin becomes maladjustment to the progressive personality-producing forces in society and in the cosmos. In every case the essence of sin is its frustration of the development of personality, both in the sinner and in his victim, both in the individual and in society.

2. THE MEANING OF SALVATION

Salvation is the victory of moral personality over the forces of nature, both within and without, which frustrate the meaning and purpose of spiritual existence. In *The Gospel and Modern Man* Mathews teaches that mechanism is overcome by achieving through Christ a new level of spiritual existence which suffering and pain cannot frustrate. The Christian can, "as a spiritual person strengthened and inspired by God, rise above the natural order, in which change and suffering are implicit, into the freedom of the sons of God; into an eternal, not a temporal order of existence; out from the kingdom of Nature into the kingdom of God."[22] Sin is overcome through the forgiveness and regenerating influence which spring from Jesus, and death is overcome through the assurance of immortality won through the triumph of Jesus over the grave.

In *The Faith of Modernism* Mathews again interprets salvation in terms of overcoming reactionary biological and social tendencies by developing right relations with God through the influence of Jesus, who points the way by word and by deed.[23] Salvation is life reoriented around the ideals and goals represented in Jesus. Love becomes the inspiring ideal which motivates the moral life. Moreover, the power of love reaches beyond the individual and remakes society also after the pattern found in the example and teachings of Jesus. By this process the whole human situation is "brought into dynamic relation with the divine Will to Love by which we are environed."[24] In Mathews' thought the Gospel is almost reduced to a simple message of moral idealism. Men are saved by being morally transformed under the suasion of the ideals of Jesus. The saved man is one whose life is motivated by good will inspired by Jesus' teaching and example. The vertical dimension is almost completely lacking. Salvation is not reconciliation with God or justification by faith. Rather, it is moral renewal in one's dealing with other men. The believer is not a rebellious sinner saved by grace but an advancing spirit whose good intentions have been strengthened by the influence of Jesus.

After the publication of *Contributions of Science to Religion* Mathews interprets salvation in scientific language as dynamic adjustment to the progressive tendencies in society and the cosmos which make for the development of personality.[25] This new adjustment, says Mathews, is aided by the inspiring example of Jesus, who is the chief exponent of adjustment. The supreme message of Christianity, then, is that men can attain to that personal adjustment with a personally responsive cosmos which Jesus achieved in his own experience.

3. THE INTERPRETATION OF HISTORY

Implicit throughout Mathews' discussion of sin and salvation is the notion of an evolutionary process in which spiritual forces are gradually overcoming the forces of nature. The cosmos itself is on the side of progress. Sin is being gradually sloughed off as moral personality comes to dominate the impulses inherited from the animals. Society is becoming more humane as moral ideals rather than animal-like selfishness come to prevail in social relations. This progressive view of history manifests itself in *The Social Gospel,* published by Mathews in 1909.[26] In this volume the goal of history is defined as the kingdom of God, that is, a new social order in which men are to be brothers to each other and sons of God. This new age is to be realized by a gradual process of social progress as men come more and more to possess the spirit of Jesus. The social principles of love and fraternity are said to represent the standard and the goal of God's immanent working with men for a better social order.

Similar convictions are expressed in more detail in *The Spiritual Interpretation of History,* published in 1916. Throughout this book there breathes a confident air of optimism which, despite the shock of World War I, sees the triumph of the spiritual values of Jesus in human society as ultimately certain. Mathews contends that an inductive study of history leads to the conclusion that there are spiritual forces at work in history which have their source in a personal God and which, despite their conditioning by economic and natural factors, are gradually bringing about an increase of human values. This view of history corroborates the teachings of Jesus, who believed in the supremacy of spiritual forces. He maintains that social evolution is a process which, "if it be prolonged, will bring the world under the sway of the ideals of Jesus himself."[27] This interpretation of history, he concludes, challenges men to co-operate with those tendencies in the cosmic process which lead to the further realization of personal values. Men who devote themselves to social reconstruction under the inspiration of the ideals of Jesus will "be the leaven of that better social order that shall make the world into the kingdom of brothers who, free spirits in the midst of physical forces and economic tensions, are the true children of God the Father Almighty."[28]

Mathews shows less restraint with regard to future historical possibilities than have any of the previous thinkers who have been considered. The eschatological element which all of them preserved in some measure is completely dissolved in Mathews' thought. He feels no discontinuity between natural evolution and moral progress. The result is an evolutionary optimism which affirms confidently that a new order of brotherhood will ultimately come to pass on earth. Both the sources which have been cited in this discussion were written before the effects of World War I were felt. Surprisingly enough, however, the immediate effect of this conflict on Mathews was to increase his optimism. In his preface to the second edition of *The Spiritual Interpretation of History*, written shortly after the war's end, he remarks that democracy "has been disclosed as an irrepressible tendency."[29] The war "released forces that will ultimately 'make the world safe for democracy.'"[30] "War is a survival we shall yet outgrow."[31] Moreover, Mathews seems to have been less affected by the catastrophes of the third and fourth decades of the twentieth century than were most of his contemporaries. An examination of his autobiography, published in 1936, does not reveal any great disillusionment with his former hopes,[32] although he does say that World War I shattered the prewar optimism of his generation.[33] However, the general impression one gathers is that basically he still adheres to the optimistic tendencies of his earlier writings with only minor qualifications. He does emphasize the fact that progress must come by gradual process and not by sudden revolution.

D. *Christology*

1. INTRODUCTION

The changing form of Mathews' thought is neatly reflected in his treatment of the person and work of Christ. In *The Gospel and Mod-*

ern Man Mathews sounds very much like an evangelical liberal, and his treatment of Christology is not fundamentally different from that found in Brown, Fosdick, Rauschenbusch, Knudson, and Lyman. *The Faith of Modernism* is a transitional book. It reflects the growing importance of method in his thought and the increasing influence of the concepts of modern science. In *The Atonement and the Social Process* his thought proceeds from a basis quite different from that of his earliest period. Mathews' grasp of reality is now informed throughout by the findings of modern science, and his terminology is strictly that of a twentieth-century American. Reason and experience, not the Christian tradition, furnish the content of his reconstruction of the atonement. All that is retained from historic orthodoxy is a formal pattern. Thus, *The Atonement and the Social Process* is an illuminating example of modernistic liberalism.

2. THE EARLY PERIOD

Mathews' first full-length treatment of Christology is found in *The Gospel and Modern Man,* published in 1910. Jesus is fully a man, but he is at the same time the incarnation of God.[34] Modern men cannot use the language of Nicaea and Chalcedon to express their valuation of Christ as God, but they can express the equivalent conviction by conceiving of him as "the immanent Spiritual Life of God focalized in a human personality."[35] Thus, Mathews is able to speak of incarnation on the basis of the principle of immanence as the other evangelical liberals did. In Jesus are to be found the spiritual qualities of moral perfection which make him the Saviour of men. He saves from natural evil (mechanism) by mediating the victory of personal spirit over the impersonal forces of nature.[36] He saves from sin by mediating the forgiveness of God. He saves from death by giving assurance to men through his resurrection that personality persists beyond the grave. Thus, men in every generation have found in the historical Jesus the Christ, the one whom God empowered by his Spirit to save men from the evils which afflict them.

3. THE PERIOD OF TRANSITION

The Faith of Modernism reflects the movement of Mathews' thought toward the modernistic side of the liberal spectrum. Mathews insists that modernism is not interested in defending any particular set of doctrinal convictions about Jesus but rather makes its appeal to Jesus himself. The starting point of Christology is "the experience of God which comes when men accept Jesus as Lord."[37] New patterns of thought must be found to express the contemporary relevance of Jesus as a revealer of God and a redeemer of men. According to Mathews, Jesus reveals God through his teaching that love is the only practicable way to live, and he saves men as they follow his example and put his teachings into practice. However, it is the moral excellence of Jesus' personality, not his teachings, which is the real secret of his saving power. Because he himself was saved, he can save others by enabling them to share his own fellowship with God and his victory over fear, despair, sin, the mechanisms of nature, and death itself. The death and resurrection of Jesus help men to understand the meaning of the evolutionary struggle from which human life has emerged. Jesus demonstrated that the life of love is superior to the impersonal world of nature. Mathews makes it clear that this interpretation of the resurrection of Jesus does not depend on the notion that the body of Jesus was literally revived. Rather, Jesus lives on in the sense that the personalities of all men persist after being freed from their animal substructure. The second coming of Jesus is a symbol of the immortality of the individual and of the triumph of the ideals of Jesus in the coming of the kingdom of God on earth.

In Mathews' reinterpretation of Christology Jesus is primarily an inspiring moral example who influences men to adopt his ideal of love as a way of life. The tendency to reduce the orthodox notion of incarnation to a simple idea of revelation is carried to its extreme by Mathews. God is not metaphysically present in Christ (except in the sense that God is immanent in all things and pre-eminently in Jesus); rather, his teachings disclose to men what God is like. In the same way, the orthodox notion of atonement is reduced to a simple idea of moral influence. The death of Christ does not satisfy the justice of God or defeat the demonic hosts; rather his whole life has persuasive power which leads men to a higher level of ethical performance. The principle of continuity has practically obliterated the distinction between Jesus and other men, between Jesus as a teacher of ethics and Jesus as divine redeemer, and between Jesus as a man and Jesus as a revealer of God.

4. THE FINAL DEVELOPMENT

The Atonement and the Social Process embodies these same reductionist tendencies but sets the whole discussion of Christology into a context dominated by scientific terminology. It represents, there-fore, a new stage in the development of Mathews' thought. In this book Mathews tests his theory that theological doctrines are func-tional social hypotheses which express Christian beliefs in contempo-rary social patterns. He concludes that each successive doctrine of atonement has "endeavored not only to set forth God's saving, for-giving love, but also to meet objections against his moral right to forgive springing from contemporary practices."[38] Christ performs whatever role is necessary to make forgiveness possible. Having discov-ered the functional value of atonement, Mathews then turns to the task of discovering in present-day terms the realities which these successive social patterns have expressed. The content of the doctrine is fur-nished to Mathews by modern science. Science has discovered a monistic universe consisting of law-abiding activity out of which per-sonality has emerged, owing to certain personality-producing factors in the cosmic environment (God). Man depends on this cosmic en-vironment for his welfare, just as every other organism is dependent on its surroundings. Salvation is achieved when men rightly relate themselves to the personality-producing factors in the cosmos. In all doctrines of the atonement God is said to have taken the initiative in the provision of salvation for men. In modern terms, according to Mathews, this means that the process which produced personality is prior to the emergence of human beings and that this process co-operates with men in the further development of the potentialities of personality. The co-working of the cosmic process with persons is perfectly epitomized in the experience of Jesus. This is the modern way of stating that Jesus had both a human and a divine nature.

In the light of this understanding Mathews believes it is possible to see great value in Jesus' experience and death. The maladjustment which caused Jesus to suffer was both social and cosmic. "It was social in that those among whom he lived were indifferent to the personal values of human life. It was cosmic because men ignored the creative process of love from which personal values emerge."[39] Jesus was per-fectly adjusted to the creative tendencies in the cosmos and was per-fectly faithful to his conviction that love guides the cosmic process. Thus, Jesus revealed in his life and by his death the real meaning of being at one with God. This redemptive scheme is completed, says Mathews, by the experience of the disciples that Jesus continued to live beyond his crucifixion, which experience they described as his resurrection. The resurrection "heralds the fact that Jesus, while suffering from others' maladjustment to personality-evolving forces of the cosmic process, triumphed through his own adjustment to those forces."[40]

E. *The Church*

Three themes repeatedly appear in liberal writings about the church. First of all, it is generally assumed that Christian experience is prior to the church. The church is made up of those who have already come under the impact of the saving power of the historical Jesus. To use the terminology of F. W. Dillistone, liberals had a "covenantal" rather than an "organic" conception of the church.[41] The "covenantal" view of the church stresses the personal response and voluntary commitments which the individual makes with other individuals and to God by which persons are bound together in a common purpose and faith. The "organic" view of the church majors on the fact that the individual is primarily a member of a social body and that he is born or baptized into a structure of given relationships which is prior to him and in which he finds his true fulfillment. In short, liberals accepted the individualistic, voluntaristic view of the church which is characteristic of most American Protestant denominations.[42] A second conviction of liberals is that the primary purpose of the church is to promote the ends of the kingdom of God. The church is a center of worship, inspiration, and training which prepares men for effective ethical endeavor in their personal and social relationships. A third belief shared by liberal thinkers is that denominationalism hinders the ethical effectiveness of the church. Greater unity, then, is an urgent need.

All three of these principles are present in Mathews' doctrine of the church. The church, he says, is the organized form of the continuing Christian fellowship. It is the community of those who are believers in Jesus Christ, and, as such, is the carrier of the Christian tradition. The continuity of the Christian faith is found in the persisting loyalty of a community of faith to Jesus and not in apostolic succession, in a common creed, or in anything of a static or institutional nature. Since the church is grounded in the experiences of its individual members and not in tradition, liberals had no interest in preserving any particular type of church order or government. Thus, Mathews affirms that the form of the church is to be determined pragmatically in such a way as to enable it best to perform its social and religious functions. In *The Faith of Modernism* he points out that the future will see the disappearance of sectarianism, ecclesiastical chauvinism, and authoritarianism. But no one can know whether the same institutional patterns will be continued or whether new organizations oriented around social service will play a more important role. It is quite clear that Mathews is not much concerned about the form of the church of the future one way or another. What is important, he says, is that "the community of those who hold to Christian attitudes and convictions will continue."[43]

The task of the church, as Mathews conceives it, is that of making the values of the Gospel supreme throughout modern life.[44] He shares the characteristic liberal idea that the church is a part of the total culture with its varied institutions and not a divine society apart from, and in tension with, society in general. The church is one among many agencies the immanent God can employ to further the growth of moral personality, which is the supreme end of all divine and human action. Mathews, then, holds what H. Richard Niebuhr has described as the "Christ of culture position."[45]

Mathews insists, finally, that the task of the church is made more difficult by the division of Christians into competing denominations and theological parties. He believes that liberals and fundamentalists could and ought to work together in the same church to make Christ supreme instead of fighting each other as enemies.[46] Moreover, he feels that the quickest road to church unity was by co-operating in common projects in a federation rather than by seeking organic union through negotiation.[47] Here is another indication of the strength of the ethical-social concerns of Mathews. What really counts is devotion to Christ expressed in practical efforts to ameliorate the life of mankind on earth.

F. Conclusion

Here, then, in the thought of Shailer Mathews is to be found the same sort of interest in the practical relevance of Christianity for the moral and religious needs of contemporary men from a modernistic perspective as was seen previously in the ethical-social liberals. However, in the later phases of his career Mathews began to put more emphasis on the role of science in providing the content of religious affirmations, thus qualifying in a sense his ethical-social orientation. While he continued to be skeptical about the possibility of attaining metaphysical knowledge of God, his reliance on scientific modes of thought relates him to the empirical thinkers who explicitly tried to fashion theological method along the lines laid down in the experimental sciences. It will be instructive now to examine the thought of D. C. Macintosh, whose major effort was to make theology into an empirical science, as another example of the way the modernists sought to find a foundation for faith not dependent upon historical revelation or tradition.

CHAPTER 9

EMPIRICAL THEOLOGY:
DOUGLAS CLYDE MACINTOSH

Douglas Clyde Macintosh (1877–1948) was born in Breadalbane, Ontario. He graduated from McMaster University, Toronto, and remained an additional year to teach philosophy. He did graduate work in theology and philosophy at the University of Chicago, receiving the Ph.D. degree in 1909. He taught Biblical and Systematic Theology at Brandon College from 1907 until he moved to Yale Divinity School. From 1909 until 1942 he served at Yale in a number of capacities: as Assistant Professor of Systematic Theology (1909–1916), Dwight Professor of Theology (1916–1932), and Professor of Theology and Philosophy of Religion (1933–1942). He was also Chairman of the Department of Religion in the Yale Graduate School from 1920 to 1938. He was an Emeritus Professor from 1942 until his death.[1]

Macintosh, like Knudson and Lyman, believes that theology must concern itself with the wider problems of epistemology and metaphysics as well as with the more restricted areas of moral faith and religious experience. There can be no ultimate separation, he feels, between the practical reason and the theoretical reason. Thus, Macintosh belongs in the metaphysical rather than in the ethical-social wing of liberalism. Because of his fundamental insistence on the experiential basis of religious thought, he is more specifically designated here as an empirical rather than as a metaphysical thinker.

Unlike Knudson and Lyman, however, Macintosh belongs to the modernistic side of liberalism. Neither the Bible nor Christ constitutes for him the norm of theology. The criterion of religious truth is not given in history but is centered completely in present reason and experience. He rejects the Christocentric principle of the evangelical, affirming that this is simply another instance of the dogmatic method.[2] Thus, the religious truths implied in the life and teachings of Jesus are not the starting point of theology but rather are affirmed after having been confirmed on other grounds. His first commitment, then, is to the methods and standards of modern thinking, although he does not feel that there is any fundamental conflict between the essence of historic Christianity and the theological theory which he is able to affirm on the basis of empirical and pragmatic grounds.

The approach of Macintosh represents a more radical application of the principle of autonomy than that found in the evangelical liberals in the sense that he grounds theology more exclusively in present experience and less in historical revelation. The evangelical liberals insist, as does Macintosh, that theology is based on experience and not on some arbitrary, external revelation. But they also insist, as he does not, that the mystical or moral experience in which Christian knowledge of God is rooted is Christocentric in the sense that the historical Jesus constitutes the universal source and norm of religious experience and truth. Thus, they maintain a firm connection between present experience and historical revelation, between faith and history. Macintosh sunders this connection. He contends that the believer cannot be dependent on anything which is subject to the relativities of historical research. Rather, he insists that a method must be devised by which it is possible to discover and verify all that is needed for a practical religious faith on the basis of general experience and reason. The revelation of God in Christ can contribute to the development of a system of religious truth, but it is not authoritative or normative in itself. Rather, it is subject to the same criteria by which all other truth claims are measured.

A. *Theology as an Empirical Science*

1. THE IMPORTANCE OF SCIENTIFIC METHOD

The modernistic liberals felt that no theological system worthy of respect could be erected which did not come squarely to terms with modern modes of thinking. Nothing in the twentieth-century world impressed the modernists more and seemed to offer greater promise for the reconstruction of theology than the remarkable achievements of modern science. If the methods of science could be utilized in the interpretation of religion, the way seemed open to avoid the authoritarianism inherent in traditional modes of Christian thinking and at the same time to give empirical validation to those elements in the historic faith which were of universal significance. No one was more convinced of the necessity and practicability of applying scientific procedure to theology than D. C. Macintosh, and no one was more thorough or conscientious in attempting to carry it out than he. He lamented the fact that theology was no longer thought of as the science of God, but he was convinced that it could once more become a science in the truest sense of the word if it could be based, at least on the ground level, on empirically gained and experimentally tested knowledge.

It is this intense concern to develop a theological system consonant with the methods and conclusions of modern science that makes Macintosh a modernistic liberal. His orientation to theology is indicated in his analysis of the types of theological method. There are basically two, he says: the conservative and the radical. The former is based on the employment of some given, external authority to which all doctrines must conform. The latter refuses to accept passively any belief merely because it is taught by some recognized book, institution, or person. Instead, the radical theologian establishes an independent criterion and includes in his system only those beliefs which are in harmony with this chosen method.[3] Macintosh apparently takes his own system to be the culmination of the attempt to define a radical methodology.

2. THE NATURE OF EMPIRICAL THEOLOGY

What precisely is involved in making theology into an empirical science? Macintosh declares that he is simply insisting that "it is possible to relate theological theory to that acquaintance with the divine which is to be found in religious experience at its best, as the physical and social sciences, with their theories as to the nature of things and persons, are related to our common human acquaintance with things and persons in sense and social experience."[4] He does not mean that all the affirmations necessary to a complete system of theology can be empirically verified. What he does mean is that at the ground level it is possible to establish a body of experimentally tested knowledge to which other rationally possible, pragmatically possible truths can be added. Empirical theology will be based on religious experience, but it will differ from the psychology of religion in at least two fundamental ways. It is interested, not in all religious experience, but only in those elements within the complex of experience which give knowledge of God. Moreover, it is a description, not of internal states of consciousness, but of the independent Object to which experience is directed. Thus, Macintosh's use of the empirical method and his adherence to a realistic epistemology lead to a strongly objectivistic interpretation of reason and experience. Subjective elements are, of course, involved in the apprehension of the religious Object, but the emphasis is on the *experienced* and not on *experience* as such. Theology deals with the former, while the psychology of religion deals with the latter.

There are several steps involved in the construction of an empirical theology as Macintosh envisions it. First of all, it must begin with certain presuppositions. Included among these presuppositions are the laws of thought and the assured results of the other empirical sciences, the established facts of the psychology and history of religion, the results of the critical study of the Bible and the life of Jesus, the moral certainty of freedom, the possibility of immortality, and the facts regarding the nature and consequences of sin. One presupposition peculiar to empirical theology is that the Object of religious experience exists. In this respect theology is no different from any other empirical discipline, since every science, he says, must assume that the object of its investigation is real and that some knowledge of it is possible. "On the basis of the knowledge of God through religious experience, one can scientifically assume *that* God is, although he may have as yet very little knowledge as to *what* God is."[5] In order to defend this assumption, Macintosh sets forth and defends a realistic epistemology, according to which the objects of experience exist independently of their being experienced but enter immediately into experience.

Beginning with these presuppositions, Macintosh proceeds to build up a system of theology composed of three levels: (1) an organized body of empirical religious data, (2) theological laws arrived at on the basis of these data, and (3) a body of theoretically permissible propositions about God which are probably true but which cannot in their entirety be subjected to empirical tests. A brief explanation of each of these levels will be helpful.

a. *Religious Data*

The data with which an empirical theology must work, according to Macintosh, are "the special facts revealed in religious perception, or again, to use the religious term, the instances of 'revelation' of the divine within the field of human experience."[6] God is experienced within a complex of elements within which the divine factor can be isolated. Just as physical objects are conceived with a complex of sense qualities, so God may be intuitively perceived as that real Object which gives rise to the human experience of moral uplift. This perception of God in religious experience as that power which morally transforms life is what Macintosh calls revelation. It is simply the objective correlate of what on the subjective side is discovery. Macintosh has carried the principle of continuity in regard to reason and revelation to its extreme limits. They are not merely harmonious; they are identical. He does regard the life and work of Jesus and the testimony of the Bible as special sources of religious data, but they simply represent the highest instances of the human experience of God. Thus, Jesus and the Bible gain their authority over human life by their inherent cogency and are judged by the same standards as all other alleged revelations.

Macintosh is not content, however, to restrict the sources of knowledge to the Christian tradition. Rather, he invites all religions to contribute whatever valid empirical data they have, although he feels that all that is of any value is already contained within the Christian revelation. Macintosh is aware of some of the same problems which Troeltsch dealt with regarding the relativity of Christianity, although he comes to somewhat different conclusions. Macintosh wants to affirm the absoluteness of Christianity; yet he is forced by his method to seek his data anywhere and to accept into his system only those elements which can be justified on the basis of his method. Macintosh, contrary to Troeltsch, believes that a universal religion is a real possibility. He is also confident that the essence of the Christian religion can be preserved on the basis of universal empirical-rational principles. Thus, he resolves the problem which forced Troeltsch to conclude that Christianity was the absolute religion only within Western culture.[7]

b. *Theological Laws*

From the data thus gathered from both Christian and non-Christian sources, Macintosh thinks that it is possible to establish an empirically verifiable body of theological laws. However, one further presupposition is necessary here. Just as all the natural sciences make the basic assumption of the uniformity of nature, so also empirical theology must assume the dependability of God to respond faithfully to the right religious adjustment on man's part. This is the constant factor in religion. The most important variable with which theological laws have to deal is the religious adjustment on the part of the individual. This religious adjustment is primarily a matter of the will, and it contains at least the following elements: concentration of attention on God with regard to some desired end, absolute self-surrender to God, absolute dependence on God, a will responsive to an active expression of God's felt will, and a steady persistence in the attitude described.[8]

Macintosh believes that there are three ways of moving from empirical data to theological laws: from ideas to facts, from facts to ideas, and a combination of both methods. According to the first, spontaneous religious intuitions are taken as hypotheses from which testable propositions are deduced and subjected to empirical tests. According to the second, the movement is from particular empirical facts to more and more general laws, using the methods of verification established by John Stuart Mill. The third, of course, employs both deductive and inductive procedures. In this way Macintosh believes that laws can be developed which make it possible to predict what God can be depended on to do, assuming the condition of a right religious adjustment.

c. *Pragmatic Theory*

Empirical theology, urges Macintosh, must take one further step. It must move from laws to more inclusive theories, i.e., from a consideration of what God *does* to a consideration of what he *is*. Three ways may be employed, separately or in combination, to develop theological theory. Theories can be constructed to account for the operation of the theological laws; prescientific intuitions as to the greatness and goodness of God may be tentatively accepted and then tested in so far as possible to determine their validity; and a view of God may be postulated which seems pragmatically necessary in the light of what the religious life requires. Such theories would deal with the moral and metaphysical attributes of God, the relation of God to men and to history, and the future of individuals and the race.[9]

Macintosh believes that if this procedure were followed, a genuine empirical theology would emerge which would displace all other rivals and establish theology on an invincible basis. All liberal theologians had a high regard for science and scientific method. No other thinker went as far as Macintosh, however, in suggesting that the procedures of empirical science could be literally applied to the realms of religion and theology. He was thoroughly convinced that theology could become an empirical science in the same sense that biology and physics are.

3. THEOLOGY AND PHILOSOPHY

Macintosh developed his theology in close connection with philosophy. Two particular problems are of importance here: his views on epistemology and his conception of the relation of theology to metaphysics. Epistemology was one of the central concerns of Macintosh, and in addition to producing two large volumes on the subject,[10] he dealt with it in some detail in all of his major theological writings.[11] The realistic theory of knowledge which he espoused is basic to his whole theological system, since an empirical theology depends on a genuine apprehension of God as an independently existing reality. He describes his particular version of realism as critical monism.[12] Macintosh was also interested in the relations between theology and metaphysics. He defines metaphysics as the synthesis of all the empirical sciences, theology included. Theology and philosophy are mutually interdependent. In order to complete the theoretical scheme, Macintosh insists that the result of empirical theology must be incorporated into a system of metaphysics, while metaphysics depends on empirical theology for some of its most valuable data. The results of each should modify and corroborate the other.

At one point or another four elements enter into the development of the total theoretical scheme which Macintosh proposes: the scientific, the pragmatic, the historical, and the metaphysical. The scientific element is found in the effort to establish theology upon a body of empirically verified knowledge. A pragmatic element is introduced in the postulation of freedom, God, and immortality as permissible presuppositions of theology and in the employment of hypotheses based on intuitions of what seems practically necessary. An appeal to history is made when the life and work of Jesus are put forth as containing a normative revelation of God in experience. Metaphysics is needed to synthesize the data from all the sciences into one systematic body of theory.

These same four elements are found in the somewhat different approach which Macintosh takes with regard to the problem of apologetics in *The Reasonableness of Christianity* and *The Pilgrimage of Faith*. In these books he takes a position called "representational pragmatism," according to which postulates that seem to be reasonable and practical are taken as representations in idea of what is actually real.[13] The content with which he begins this procedure is the assumption of moral optimism, which is the affirmation that the world can be made better by human effort directed by good will and that the cosmos supports such striving.[14] He identifies this assumption with the essence of Christianity and affirms that it leads to the postulation of freedom, God, and immortality.

B. *The Doctrine of God*

1. THE EXISTENCE OF GOD

One of the problems to which liberals devoted a great deal of attention was the question of God's existence. This problem became particularly acute at the height of the humanist movement during the third and fourth decades of this century. To a great many people the methods and conclusions of modern science seemed to make belief in God not only indefensible but unnecessary. A naturalistic world view, with a concomitant confidence in the sufficiency of men to meet all human needs through the exercise of creative intelligence, seemed to the humanists to furnish a firm foundation for a new religion without God. Liberal theologians, who could no longer appeal to the Biblical revelation in support of theism, felt called on to show the inherent reasonableness of belief in God by an appeal to experience and philosophical argument.

Macintosh makes one of his most important contributions to this problem in his conversation with Max Carl Otto and Henry Nelson Wieman in *Is There a God?*[15] In the procedure which Macintosh follows in this instance, he gives an excellent illustration, not only of the factors which enter into his theological method, but also of some of the major elements which enter into all liberal thinking. Among these latter factors four are of special importance: respect for science and scientific method, emphasis on religious experience as the locus of the self's encounter with God, tentativeness regarding theoretical conclusions, and primary interest in the practical rather than in the intellectual side of theological doctrines.

Macintosh begins by stating simply that there *ought* to be a God; i.e., it would be well for men if there were. Moreover, there *may* be a God; i.e., it is theoretically possible, and many tendencies in modern scientific knowledge seem to point to the existence of an immanent, rational, purposive factor at work in the cosmos. Appeal is made here particularly to the scientifically based philosophies of Bergson, Whitehead, Morgan, and Alexander as giving some aid and comfort to belief in a Cosmic Mind. Furthermore, there *must* be a God if moral optimism and the way of life exemplified by Jesus are valid approaches to life and to reality. Here he states the pragmatic principle that "we have a moral right to believe as we must in order to live as we ought."[16] Finally, it can be affirmed that there *is* a God who is known in the personal experience of moral transformation.

2. THE BEING AND NATURE OF GOD

The most systematic development of Macintosh's doctrine of God is found in *Theology as an Empirical Science*. The scientific theology which Macintosh espouses presupposes the existence of God on the basis of a prescientific experience of God. He is defined in a preliminary way as "a Power, not identical with our empirical selves, which makes for some dependable result (e.g., righteousness) in and through us, when we relate ourselves to that Power in a certain discoverable way."[17] Or, lacking this experience, the existence of God may be postulated as a hypothesis to be tested on the pragmatic assumption that there is actually in existence a Being great enough and good enough to be sufficient to meet man's religious needs. The classical arguments for God's existence—the moral, the cosmological, the teleological, and the ontological—are found by Macintosh to have some value. But, he says, they are insufficient in themselves, since none of them really offers proof of the existence of the Object of religious faith apart from the actual experience of God in the moral life. However, when completed by the empirical argument, they may add further dimensions to the knowledge of what God is.

When sufficient empirical data have been gathered from personal experience, from the special sources of revelation in the life and work of Jesus, and perhaps from other religions, Macintosh affirms that certain laws may be formulated which accurately describe what God may be expected to do within human life when certain religious adjustments on man's part are made. The simplest of these laws has to do with the answer to prayers in which certain spiritual results are desired. This law is stated by Macintosh as follows: "On condition of the right religious adjustment with reference to desired truly moral states of the will (such as repentance, moral aspiration, and the moral elements in self-control, courage, victory over temptation, faithful service and patient endurance), God the Holy Spirit produces the specific moral results desired."[18] Other similar laws state what God will do with regard to the production in the individual of regeneration, sanctification, perseverance, etc. In addition to these volitional effects, God will on the condition of certain definable requirements produce certain emotional, intellectual, and physiological states. Still other laws define what God will do in the church or in society when men meet the required conditions.

Macintosh admits that when theology moves from the level of law to the level of theory, that is, from a consideration of what God does to a consideration of what he specifically is, the degree of certainty that can be attained decreases, and some element of pragmatic postulation replaces strict empirical procedure. The fundamental assumption or postulate at this level, he says, is that God is absolute. This absoluteness "is to be interpreted in a pragmatic and empirical sense, as meaning absolute satisfactoriness as Object of religious dependence, absolute sufficiency for man's religious needs."[19] This affirmation is intuitively certain from the standpoint of religious experience; it is pragmatically imperative from the standpoint of man's religious needs; and it is theoretically required to explain the operation of the theological laws which have been discovered and verified in actual experience.

Macintosh applies this postulate first to the moral attributes of God and then to the metaphysical attributes. The moral absoluteness of God means that he is morally perfect, an affirmation which is analyzable into the immanent attributes of holiness and love. With regard to the positive metaphysical attributes, Macintosh affirms that God is a self-existent, self-conscious, rational, purposive Being who is powerful enough, wise enough, and present enough with all reality to be man's completely adequate Savior. He is present in the world as the human self is immanent in its own experience and distinct from the world as the self is transcendent to the objects of its experience. From the point of view of a pragmatic theology Macintosh contends that it is not necessary to come to any decision regarding ultimate origins or to affirm that God created the world, as long as it can be maintained that God has adequate control over the world to guarantee man's well-being. However, his metaphysical point of view allows him to set forth a doctrine of origins along the lines laid down by Bergson in his theory of creative evolution.[20]

3. SUMMARY

Macintosh is an ethical intuitionist. He affirms that God is known primarily through the self's experience of moral transformation. Thus, Macintosh, like every liberal thinker, adheres to the principle of autonomy, according to which theological knowledge is grounded in experience rather than in revelation. Macintosh, however, does not give a Christocentric interpretation of moral experience. Knowledge of God sufficient unto salvation can be attained in present experience apart from the existence of the historical Jesus or without reference to his teachings. There is no necessary connection between Christian experience and history. This is a proposition which no evangelical liberal could accept. The principles of immanence and autonomy have combined to dissolve the concept of revelation in Macintosh's theology in a way that is not the case with the more moderate liberals.

In such a theology as this the doctrine of the Trinity can play no vital role. The connections of Macintosh's interpretation of this doctrine with the historic tradition are tenuous indeed. It is clear that the trinity of aspects to which he refers by no means refers to any real distinctions within the internal being of God.[21] Rather, they arise only from man's point of view and refer to various ways that God is known in experience or thought of by the intellect. The most decisive point, however, is that the existence of the historical Jesus logically is not necessary to establish the three aspects of God to which he refers. Historically, of course, the doctrine arose for no other reason than to account for the relationship between the unitary God of Hebrew monotheism and the God who was incarnate in Jesus Christ. Since he rejects the traditional view of the role of Christ, he has radically undermined the grounds by which the doctrine has historically been established. This amounts, as Welch points out,[22] to an explicit rejection of the doctrine, regardless of the similarity of some of his language to the orthodox formulas.

Despite the vast gulf between Macintosh and the orthodox Christian view of God, however, he is still closer to traditional theism than either of the other modernistic liberals. Although he interprets the moral and metaphysical attributes of God pragmatically, he believes firmly that God is absolute and that he is in some sense transcendent to the world process. He alone thinks of God as a living personal being. In fact, he is the only genuine theist in the group. Mathews and Wieman are fundamentally naturalists who apply the term God to some aspect of the evolutionary process. Some interpreters classify these two as theists of a sort,[23] but their fundamental loyalties bind them to a scientific naturalism.

C. *The Doctrine of Man*

1. THE NATURE OF MAN

The most characteristic way of defining man in liberal theology has been in terms of moral personality. This inheritance of American theology from the Kant-Ritschl tradition can be seen to some extent in every theologian dealt with thus far, and it is clearly present in D. C. Macintosh. Implicit in all that Macintosh says about man is the conception of a being who has arisen out of the evolutionary process of nature and yet who distinguishes himself from nature by virtue of his spiritual capacities. What man seeks in religion is power to develop the potentialities of personality to the fullest. This involves both the attaining of freedom from the evil inherent in the vicissitudes of nature and the realization of the moral ideal. "The God of moral optimism is that Factor which can be depended upon for conservation of the highest values for persons of good will, in spite of anything the forces of nature can do."[24]

Macintosh affirms that God aids man in his search for fulfillment through both general and special providence. General providence is defined by Macintosh as the provision of a law-abiding world in which men can learn by trial and error through the operation to the pleasure-pain principle and the laws of cause and effect what the true values in human life are. Special providence is the provision of divine aid, upon the right condition of a right religious adjustment, which enables men to triumph over nature and to attain the moral ideal.[25]

Macintosh argues that from the concept of man as a moral personality it can be postulated that man is free and probably immortal. The freedom of man does not mean, he says, complete indeterminism or the "liberty of indifference" but simply that the will itself is one factor among those which determine the actions of men. No known fact makes this kind of freedom impossible. Freedom is the necessary correlate of moral personality, and its reality is derived from the ordinary human consciousness of moral responsibility. Macintosh accepts the Kantian dictum that "I ought implies I can." Without freedom there could be no moral responsibility. Thus, freedom is seen to be theoretically possible, morally imperative, and intuitively certain.[26] Immortality can be pragmatically postulated on the basis that it is morally necessary on the assumption that personality is of infinite value.[27] Moreover, if moral optimism be a valid approach to life, immortality would seem to follow as a moral necessity also because the highest values of men cannot be realized otherwise.[28] The final assurance of immortality is not attained, however, until these pragmatic postulates have been validated on the basis of the personal experience of God and the consequent analysis of the character of God, which is the final guarantee of man's immortal destiny.[29]

2. THE MEANING OF SIN AND SALVATION

Macintosh discusses the nature of sin and salvation on the basis of the principle that personality is of infinite value. Sin is the violation of those moral ideals which constitute the good of persons.[30] Sinful action is seen by Macintosh to be made up of four constitutive factors: sensuousness, selfishness, ignorance, and indolence. Given the theory of evolution which tells of man's emergence from animal background, Macintosh feels that the origin of moral evil is not difficult to understand. The beastly impulses in man constitute a drag on his developing moral sense and make it difficult for him to discipline his passions and overcome his animal greed.[31] Here once again is an instance of the universal liberal belief that the understanding of sin in terms of the conflict between nature and spirit can account for wrongdoing without recourse to a belief in the corruption of the will or in a supernatural evil power.

One interesting feature of Macintosh's thought is that the concept of sin is derived from an analysis of the human situation apart from revelation or any experiential knowledge of God. The idea of sin is included among the presuppositions of theology. In this analysis there is no reference to the will of God as the norm in terms of which conduct must be measured. The concept of salvation, however, is developed in the light of the actual experience of God and is included among the empirical data of theology. The point at which, and the principle by which, Macintosh connects sin with the will of God in accordance with his own theological procedure is by no means clear, although he says that in the ordinary mind this connection is made as a matter of course. This way of dealing with the concept of sin represents a curious combination of the principles of autonomy and continuity. Sin is defined exclusively in terms of reason and experience and with reference to human relationships only. Moreover, he assumes a continuity between the state of sin, which can be defined apart from religious experience, and salvation, which presupposes an encounter of the self with God. Likewise, there is continuity between the moral ideals of Jesus, which to follow is salvation, and those ideals known discoverable by reason, which to violate is sin. He can move without difficulty from the human moral ideals which theology presupposes to the will of God which constitutes the standards of the redeemed life.

Salvation is defined by Macintosh as deliverance from evil, actual or potential, through the divine agency. To be at one with God is virtually to be saved, although the actual deliverance from evil may take a lifetime. The positive content of salvation is becoming Christlike in character through the agency of the Holy Spirit, which is the power of God in human life. The process of salvation includes a preliminary conviction of sin characterized by moral dissatisfaction together with a sense of need for atonement. This is followed by conversion, which consists of a turning away from sin (repentance) and a commitment to the will of God (faith). Following conversion, which is accomplished by a sense of forgiveness, peace, and assurance, a process of growth normally ensues in which the Christian character is strengthened, and new heights of attainment become possible. Macintosh is highly optimistic with regard to man's capacity for moral achievement. He affirms that "there is no evil resting upon individual or corporate delinquincy which may not also be finally uprooted and destroyed."[32]

In this view salvation is primarily a present reality, the essence of which is an internal moral transformation in which the self is organized around the moral ideal defined by the example of Jesus. There is little that is new or different in this interpretation of salvation. Actually, despite his radical method Macintosh retains many features of evangelical Christianity. His doctrine of the way of salvation is an instance of this. His own wholesome religious experience and his evangelical background no doubt were strong influences at this point. Thus, he insisted strongly on the centrality of personal conversion, repentance, faith, and a warm devotional life. There is little or no divergence at this point between Macintosh and the evangelical liberals.

D. *Christology*

1. CHRISTIANITY AND HISTORY

Christology was not a central concern of the modernistic liberals. The revelation of God in Jesus was considered to be normative only in the sense that the life and work of Jesus were illustrative of principles which could be discovered on grounds which were independent of the Christian tradition. This way of looking at the significance of Jesus is reflected quite clearly in Macintosh's statement to the effect that while the historical Jesus may be *psychologically* necessary for some people, his actual historicity is not *logically* necessary in order to establish or to validate the essence of Christianity.[33] There is an advantage, he urges, in showing how it is possible to justify the essentials of Christian belief without recourse to particular facts from the past. To make Christianity dependent on the findings of the historical critics infects belief with relativism and uncertainty.

These conclusions of Macintosh reflect his attempt to escape the relativism and skepticism which seemed to be the inevitable result of trying to ground theology in particular facts of history. Macintosh felt keenly the impact of those questions which were being raised by Troeltsch in Germany and by G. B. Foster in this country regarding the finality of the Christian religion and the relation of Christian faith to history.[34] The history of religions school and the uncertainties of contemporary New Testament scholarship threatened to undercut the attempt of much of liberalism to go behind theology and faith to the historical Jesus. Macintosh concluded that the only way out of these difficulties was to detach the essence of Christianity from dependence on history and base it squarely, at least on the ground level, in verifiable scientific fact.

This separation of the doctrine of God from Christology and the sundering of faith from history distinguishes Macintosh at a vital point from the evangelical liberals. Brown's principle from first to last was "Back to Christ." Fosdick understood the essence of Christianity in terms of reverence for personality, but he could not conceive of this principle apart from the historical Jesus. Rauschenbusch founded the social gospel solidly on the teachings and example of Jesus. Knudson rejected the Chalcedonian creed on both philosophical and theological grounds, but he attempted to preserve the essence of that doctrine in his own personalistic reinterpretation. Lyman's conception of Christian experience is bound up with his "Christ mysticism." In contrast to this Macintosh, Mathews, and Wieman disassociate their thinking from historical revelation and base their theology solely in reason and experience. Their only connection with the Christian tradition is that they affirm that the essence of Christianity is compatible with their findings.

2. THE SIGNIFICANCE OF JESUS

Despite the fact, however, that Macintosh does not base his theology at its center on the revelation of God in Christ, he still insists that Jesus is important. Jesus may be psychologically necessary for the promotion and development of the Christian experience of salvation. His moral example and his religious achievement have tremendous pedagogical value in helping others to attain a saving experience of God. Moreover, Jesus has considerable logical value in offering the supreme verification of the Christian moral ideal and the redeeming power of God in human life. Furthermore, he feels that enough can be known historically about Jesus to make it possible to evaluate his person in terms of a genuine revelation of God.

Macintosh emphasizes three divine elements in the person of Jesus: the quality of his life, the function which he performed, and the immanent presence of God within him. The quality of his personality is seen in his complete devotion to the highest moral ideals. His divine function is exercised in the effect of his life and work in leading men to an experience of moral salvation through dependence on God. From the divine quality of his personality and the divine function which he performed, it may be concluded, says Macintosh, that God was present in him to a unique degree. If Christ is Godlike, then God must be Christlike and therefore must be doing a Christlike work for the salvation of men in Christ and in all the Christlike. The divinity of Christ, then, simply means that in the human Jesus we find the supreme example of the immanence of God, the God who is present in every man to the extent that he approaches the right religious adjustment.[35] The work of Christ, according to Macintosh, is not that of making an objective atonement between man and God by bearing the sins of the world at Calvary. Rather, it consists in the influence of his life, his teachings, his example, and his personality in leading men to an experience of God. In revealing the love of God and the true moral ideal, he inspires men to repent of their sins and to seek that reconciliation to God which they see in Jesus.[36]

It may be seen from this analysis that Macintosh's approach to Christology is more radical in principle than it is in content. His view of Christ as a unique moral personality who leads men into a right relationship with God does not differ essentially from the point of view expressed by the evangelical liberals. Macintosh and the evangelical liberals interpret the divinity of Jesus in terms of the perfection of his humanity and agree that the difference between Jesus and other men is one of degree. The essential difference between them is that the evangelical liberals insist on a connection between Christian experience and historical revelation which Macintosh thinks is untenable if theology is going to escape from relativism and uncertainty.

E. *The Church*

The church is more neglected in the thought of D. C. Macintosh than in any other thinker under consideration. In fact, the doctrine is almost completely ignored. No chapter in any of his major books written before 1935 concerns itself with the church, and only a few passing references can be found here and there. In referring to the formulation of theological laws in the realm of ecclesiology, Macintosh points out that by the church he means "the community united on the basis of vital religious experience shared in common."[37] In listing those factors which are necessary to the well-being of religion, he says that "it would seem essential for the most effective preservation and propagation of experimental religion, that there should be an institution, a social religious organization, devoted primarily and specifically to these ends."[38] He adds that the church is such an institution and that the best church is the one which most effectively promotes experimental religion. The individual in this scheme of thought is free to draw up his own personal confession of faith containing whatever elements he deems necessary, and the church is free to adopt any form of church government which it deems most practicable. This pragmatic conception of the church which frees it from the traditions of the past is typical among liberal thinkers. The religious experience of the individual is clearly prior to the community; the community arises on the basis of the shared experiences of individuals. Individuals are free to join or not to join. The church is free to organize itself as it chooses and to believe as it chooses. It is one organization among many which has its peculiar function in being that institution which expresses and promotes the religious interests of its individual members.

Macintosh does include a chapter on the church in *Personal Religion,* published in 1942. In this volume he defines the marks of the true church as "the participation in an evangelically Christian religious experience and the propagation of that experience in individual and social life."[39] The sacraments are defined as potential means of grace which become actually effective in the lives of those who receive them in true faith and who are spiritually strengthened thereby. He approves the ecumenical movement and points out that "we need organization for more effective co-operation, with freedom to differ on many points within the limits of an essential working union."[40] The present task, he feels, is to work for more outward unity without enforcing uniformity.

F. *Conclusion*

The tendency among the modernistic liberals was to move far away from traditional Christian modes of thought, sometimes even to the point of abandoning theism. Of the three modernists here considered Macintosh perhaps remained closest in terms of content to the evangelical liberals, although in methodology he was as radical as either Mathews or Wieman. He was the only one of the three, however, to retain a recognizable theism. It is at this point that he differs most from the next man to be dealt with. Henry Nelson Wieman moved completely and explicitly into a philosophical naturalism to which Macintosh strenuously objected. This naturalistic alternative to the theism which Macintosh thought could be supported on rational grounds must now be considered.

CHAPTER 10

THEOLOGICAL NATURALISM:
HENRY NELSON WIEMAN

Henry Nelson Wieman (1884–   ), a native of Missouri, received the A.B. degree from Park College in 1907 and graduated in 1910 from San Francisco Theological Seminary. After studying in Germany at Jena and Heidelberg for two years, he returned to this country to earn the Ph.D. at Harvard University in 1917. Subsequently he served for ten years in the Philosophy Department at Occidental College in Los Angeles. In 1927 Wieman moved to the University of Chicago Divinity School, where he taught in the field of Philosophy of Religion until his retirement twenty years later. Since that time he has taught Philosophy at the University of Oregon (1949–1951) and at the University of Houston (1951–   ).[1] Wieman and Fosdick are the only two of the theologians considered here who are still living.

Among the theologians dealt with in this volume Wieman represents the extreme left; that is, he is furthest from the methods and conclusions of traditional Christian theology. He is a modernist because he begins with a set of presuppositions which are derived from twentieth-century American culture and not from the historic faith. He will accept no belief which cannot be validated on the basis of observation and reason. He considers that his method preserves what is really essential to Christian belief and that he is a loyal Christian. However, this loyalty does not include any obligation to accept any item of belief on the authority of the Bible or Christian tradition alone.

It has been remarked earlier that William Adams Brown retains more of the traditional language than any of the other men under consideration. It may be said now that Henry Nelson Wieman stands at the opposite extreme in this regard. In order to understand him, one must be prepared to learn a new terminology. In *The Source of Human Good,* published in 1946, Wieman makes more effort than he had before to connect his distinctive language with the corresponding terms in historical theology. Nevertheless, in spite of this movement toward more traditional ways of expression, his views of God, man, sin, salvation, and the church are set within a basic orientation which is alien to what has generally been thought to be essential to Christian belief.

What is most distinctive of Wieman is his attempt to reformulate Christian theology within the context of a naturalistic world view. With the exception of Mathews in his latest period, every liberal thinker considered here has insisted that theism is essential to the Christian outlook. Wieman, however, is thoroughly convinced that every form of supernaturalism has been outmoded by modern science. The doctrine of immanence is taken by Wieman to its ultimate conclusion. The discontinuity between God and nature is completely overcome. God is simply one aspect of the all-encompassing reality men call nature. While other liberals have insisted that the traditional dualism between God and the world must be reinterpreted in the light of the doctrine of immanence, none but Wieman has been willing to abandon theism completely for an openly avowed naturalism.[2]

In the intellectual autobiography which he contributed in 1932 to the symposium edited by Ferm, Wieman contends that his basic aim in theology is to promote a theocentric religion over against the prevailing anthropocentrism. The first requirement of such a religion, he maintains, is that the reality of God himself and not ideas about him be made the object of love and devotion. This means that men's ideas about God must be shaped by objective evidence and not by wishful thinking. In short, one must detach himself completely from traditional theological ideas and subjective wishes and desires and seek to learn about God strictly on the basis of scientific method. All beliefs must be subjected to the tests of observation and reason. In this sense there is the same strong note of objectivity in the thinking of Wieman which has already been noted in Macintosh. Both are attempting to ground theology in a solid foundation of objective fact discovered through empirical inquiry and rational analysis. Both hold to realistic views of epistemology, and both are trying to escape from an interpretation of religion based on feeling and internal states of consciousness. They want to describe the *realities* over against men which give rise to religious knowledge, not the *experience* of God within the soul. This objective note becomes stronger in Wieman after about 1930. Before that time he had given more emphasis to the significance of occasional, special states of mystical awareness out of which fresh insights are developed.

The discussion of Wieman's thought which immediately follows is based almost exclusively upon those books and articles which appeared before about 1939. A postscript will deal with further development in Wieman's outlook after this period down to the publication of *The Source of Human Good* in 1946.

A. *Religion, Empiricism, and Naturalism*

There are three particular aspects of Wieman's thought which, when taken together, make him unique among the theologians thus far considered: his value-centered religion, his adherence to a strict empiricism, and his naturalistic world view. An explanation of each of these factors is in order.

1. RELIGION AND VALUE

Religion, according to Wieman, is the way man adapts himself to the ultimate facts of existence in order to achieve the greatest good.[3] In the background of this view of religion is the conception of man as an organism interacting with his natural environment.[4] Man is dependent on those factors about him which produce, sustain, and increase value. Whatever plays this role is God. Religion is the search for the source of human good (God) and the effort to increase human good by proper adjustment to value-producing factors in the cosmos.[5] In *The Wrestle of Religion with Truth* Wieman maintains that religion consists of three interrelated phases.[6] First of all, there is a realization of one's maladaption to the universe and an emerging sense of need. Secondly, there is the discovery of the hard facts of existence to which life must be adapted, a discovery which judges one's present behavior and demands the reorganization of personality. Finally, there is the attainment of peace, joy, power, and integration of personality following from the proper adaptation of the self to the cosmos.

Religion, then, is devotion to value or human good. But what is value? Wieman has at one time or another in his career defined value as the fulfillment of human interest,[7] as the connection between enjoyable or appreciable activities,[8] and as qualitative meaning.[9] Whatever differences of emphasis may be involved in these changes in terminology, there is a common factor running through all of them. Human good is always to be found in a context in which enjoyable activities are connected with other activities which affect human life in such a way that a meaningful structure is built up in which each activity is organically related to the total system of activities which constitute human living. Value, then, is "that connection between appreciable activities which makes them mutually sustaining, mutually enhancing, mutually diversifying, and mutually meaningful."[10] Appreciable here means what would be enjoyed if its contribution to human life were fully understood. Activity here means a change which contributes to the organization of the system to which it belongs.

Increase of human good occurs when there is an increase in the connections between those activities which affect human life. This connective growth makes possible new dimensions of enjoyment and meaning, integrates further the parts of experience with the whole of life, and opens up still further possibilities of creative growth. Some types of growth, however, may be evil. An example is a cancerous growth. Growth is good only when it is constructive, i.e., when it makes for the unlimited continuation of the integration of meaningful activities without destructive conflicts and frustrations. Evil is, on the one hand, stagnation or cessation of growth and, on the other hand, competitive, self-centered, disintegrative growth.[11]

This concept of religion as the effort to realize human values connects Wieman with the fundamental concern of liberalism for the development of human personality. Religion in liberal theology is man-centered in the sense that its aim is not primarily to glorify God but to develop personality. God is the source of human good and thus is indispensable to the human venture. Wieman represents an extreme example of this man-centered outlook in that he defines God in terms of his function in relation to the increase of human good. By definition God is relevant to the development of personality.

2. EMPIRICISM

If religion is the search for human good, how can the truth necessary to this venture be discovered? According to Wieman, the only way that men can discover the source of human good and learn how to relate themselves to it productively is by adhering strictly to the empirical method. This simply means that God must be known in the same way that any other object is known, that is, through the data provided by raw experience, conceptualized, interpreted, and systematized by reason.[12] The concepts derived by reason from experience must then be subjected to experimentation in actual human living in order to test their validity.

This means that God must be an object of sense experience, and that is precisely what Wieman affirms.[13] Two essential factors must be combined, according to Wieman, before one can perceive God in immediate experience in such a way that new insights about values and the way to realize them are forthcoming. First of all, one must develop the right religious adjustment to the divine value-producing factors in the universe.[14] The life of prayer, worship, and active devotion to known values and an openness to new values opens the door to increased knowledge of God. This intense cultivation of values will occasionally and continually yield intuitions, mystical experiences, moments of unusual awareness, and sudden visions of unattained possibilities of good. These rare experiences provide the raw data out of which new knowledge of God comes. In the second place, one must develop the proper tools of critical thought in order to interpret the data which religious experience provides. The concrete sense data must be organized by reason into concepts, and these concepts must be related to the total system of concepts which constitute the person's present range of knowledge. When these concepts are organized into concrete beliefs, these beliefs must then be subjected to the tests of actual life in order to seek if they hold true in practical experience.

What Wieman is calling for here is experimental living which alternates between the having of creative religious experiences and the interpretation of them in order to achieve a gradually increasing body of reliable knowledge about God. He refers to these two facets of the religious venture in a number of widely differing ways, but he always makes the same point. He speaks of the life of contemplation which alternates between mystical experience and scientific analysis,[15] of human creativity which alternates between discovery and theorizing,[16] of religious experience which provides the concrete data which are organized into concepts by philosophy of religion,[17] of scientific method which consists of observation and reason,[18] and, finally, of the sides of the ladder of truth consisting of immediate experience and experimental verification.[19]

In his first books Wieman attributed great importance to mysticism as the form of human experience in which God is apprehended. In ordinary experience, he says, certain objects and ideas are selected out of the total mass of conscious experience for attention and response; all else is excluded. In mystical experience this routine selectivity is interrupted (sometimes under stress, confusion, and unusual excitement), and wider ranges of data are immediately experienced. The self is flooded with an undifferentiated mass of data so rich, so full, and so overwhelming that all perception and cognition are drowned in a sea of sensuous awareness. Mystical experience is confrontation with a total event beyond the ordinary interpretation people give it. The immediate experience is meaningless, but from this experience new insight and power come. A transformation takes place in the self, a moral renewal, in which old habits and patterns are dissolved and are integrated about a new center.[20]

In Wieman's writings after about 1930, however, considerably less emphasis is put upon mysticism, and criticism is raised against religious experience as such as a guarantee of religious truth.[21] He now maintains that neither the subjective effects of beliefs nor any particular content of consciousness gives assurance that anything objective has been apprehended.[22] Stress is increasingly put upon the necessity for observation which tests the subjective insights and intuitions of the mind. While a significant change of emphasis is apparent during these later years, no real change in principle is indicated, since he had insisted from the beginning that experience must be interpreted and tested in order to attain dependable knowledge. However, Wieman does seem to be putting emphasis now on the objective referent rather than on the subjective apprehension of objects. This change of emphasis no doubt represents the influence in Wieman's thought of religious realism, which was making its influence felt in America in the years after 1930.[23]

Wieman, then, is a strict empiricist. There is, of course, no place in this scheme for the concept of revelation. Wieman dismisses revelation simply by identifying it with inherited beliefs drawn from the Bible, the church, or traditional systems of theology. Theology, according to him, has no special sources of data or any methods peculiar to itself. Rather, it is identical with philosophy of religion. All attainable truth is available through the method of observation and reason. This procedure represents a radical application of the principle of autonomy. Theology is completely divorced from history and is grounded solely in present experience. As has been pointed out previously, this marks a significant distinction between the evangelical and modernistic liberals. The latter, unlike the former, find no norm in the historical Jesus to which all Christian thinking must conform. Wieman can define his theological method without once mentioning the authority of Christ.

3. NATURALISM

Wieman's value-centered view of religion and his adherence to a strict empirical methodology are set within the context of a naturalistic world view. Naturalism affirms that there is but one reality, and that is the reality which is open to observation and testing by the scientific method.[24] There is no reality beyond the reach of the senses. The naturalism of Wieman is not a reductive materialism which denies the reality of mind, consciousness, values, and God. It denies nothing that is a genuine part of human experience. It simply denies that mind, consciousness, values, and God belong to another realm or dimension of reality than that which can be observed by the senses.

Wieman is a naturalist who belongs to that group of thinkers who make process ultimate. Not static perfection but ceaseless change, not being but becoming, is the last word about reality. All existing things are processes having a structure.[25] The influence of Dewey, Whitehead, and Bergson is clearly evident in this emphasis on the ultimacy of process. This process is taken as is, as a going concern, as dynamic existence, which neither can be nor need be explained by reference to a transcendent creator or purposive mind.[26] The world process, however, is not simply dynamic; it is also creative. There are progress and growth in the world. New meanings and values emerge; new levels of being are produced; and ideal possibilities constantly become realities. But here again growth is in and of nature and is not the work of some ontologically transcendent power.

Wieman's naturalism represents a radical application of the principles of continuity and dynamism in the same way that his empiricism represents a radical employment of the principle of autonomy. All liberals insisted on the immanence of God in that they described God primarily as the Christlike Spirit who pervades the whole of reality and who is actively present at all times and places, working out his creative purposes. Nevertheless, with few exceptions they never denied a real distinction between God and the world. Dualism was rejected, but a duality remained. This is true of all the evangelical liberals surveyed in this inquiry and also of Macintosh. Mathews' view is similar to Wieman's. Wieman, however, takes the principle of continuity and applies it in such a way that even the duality between God and the world is overcome. Nature encompasses the whole of reality. This does not mean that God and the world are identical (pantheism), but it does mean that God is himself a part of the natural process and not something other than, or different from, nature. Wieman also goes further with the liberal emphasis of the dynamic aspects of the world. He does not affirm simply that the present state of the world is a result of a long process of development but that reality as such is a process. There are no static things which change. All beings *are* structured processes, including human persons and God. In short, dynamism is interpreted in metaphysical as well as in historical terms.

B. *The Doctrine of God*

1. THE DEFINITION OF GOD

Wieman's doctrine of God is developed within the context defined by his value-centered religion, his empirical method, and his naturalistic world view. The experienceable world—which is the only reality men can know—is a dynamic, creative process. This process has produced human beings who are dependent upon a right adjustment with the environing conditions for their security and welfare. Among the multiple, complex activities which make up the total human environment, certain of them are of critical importance for human life. These activities are those which produce, sustain, promote, and increase human good. This behavior or activity which constitutes the value-producing factor in the universe is God. God, then, is a reality in nature, knowable in experience, which functions as the source of meaning and value.[27]

An important clarification in Wieman's attempt to arrive at the precise meaning of the concept of God came in his encounter with John Dewey in *The Christian Century* in 1934. The debate began with Wieman's enthusiastic review of Dewey's book, *A Common Faith*.[28] Wieman made it appear that he and Dewey were thinking of God in essentially the same way. He attributes to Dewey the belief that the idea of God involves reference to a superhuman reality consisting of activities in nature which generate and support values. According to

Dewey, he says, this reality operates in the world beyond human power but in co-operation with men to promote human good, i.e., to unite the ideal and the actual. In a later issue E. E. Aubrey, Wieman, and Dewey contribute letters which bring the matter to a head.[29] Aubrey challenges Wieman's interpretation of Dewey, insisting that "the integrative power binding actual and ideal is still restricted, in Mr. Dewey's thought, to human imaginative intelligence."[30] In his response Dewey accepts Aubrey's rebuttal of Wieman, agreeing that Wieman "has read his own position into his interpretation of mine."[31] Dewey then makes it clear that the union of ideal with the actual of which he speaks and to which he cautiously applies the term God is a union "accomplished in human imagination and to be realized through human choice and action."[32]

The conclusion which emerges from this exchange is that Wieman had simply been overzealous in his attempt to claim Dewey as an ally. Dewey is patently a humanist, and he interprets God purely in human terms. In a final letter Wieman reluctantly admits that he has been wrong about Dewey's intended meaning and now accuses Dewey of failing to carry out the implications of his thought to its logical result. He expresses stunned disbelief that Dewey can really believe that the term God refers only to the work of human imagination and effort, when it is so obviously clear that possibilities of value are generated, sustained, and promoted by certain activities in the cosmos itself. In other words, Wieman ends by maintaining that while Dewey apparently does not agree with him, he ought to if he is to be consistent with his own implicit position and the obvious facts of experience.

The significance of this discussion was that it made it apparent to Wieman that in defining God to refer to some kind of operative reality in nature itself, he could not expect the support of the empiricists in the naturalistic, humanistic wing of American philosophy of religion. In other debates with D. C. Macintosh and Robert Calhoun it became evident that he could not expect support from those on his theological right in the theistic camp. Neither group by and large seemed able to understand or to accept his attempt to be both a naturalist and a theist.

2. THE NATURE OF GOD

What God may be in the fullness of his concrete being, Wieman contends, is beyond the present range of man's knowledge,[33] but some

additional conclusions about God can be reached. One further speci-
fication about God emerged in connection with the criticism that Wieman's "immediate empiricism," in which objects are taken to be just
what they are experienced as,[34] leads to a "theological behaviorism."
According to this "theological behaviorism," so the criticism runs,
God is defined as a kind of growth or interaction or activity without
reference to any kind of substance or being or mind which is the subject of these functions.[35] Wieman's general reply to this criticism is
that all existing things are processes or interactions having a certain
form or structure. There is no hidden something behind the process
itself. The structural process, including the possibilities which inhere
in this process, is itself the concrete reality.[36] Wieman's most effective
response to the charge of "theological behaviorism" was developed in
a debate with Robert Calhoun in *Christendom* in 1936–1937. He
admits a willingness to declare that God is a substantial agent if substance be defined in one or a combination of three ways, (1) as "the
most inclusive system of all internally related activities, actual and
possible, which make up an organic whole,"[37] (2) as "an activity
which underlies all others" in an organic whole,[38] or (3) as the "order, form structure, principle," the "timeless, eternal, changeless factor found in all change."[39]

Regardless, however, of whether God be referred to as a substantial agent or simply a certain kind of structured process, Wieman
resolutely denies that his value-producing reality can be called mind
or personality in any meaningful sense.[40] He has stated his objections
to referring to God as a personality in a variety of ways. (1) God
cannot be a person because personalities develop only in a society of
interacting persons, and this cannot be true of God.[41] (2) The greatest good is realized only in interaction between persons, and since
God is the greatest good, he cannot be a person himself.[42] (3) "God
is more than a personality because the parts between which that interaction occurs which is God are personalities."[43] (4) The function
of God is so important, and personality is so little understood, that it
is unintelligible to speak of God as a personality.[44]

The most important reasons for denying personality to God came out
in his debate with Calhoun, to which reference has already been made.
Wieman maintains that while process and interaction apply to all existing beings, including God, mind and personality are limited, re-
strictive characteristics which appear only at the summit of those

beings which possess them. Therefore, if God is mind or personality, he cannot be more than this, whereas Wieman wishes to maintain that God is infinitely more than mind.[45] Lastly, and of most importance, is the distinction made by Wieman between the work of minds and the work of God. Human minds can make only mechanisms, that is, entities characterized by external relations. God makes only organisms, that is, entities characterized by internal relations.[46] This distinction between man's work and God's work, Wieman insists, makes mind totally inappropriate as a description of God.[47]

3. GOD AND NATURE

Wieman has a great deal to say about the relation of God to nature. God is not more than nature or outside of nature in any sense. Thus, he denies supernaturalism. But neither is God identical with the universe itself. In this way he avoids pantheism.[48] God is one direction of movement or system of activities within the universe. Thus, Wieman is a pluralist.[49] God does not control all of existence, and so far as Wieman can judge, nothing does. There are many directions of movement within the world, and this allows for an element of freedom, change, and indeterminacy. However, God is unitary, because it is that integration of many activities into a connected system which makes for value.[50] Evil is competitive, multiple, divisive, and destructive, and since the work of God is that of integrating and unifying, evil cannot be the work of God.[51] God works at every level of nature. Since value at the human level depends on physical, chemical, biological, and psychological factors, the integrating activities of God go on at these lower levels also.[52] God's being, then, includes not only the actual structured processes which now serve to connect human enjoyments but also those unrealized possibilities which inhere in these processes.[53]

4. TRANSCENDENCE AND IMMANENCE

Wieman affirms that God is both transcendent and immanent, but care must be taken to see precisely what he means in each case. If God is one system of activities within nature, it would seem that he could not be transcendent to nature taken as a whole. From this point of view, then, God is purely immanent within nature, and in no sense is he more than, apart from, or creative of, the world. Furthermore,

God is not transcendent to his own actions. God as a substantial agent is simply the total system of activities which is constitutive of his being or the whole of his activities which underlies one part of his activities. There is thus no distinction between the agent and his actions.[54]

However, there are certain ways in which God is said to be transcendent. At least five such ways can be enumerated. (1) God as eternal, changeless form is transcendent to the temporal process.[55] (2) God's work is superhuman. Growth of meaning and value is always the work of God and not of man. Furthermore, God works beyond, ahead of, and sometimes contrary to, human purposes to achieve the greatest possible integration of meaningful activities.[56] (3) The nature of God's absolute being and the details of how he works are beyond human comprehension.[57] (4) Again, God's being is utterly different from ours.[58] (5) There are unrealized possibilities which inhere in the present reality of God. These possibilities are patterns in the being of God which do not now exist as actual achievements.[59]

5. COMMENT

Wieman has set forth a doctrine of God which is far removed from the main line of the historic Christian tradition. The most fundamental difference between Wieman and Christian tradition is that he is able to arrive at a conception of God without any reference whatsoever to the Christian revelation. Not once does he appeal to the authority of the Bible or to the revelation of God in Christ as a source of truth. He appeals only to experience and reason. This procedure is simply the logical outcome of the radical application of the principle of autonomy, and the result is that the concept of revelation disappears altogether.

Given his empirical method and his naturalistic world view, Wieman arrives at a view of God which has but faint resemblance to the classical Christian treatments of the doctrine. No longer is God described as the Almighty Creator of the world and the Sovereign Lord of history. There is no mention of the Trinity of Father, Son, and Holy Spirit. Nothing is said about the self-manifestation of God in history to Israel and in Christ. It is denied that God is a personal being with the attributes of mind and personality. He is not absolute, nor omnipotent, nor even in any real metaphysical sense transcendent. This list could be indefinitely lengthened, but it is obvious that Wieman has cut himself completely loose from the Christian tradition and has struck out on his own to construct a view of deity which can be affirmed by a man thoroughly immersed in modern scientific culture.

C. *The Doctrine of Man*

1. THE NATURE OF MAN

Wieman's doctrine of man is based upon an organism-environment scheme in which the concept of adjustment becomes the key to sin and salvation.[60] Upon this basis Wieman proceeds to investigate empirically the nature of the human organism and the nature of its environment in order to discover how man may adjust himself to reality (the total natural environment) to achieve the greatest possible human good. Human behavior itself as it appears under the searchlight of observation and reason is the object of study. From the standpoint of the methods employed and the concepts used in this investigation of human nature and human behavior, Wieman's doctrine of man takes the form of a psychology of religion.

The human person or the self is described by Wieman in dynamic terms as a living, acting organization of habits, drives, and impulses oriented to the attainment of certain goals which give direction to its vast potentialities for growth.[61] The problem of human life is to organize one's habits in such a way that they are integrated around those goods and goals which are in harmony with the increase of meaning and value in the world.[62] What is called for is continual growth in which new and better habits are developed and which extend the range of human response to the lure of the indefinite possibilities of good. The continual transformation of the organized responses of the individual to those value-producing factors in the environment is the clue to the abundant life.

2. SIN AND SALVATION

Given this scheme, sin and salvation come to be interpreted in terms of maladjustment and adjustment. Sin "is failure to make that adaptation to God which the growing life requires."[63] The ills that result from this failure to grow are three: mental misery, wrongdoing, and impoverished life.[64] In a later book sin is defined in a more theocentric fashion as disloyalty to God, but the meaning remains the same.[65] Salvation means attaining that proper adjustment of the growing personality with those increasing possibilities of value by which life is integrated and attains its proper fulfillment.[66] In *Normative Psychology of Religion* Wieman speaks of the process of salvation in terms of guilt, confession, forgiveness, and conversion.[67] Disloyalty to the growth of meaning and value produces a sense of guilt. Confession purges the soul from its disloyalty, keeps the conscience sensitive to the fine distinctions between better and worse, and enables one to yield himself more completely to the purging process of growth which is God. Forgiveness is made possible by the fact that God constantly seeks to weave the individual and his activities into that web of meaning and mutual support in which all value lies. Conversion, as defined by Wieman, is that change in a person's life which integrates him into that process by which God fulfills life through connective growth.

3. SUMMARY

Two of the principles which are fundamental to liberalism are particularly noticeable in Wieman's doctrine of man. The principle of continuity is radically applied in that man is an emergent out of nature, while God is a process within nature. There is, then, no sharp division between nature, man, and God. The principle of dynamism is also very much in evidence. Man has emerged out of an ongoing world process, owing to certain personality-producing activities in nature. Man himself is a dynamic creature consisting of a complex organization of habits, drives, and processes. He finds his true fulfillment by adjusting himself to those creative processes in the cosmos which are knitting together possibilities of meaning and value. Activity, growth, process, change, development—these are everywhere key words for Wieman.

The resulting doctrine of man is scarcely recognizable as far as specific Christian content is concerned. All that man needs to know about himself, his world, and his relationship to ultimate reality is available to him through the use of scientific method and without reference whatsoever to the Christian revelation. The organism-environment scheme which informs his understanding of man is taken from the biological sciences and is closely related to the instrumentalism of John Dewey. Completely missing in Wieman's account is any reference to the *imago dei,* original sin, the future life, and many of the other staple concepts of historic orthodoxy. Sin and salvation are no longer understood in terms of man's relationship to a transcendent, personal Creator, Judge, and Redeemer but in terms of man's adaptation to the impersonal processes of nature. Wieman's view is that of a thinker completely emancipated from the historic faith.

D. *The Significance of Jesus Christ*

1. PRINCIPLES VERSUS PERSONALITY

Wieman's theology is not Christocentric. This has already become patently clear from the foregoing discussion. He "draws upon all that tradition may declare concerning God, but cannot accept any belief unless it can be supported by what can be actually found going on in the world."[68] This is not to say that Wieman finds no significance in Jesus, but it is to say that whatever significance he does find is in the fact that Jesus is illustrative of principles and truths which are inherent in his own scheme of thought. This point of view regarding Jesus clearly identifies Wieman as a modernist.

The modernistic outlook is well illustrated by an article by Wieman in *The Christian Century* in 1930 entitled "Appreciating Jesus Christ."[69] The thesis which he defends is that what is really important in Jesus is not his individual, unique personality but the principles which he advocated and the specifications which are involved in attaining the kind of life he represents. The appreciation of Jesus, he admits, may contribute more personal enjoyment to individuals in the form of a warm emotional glow and ecstatic exhilaration, but it gives little aid in reproducing that experience in other lives, except as admiration of Jesus may lead to an imitation of his principles. Moreover, Jesus himself did not advocate the appreciation of himself, according to Wieman, but urged that certain principles be put into practice. In short, what is called for is patient, laborious investigation of the good life by means of observation and reason in order to discover those principles and specifications which make the good life possible and attainable. Jesus is of value only as he helps us in this empirical venture. Furthermore, it is the fact that the principles of Jesus are right and not the fact that Jesus practiced them that is primary. The principles themselves are universal and belong to all mankind, not merely to Jesus alone.

2. THE UNIQUENESS OF JESUS

But what precisely is it in Jesus which makes him unique in human history, so that we must turn to him to find those principles whose practice will further the growth of human good? Wieman answers this question in another article in *The Christian Century* entitled "Was God in Jesus?"[70] Jesus is unique because there is more of God present in him than there is anywhere else. God is the superhuman growth of organic connections which produces, sustains, and increases human good. God is present in Jesus in terms of a reality functioning in him to further this integrating process among men. Thus, Wieman concludes, "the identifying mark of God is organic unity, found functioning pre-eminently in Jesus, which operates in the world to make us brothers, that is, functional members one of another."[71] The presence of this reality in Jesus was and is unique, but this uniqueness is attributed to fortuitous, favorable historical circumstances and not to a special act of God which breaks the continuities and regularities of the historical process. Moreover, this reality manifests itself in other persons and events in such a way that would seem to differ only in degree from the revelation found in Jesus. The work of Jesus, then, would seem to be reducible to the illuminating revelation of the growth of organic connections in the person of Jesus and to the actual, empirically verifiable, historical effects of his life and work which have persisted down to our own age and still continue.

3. SUMMARY

Jesus is not the way, the truth, and the life; he is merely illustrative of it. He is not the source of the Christian experience of redemption; he is merely its exemplification. Jesus is a very, very good example of principles, values, and realities which have been discovered and found to be of supreme importance independently of himself and on grounds other than his intrinsic authority. Had Jesus never lived, observation and reason could have discovered the nature of God and the way to attain human good elsewhere, although Jesus is of great significance because of his revelatory function and his actual empirical influence within history. Jesus is valuable, but not indispensable.[72]

E. *The Church*

Wieman nowhere gives an extended, systematic treatment of the doctrine of the church. What he says regarding the church appears incidentally along with more central concerns. As is true in most liberalism, the church is a peripheral interest. Wieman's view of the church has to be developed from occasional comments scattered here and there throughout his writings.

Wherever Wieman treats of the church, it is from the standpoint of its functional significance. The church seems to be thought of largely as a bearer, sustainer, promoter, and interpreter of the religious worship and fellowship of individuals. In his earliest period Wieman connects the purpose of the church closely with the stimulation and interpretation of mystical experience.[73] It is also an agency of action and a personality-building association.[74] In Wieman's later books the emphasis comes to be more upon function of the church in promoting organic relationships between its members and in furthering loyalty to the creative value-producing processes at work in the world (God) and less on the stimulation of mystical experiences. There is a turning toward the objective factors in religious growth in Wieman's writing after 1930, and this change of emphasis is reflected in his teachings regarding the church. In *Normative Psychology of Religion,* published in 1935, the function of the church is said to be "the fostering and promoting of loyalty to that which is believed to be supremely worthful for all human living."[75]

Wieman shares the typical liberal disregard for the traditional forms, ceremonies, and beliefs of the church and manifests a disdain for denominational divisions and ancient doctrinal squabbles. In discussing the present-day problems of the church in *Normative Psychology of Religion,* the main note of emphasis is that the church must be modern in belief and structure in order to function effectively in the modern world.[76] Finally, Wieman strikes one note which is somewhat different from the usual liberal view regarding the function of the church within society. It is commonly said among liberals that the church is the agent by which the kingdom of God is to be realized on earth. Wieman gives a sociological reason why the church as such cannot perform this function.[77] The church is an organic part of the society in which it exists and is shaped by the mores, customs, and values of that society. It can work to change the patterns of groups which are contrary to its own, but it cannot transcend its own values, which are themselves socially derived. The church as a whole can conserve, but it cannot revolutionize. The prophets and the reformers must operate as catalysts within the total church. This emphasis upon creative individuals and small groups within the larger fellowship as the real dynamic within the church is typical of Wieman.[78]

F. *Postscript*

What has been said thus far is an attempt to state the basic themes of Wieman's thought as it had developed to approximately the year 1939. Since his thought was undergoing change at that time, a brief statement regarding the later developments may be helpful. In his contribution to the series of articles in *The Christian Century* on "How My Mind Has Changed in the Third Decade,"[79] Wieman indicated that certain blind spots had been removed, owing largely to changes in the social environment and to certain conversations he had had with other thinkers, notably R. L. Calhoun, John Dewey, D. C. Macintosh, Max Otto, in addition to the writings of Barth, Brunner, Tillich, and Berdyaev. He indicated six changes. (1) He now uses Christian symbols more because they carry a depth and scope of meaning developed over the centuries which no other words can match. (2) Sin is now viewed not as "the disparity between our conduct and our highest ideals," but as "the disparity between our highest ideals and the concrete goodness in the immediate situation which is the offering of God and his demand."[80] (3) Grace is seen to be "the good which God puts into each concrete situation over and above all that man can do or plan or even imagine."[81] (4) The grace of God is the living Christ. The incarnation of God in Christ initiated a tradition which has been profoundly creative of human good from the first century until now. (5) The church is really the same thing as the living Christ. It is the influence of Christ made effectively continuous through fellowship. (6) God is seen with increasing clarity to be utterly different from man. Human persons and minds cannot give rise to growth. Only God can work in this concrete way.

In *The Source of Human Good,* published in 1946, Wieman gives a systematic statement of his views on religion which incorporate changes in his thought up to that point. In this book are to be found the same three elements which have previously been specified as being basic to his thought: a value-centered religion, an empirical method strictly adhered to, and a naturalistic world view. The interrelated structure of appreciable activities which constitute human good and in which any single activity becomes a reminder or sign of the meaning of the whole is now called qualitative meaning. That value-producing activity within nature which increases qualitative meaning is the creative event. This source of human good is God. Qualitative meaning now actually functioning is created good. The creative event with reference to the increase of created good is creative good.

Within this framework Christian doctrines are given their meaning. The creating, preserving, and saving work which has been attributed to the transcendent God of traditional Christianity is seen to be identical with the creative event. Sin is the domination of the life of man by created good. Salvation is the reversing of this domination of created good to domination by creative good. Salvation is accomplished through Christ, who represents the domination of the creative event made continuous in history. To be saved is to be incorporated into this continuous movement initiated in history by Christ.[82]

In this book certain of those newly emerging tendencies which appeared in the 1939 article in *The Christian Century* are clearly in evidence. Of particular importance are: (1) his increased employment of traditional Christian terminology, (2) his new emphasis on the meaning of the living Christ as a tremendously potent creative factor within history—equaled only by the creation of the living cell and the emergence of the human personality—and, (3) the emphasis on the church and the embodiment of the influence of the Christ in a continuing community through which salvation is mediated. Both the depth of sin and the reality of God's grace in Christ receive more attention. However, the result is still determined by a perspective drawn from modern culture centering in a value-centered, religious version of a naturalistic process philosophy erected by means of an empirical method—all of which are distinctly modern—and not from the stream of Christian tradition.

Beginning with William Adams Brown, who attempted to unite the old evangelicalism with the new theology, this survey has touched upon the major varieties of liberalism and has now reached the other extreme represented by Henry Nelson Wieman, who abandoned the old theology for the distinctly new and modern. Two tasks now remain. First, the liberal theology which has been described must be summarized, evaluated, and, finally, the impact of liberal modes of thought upon the continuing theological enterprise must be assessed. The remaining chapters are devoted to these problems.

PART FOUR

CONCLUSION

CHAPTER 11

THE ESSENCE OF LIBERALISM
AND ITS VALIDITY

I. THE ESSENCE OF LIBERALISM

The purpose of this chapter is to offer, by way of summary, an outline of the basic structure of liberal theology. Since it is necessary to
speak in broad, general terms, the portrait of liberalism that is drawn
may not be entirely fair to the views of any particular liberal theologian. However, what is said is a true description of liberalism as
a distinct theological perspective, within which there are divergences
of emphasis with regard both to method and to content.

Liberalism was dominated by a world view which tends toward
monism. Reality is fundamentally one realm, one process, one structure of activities. There is continuity between the world and God and
between nature and man. God is thought of as the Immanent Spirit
or as the Purposive Power at work within nature and history. The
organism and not the machine is the best analogy of the world, and
God is as much the Soul of the world or its Living Spirit as he is its
creator. God has been at work over a vast period of time to bring order out of chaos and to create ever new and higher levels of being.
Out of inorganic matter has come organic life, and from lower types
of organisms has emerged a creature possessed with mind and spirit.
Man is the crowning achievement of God's creative work, and, because of the divine image implanted within his being, he is capable
of joining with God as a partner in the task of making an even better
world. This creature is of infinite worth, and the goal toward which
God now supremely works is the perfection of man's moral person-

ality through the establishment of the rule of love among men.

The clue to the nature of this Immanent Spirit who is at work in all things is to be found in the person and work of the historical Jesus. The meaning and goal of the long evolutionary process have been made manifest through his life. In him the nature of the divine purpose which activates the world is revealed with great clarity and power. The end toward which God has striven is the creation of a society of persons whose lives are patterned after the ideal represented in Jesus. He is the light of the world through whom men can come to know who God is and what he is like. In short, the universe is a unified, dynamic process activated by an immanent Christlike Spirit whose supreme goal is the establishment of a kingdom of love and brotherhood on earth.

It follows from the immanence of God that he can be discovered in all natural and historical processes. Since God is actively present in all things, no special, miraculous revelations are necessary. Rather, the divine purpose can be seen in the evolutionary process of nature, in the long upward development of men from beasts to moral personalities, in the strivings of humanity for a better world, and in every moral and spiritual advance of the race. Men also know God in their own personal experience. In the apprehension of moral values, in the awakening of compassion in response to human needs, in the demands of the conscience, in the invasion of the soul by the divine Spirit which kindles love for God and man, fortifies the self with strength to meet all crises, and floods the self with peace, joy, and power, in the kindred responses of men to truth, goodness, and beauty—in all these ways men make contact with God.

It is, of course, through the experience of the Hebrew people that the highest religious insights have come, for they have been especially responsive to the divine impulses which are dormant in all men. Jesus represents the climax of the religious development of his people, and the Christian religion which he founded is the most complete and perfect of all the world religions. The Bible is a testimony to the way these pioneers of the true faith met, knew, and served God in their own generation. It traces the development of the Hebrew religion from the primitive polytheism of the Patriarchs to the lofty ethical monotheism of Jesus. Through its witness to the remarkable achievements of these spiritual geniuses—and supremely to Jesus—the Bible awakens, stimulates, and clarifies the experience of God in the present age.

It helps men now to attain the ideal represented in the life and teachings of Jesus. Its ancient categories must be revised in the light of new knowledge, but its insights into the abiding experiences of faith, love, and obedience are of universal significance. In this way revelation is seen to be continuous with reason and experience. In fact, the gulf between them is so reduced that they often tend to be identified. Christianity is fundamentally reasonable, and it appeals to the highest and best in human nature. The truths of the Bible help to clarify the meaning of the present experience of God, while religious experience confirms the best of the Biblical insights as these are measured by the supreme achievement of Jesus.

The dynamic, monistic outlook of liberalism provided the clue for the understanding of the human problem. Human beings are moral personalities who have emerged out of nature. Their greatest problem is that they are not fully emancipated from the animal background out of which they have come. Moreover, the mechanisms of nature subject men to pain, suffering, and death. The beastly passions within and the indifference of nature to personal values without constitute a barrier which must be overcome if moral personality in man is to attain its highest potentialities.

The liberal gospel is that the victory of spirit over nature may be won if men will appropriate the light and life which are mediated to them through the impact of the historical Jesus. Under his influence the native capacities of reason, conscience, and good will in men can be so strengthened and developed that a quality of life is made possible in which moral personality is fulfilled. When men are morally renewed by the inspiration and example of Jesus and fortified by the spiritual resources which flow into life from him, nature no longer holds for them any terror. Moreover, they are able to overcome the atavistic drag of their animal impulses. The highest human good is realized as individuals join together in the creation of a community based on mutual love, sacrificial service, and universal brotherhood. The achievement of this perfect society is the highest moral demand which is laid upon men.

The principle of immanence provided a basis for the understanding of Christ. He represents, not the incarnation of the second Person of the Trinity, but the perfection of human personality. His divinity is his perfect humanity. His life is the supreme moral and spiritual achievement of human history, and this uniqueness makes him both the revealer of God and the savior of men. He is a window through whom men catch a glimpse of the divine nature. Moreover, Jesus, as the embodiment of the ideal human personality, constitutes the normative pattern toward which all men should strive, and the impact of his life upon men helps them to attain this goal. Finally, the teachings of Jesus define the standards of the kingdom of God, which is the highest good of men and the supreme goal of God.

Through the spiritual light and moral power which were released into the stream of history by the life and influence of Jesus, new levels of human fulfillment have become possible. One result of his work was the establishment of a community of men committed to the way, the truth, and the life which he advocated. The church exists to further the ideals of Jesus and to permeate every aspect of human life with his spirit. It is a center of worship, training, fellowship, and inspiration which prepares men for Christian service, and, as such, is the divinely established agency through which the kingdom of God will be established on earth.

The heart of the matter can be put even more briefly than the preceding paragraphs have indicated. The idea of a dynamic, unitary world in which Spirit is gradually permeating nature with meaning and value is fundamental to the modern understanding of reality.[1] It is this basic grasp of things to which the liberals felt called to accommodate the historic Christian religion. This scheme provided a convenient way of interpreting the main elements of Christian belief. Since God is immanent both in men and in the world, experience is taken to be the locus of the self's awareness of God. The Bible is viewed as the story of man's developing religious consciousness. Christ is both the ideal man and the revelation of God, and he represents the goal toward which the creative process is tending and the means of directing the human race toward this end. Man is a finite spirit who has evolved from lower organic forms of natural life. Sin is the drag of man's natural substructure on his weak but advancing spirit. Salvation is the gradual triumph of spirit over nature made possible by the truth and power which flow from Christ. History is the story of the progressive triumph of the kingdom of God on earth. The church is the agency which promotes the advance of the kingdom. The validation of this whole scheme of thought is found in the actual progress which is being made in the lives of individuals and in society.

The basic themes which have just been enumerated constitute the heart of liberal theology. In varying degrees and in a variety of ways, they have appeared in the thinking of every theologian considered in this undertaking. To summarize even further, it can be said that liberal theology is essentially a Christian version of the way in which the divine Spirit is gradually permeating and imparting its own qualities to the realm of nature and to the structure of history. This fundamental scheme is epitomized in the emergence out of nature of a creature possessed with the qualities of mind and spirit and capable of unlimited possibilities of spiritual development. The supreme achievement of Spirit is the personality of Jesus, who both mirrors the nature of the ultimate power and purpose and is the prototype of man as he is to be. A time will come when the ideals of Jesus will dominate, and spirit in man will achieve its full victory over nature. Liberals believed that great progress could be made toward this ideal on earth, and most of them looked beyond death toward an unending life in glory consisting of continuous growth toward moral and spiritual perfection. In short, liberal theology is the account of how an immanent God works in the universe toward the creation and perfection of a finite spirit who shares the divine image.

II. An Evaluation of Liberalism

The primary purpose of this inquiry has been to understand the origin and nature of liberalism rather than to judge its validity. Nevertheless, every interpretation of a complex historical phenomenon is inevitably affected to some degree by the orientation of the interpreter, and certain value judgments have been implicit throughout. It is only fair that the perspective from which these judgments have proceeded should now be made explicit. Moreover, the project would not be complete apart from some attempt to assess the authenticity of the liberal reconstruction of the Christian message. Since the theological outlook of the writer has been shaped by the dominant developments in postliberal theology, this evaluation will reflect to a large extent the trends to be discussed in the concluding chapter.

While every attempt to judge a past theology is likely to be as partial in its comprehension of the total Christian Gospel as the theology which is being judged, it is nevertheless true that subsequent generations can often see shortcomings and aspects of truth which were not obvious to their predecessors. It is on the basis of such a recognition that the evaluation of liberalism must proceed and not on the grounds of any claim to absolute knowledge.

Every historical movement must be understood and evaluated, at least in part, in the light of the context in which it appeared. When viewed in this way, it must be said that liberalism arose in an attempt to meet a vital need. In its effort to reinterpret the ancient Christian message in terms which were relevant to modern men, liberalism was facing up to one of the essential tasks of theology. One is compelled to agree with Henry Churchill King at the turn of the century that reconstruction in theology was needed. This reconstruction was demanded not only by the challenge of science and secular thought but by the needs of living faith and by developments within the Christian community itself.

A growing number of sensitive Christians found themselves unable to express their deepest convictions about God and man within the categories of Protestant orthodoxy. Moreover, the moral and spiritual needs of the time seemed to call for something more than was offered by the Christianity which then prevailed in most of the churches.

Now this may mean that Christians had succumbed to modern secularism and were really demanding a revision of the substance of the faith rather than a reconstruction of its form. While this is no doubt part of the truth, it is not the whole truth. A more adequate explanation is that the Protestant orthodoxy which had been shaped to meet the needs of an earlier situation could no longer speak effectively to the new social, intellectual, and spiritual state of affairs which had emerged. Thus, while it may be that liberalism in reinterpreting the faith also distorted it in various ways, it can be said unequivocally that reconstruction of some sort was vitally necessary. Christians simply had to rethink their faith if they were to maintain their intellectual integrity and to present a message to the world which could compete successfully for the loyalties of well-informed modern men. Liberal theologians tackled this problem honestly and courageously. Theology must always be on guard against dissolving the Christian revelation in the thought patterns of the age, but it must attempt in every age to make the timeless Gospel relevant to contemporary needs.

Liberalism, then, attempted to speak to its age, but did it speak Christian truth or some other truth? The position of the writer is that a double evaluation must be made at this point. On the one hand, liberalism served as a needed corrective in that it called attention to aspects of the Biblical faith which had been neglected in the prevailing orthodoxy. Moreover, the liberals attacked traditional problems from a fresh perspective and threw new light on old problems. Many of the issues which are in the center of contemporary theological debate were first formulated by liberal thinkers. In these ways liberalism made a significant contribution to the continuing theological enterprise. On the other hand, in its enthusiasm for modern modes of thought, liberalism lost sight of much that was of permanent validity in the historic tradition. Liberal thinking was too greatly influenced by a cultural faith centering around an exaggerated confidence in the goodness of men and in the redemptive nature of history. Any theology which attempts to speak to an age in its own language runs the danger of compromising the eternal message of the Gospel with the temporarily plausible conviction of the time. Liberalism did not escape this peril, and as a result liberal thinkers offered to the world a compound of truth and error.

A. *The Strength of Liberalism*

The rest of this chapter will be devoted to the elucidation of this double evaluation. Several strong points in the liberal version of the Christian message need to be noted.

1. Liberalism brought to theology a strong emphasis on the authority of Christian experience. This stress was an inheritance from the pietism and revivalism of the preceding century which had already shifted attention from doctrines to life and prepared the way for the breakdown of Biblical authoritarianism. At a time when scientific knowledge, higher criticism, and a skeptical philosophy were undermining the authority of the infallible Bible and a rational knowledge of God, liberalism affirmed the conviction that the surest ground of Christian confidence lies in a personal experience of God. While this emphasis tended to lead to a subjectivism which neglected historical revelation, it did bring to the attention of Christians the fact that God and experience go together and that no faith can endure which is based merely upon some external authority and not upon the inner certitude of the believer. Recent theologians of the stature of Emil Brunner and H. Richard Niebuhr are continuing to emphasize the fact that Christian truth arises out of the encounter of the self with God and consists of a testimony to a personal truth appropriated through experience and decision.

2. Another genuine Biblical note in liberal theology was its ethical passion. The moral fervor reflected in the attempt of the social gospel movement to subordinate all of life in both its individual and corporate dimensions to the ethical will of God represented a rebirth of the prophetic spirit in the church. Liberals stood for that side of the Biblical tradition which stresses the union between a man's moral life and his relationship to God. They reflected the outlook of the Old Testament prophets when they pointed out that adherence to correct dogma, formal religious practices, and pious feeling are abominations to God apart from the embodiment of love in personal relations and an effective dedication to the struggle for justice in society. There is something in this stress on the moral side of religion that is essential to the Christian understanding of God and man. While in some thinkers this ethical passion tended to dissolve the Gospel of grace into a moral idealism which spoke only of human striving, it is nevertheless true that the insistence that only those who do the will of God can expect to enter the kingdom of God is genuinely rooted in the Biblical faith.

3. Liberal thinkers also contributed to the church a new sense of the concern of God for all of life. Liberalism stood for the truth that man's life is a unity and that the Gospel is addressed to man as a whole. Liberals rightly saw that the spiritual health of personality in the individual is intimately connected with the social and material context in which it exists. This means that the church must be concerned about social justice as well as individual piety and about the material welfare of men as well as the security of their souls for the life beyond. The social gospel movement reflected the liberal insight that the Christian message is relevant to the whole complex struggle of man to find meaning and fulfillment for his total being here and now. Moreover, Rauschenbusch and others rediscovered the Biblical idea of the corporate nature of the kingdom of God, a truth which had been neglected in orthodoxy's concern to save souls one by one for a future life of bliss. At these points liberalism has made one of its finest contributions to theology. More recently theologians have criticized the optimism of the social gospel and its naïveté about the sinfulness of man, but they have continued to stress the relevance of the Gospel for the whole man and for his total life in society.

4. Again, liberalism rightly insisted upon some of the legitimate rights of reason and of moral feeling. Liberal theology was imbued with a spirit of freedom which insisted on the right of men to question

even the most sacred of dogmas if they seemed to be unreasonable or offensive to the moral sense. A new understanding of the process by which the Bible came into being relieved liberals from the necessity of regarding the lower levels of moral and religious insight in the Scriptures as the verbally-inspired word of God. Moreover, they raised serious questions about the validity and moral justification of some of the harsher doctrines of historic Christianity, such as eternal punishment and double predestination. Liberals refused to admit that any belief which offended the enlightened Christian mind and conscience could possibly be true of God as revealed in Jesus Christ. A revised estimate of the Scriptural revelation also freed the liberals from the necessity of defending the scientific world view of the Bible against the convincing evidence of the empirical sciences. One can concur with the following remark of John Bennett made in 1933:

... liberalism has been a cleansing force in Christian history. It has overcome much that our age rightly regards as incredible. It has removed a great deal of excess baggage, especially all that went with biblical literalism. . . . So today there are few Christian groups which hold a doctrine of God which offends the moral sense.[2]

5. One of the most important contributions of liberalism was made at the point at which it called for a re-examination of the whole question of the authority of the Bible and the meaning of revelation. Liberal thinkers rightly perceived that modern science and higher criticism had rendered forever untenable the idea of Biblical infallibility upon which orthodoxy had relied. They saw that the Bible contained not one system of pure doctrine from cover to cover, as classical Protestantism had generally assumed, but rather reflected a wide diversity of perspectives which developed over a long period of time. New studies of the history of Christian doctrine revealed a similar diversity in the theological categories that had been employed over the centuries to interpret Christian truth. Thus, liberal thinkers came to recognize that all theological ideas, including those of the Bible, are historically and culturally conditioned. This means that theology must now face squarely the difficult problems having to do with the diversity of thought within the Bible and with the radical differences between the world view of the Bible and the intellectual outlook of modern men.

The recognition of the principle of historical relativity means that no system of doctrine in the Bible or outside the Bible can ever be a final statement of truth for all men everywhere. How, then, can one separate the eternal truth of the Christian revelation from its culturally conditioned framework in Biblical and historical theology? Or to state it differently, how can one set forth in the relative categories of modern thought a message which incorporates the essential truth contained within the Biblical categories? This problem of translating the ancient faith into the modern idiom without sacrificing either its truth or its relevancy defines one of the fundamental issues of theological discussion in the twentieth century. This way of putting the problem is a heritage from liberalism.

While liberal thinkers did not solve all the complex problems involved in the new approach, they did succeed in freeing themselves from the inadequate ideas present in orthodoxy and in formulating the questions which are now in the center of contemporary theological discussion. Moreover, the contemporary wrestle of theology with the authority of the Bible and the meaning of revelation presupposes some of the fundamental principles which liberalism first brought to light. Therefore, it should not be forgotten that the more adequate treatment of these problems in recent theological writings has been made possible in part by the prodigious labor and insight contributed by liberal theologians.

6. Closely connected with the preceding point is liberalism's emphasis upon the historical nature of the Christian faith. Protestant orthodoxy had tended to look upon Christianity as a body of doctrines contained in the Bible. It was not unrecognized that Christianity had a historical basis in the great events which constitute the object of the Biblical witness, but a static, propositional view of revelation took attention away from the dynamic historical process by which the Christian faith had come into being. Under the influence of higher criticism and a new historical consciousness liberalism came to recognize that the fundamental beliefs of the Biblical faith had developed over a long period of time out of the wrestle of the Hebrews with the great issues of life. In Jesus of Nazareth the liberals discovered both the culmination of the Hebrew experience of God and the emergence of a new faith based on the excellence of his moral and spiritual life and the sublimity of his teachings.

The application of an evolutionary scheme to the development of Biblical religion and the stress of human experience rather than divine revelation resulted in a one-sided picture of the historical process out of which Christianity came. Certain crucial events in this history are now seen to have been of special revelatory significance in that they provided the clue to the nature of the whole historical drama. Nevertheless, liberalism did succeed in shifting the emphasis from the doctrines of the Bible to the encounter between God and men on the plane of history out of which the doctrines came.

7. One of the finest contributions of liberalism is closely related to the above point and consists in the recognition of the dynamic nature of history. The principle of dynamism is a sound one, and it is rooted ultimately in the Biblical view of God's relationship to the world. Christianity, almost alone among the world religions, recognizes the importance and the meaningfulness of history. What makes history important is that it is the unique product of man's freedom and creativity, which together define the essential qualities of men. History is the locus of the encounter between a free, Sovereign God and free, finite persons. The fundamental content of history is made as God and men mutually act and respond to each other as time moves. The meaningfulness of the historical drama is found in the fact that it is the stage upon which God works out his purposes. The promise of the Bible is that a consummation is in store in which good will overcome evil, and the fragmentary meanings and fulfillments of this life will be made complete. Liberalism tended to identify process too easily with progress and to lose sight of the transcendence of God over history, but the emphasis on development in history grows out of a profound, and ultimately Biblical, understanding of its nature.

8. Liberalism took another step in the right direction in regarding the humanity of Jesus seriously. The church has always insisted that Jesus Christ was fully man, but it has hesitated to carry out all of the implications of this belief. A subtle docetism has always haunted the theology of the past, even when its more obvious forms were denounced. Liberal thinkers overcame this hesitancy to regard Jesus as fully man and called the attention of the church to the truth that whatever else he was, he was a human being in the fullest sense of the word.

D. M. Baillie has pointed out that this conviction of liberalism is common ground today even among those theologians who have revolted against the Jesus of history movement and who want to affirm the full deity of Christ after the fashion of Chalcedon.[3] On all sides theologians are taking into account the limitations of the knowledge of Jesus and the human character of his miracles and his moral and religious life. The Christological question that faces theology today is how this man, completely human in every respect, could also have been the incarnate Christ. While the liberal solution to the problem of Christology had its limitations, liberalism did make a substantial contribution to theology by putting an end to docetism. This has led to a new formulation of the Christological question which really takes seriously the genuinely orthodox affirmation of the humanity of Jesus.

9. Finally, liberalism has generally been characterized by a liberal spirit. The open-minded, tolerant attitude which liberalism fostered lives on in most contemporary theologians. With few exceptions theologians confront each other today with mutual respect and display a willingness to be criticized by others and to be taught of them. This is not to say that the liberal spirit was unknown before the nineteenth century or that no liberal thinker was illiberal in attitude. It is to say that the emancipation of liberals from the necessity of defending some particular set of doctrines as final and ultimate truth and their realization that all theologies are relative to time and place have been productive of a humility which is altogether becoming to finite, fallible men. Moreover, the emphasis on religious experience reduced the seriousness of doctrinal disputes.

B. *The Weaknesses of Liberalism*

In all the preceding ways liberalism has made a contribution to modern theology. Yet, in spite of the insights which liberalism contained, most of them stand in an ambiguous relationship to an adequate interpretation of the Christian message. Its truth is mixed with error in a complex fashion which makes its necessary to qualify most every positive remark which is made about it. The explanation for this is that the overall understanding of reality which informed liberalism is faulty, and this introduces a distortion at the center of the liberal outlook which affects the whole theological system.

This means that what is fundamentally necessary is not a critical evaluation of the separate doctrines of liberalism; rather, what is needed most is an examination of the underlying foundation of liberalism which conditions the form and substance of each individual doctrine. Once this aberration at the center is corrected, it will be relatively easy to see what detailed modifications are called for.

1. THE ATTACK UPON LIBERALISM

It will contribute to the understanding of the fundamental weakness of the liberal perspective to look briefly at the charges which have been brought to bear against liberalism by two of its most profound critics.

In Europe the revolt against liberalism was led by Karl Barth at the close of World War I. Barth lashed out against the principle of immanence, declaring it to be the fundamental defect of liberal thinking. In the preface to the second edition of *The Epistle to the Romans* Barth stated that if he had a system

. . . it is limited to a recognition of what Kierkegaard called the "infinite qualitative distinction" between time and eternity, and to my regarding this as possessing negative as well as positive significance: "God is in heaven, and thou art on earth." The relation between such a God and such a man, and the relation between such a man and such a God, is for me the theme of the Bible and the essence of philosophy.[4]

Rejecting the immanent God to which the liberals pointed, Barth spoke of the wholly Other, a God completely hidden from human vision except at the one point at which he invaded history in the Word Incarnate to shatter the darkness of man's ignorance and impotence. "The Gospel proclaims a God utterly distinct from men. Salvation comes to them from Him, because they are, as men, incapable of knowing Him, and because they have no right to claim anything from Him."[5] Christ he interpreted as a sheer vertical intrusion into the horizontal plane of history from above, touching the world as a tangent at this single point. Here and here alone is a connection established between the unknown world inhabited by the transcendent God and the known world inhabited by the fallen race of man. This is a clear and decisive rejection of the liberal principle of continuity, which is at the heart of the liberal perspective.

In America the leading critic of liberalism has been Reinhold Niebuhr. Niebuhr attacked the liberal view of man, declaring that its gravest weakness was here. Liberalism erred fundamentally by rejecting the doctrine of original sin and by substituting for it a notion of man's inherent goodness and perfectibility derived from modern secularism. Liberalism's optimism about man has led, he insists, to a false confidence regarding the possibilities of moral attainment in the individual and to a naïve faith in the redemptive nature of history. As a corrective to these illusions about man Niebuhr has sought to recover the insights of the Augustinian view of the human predicament. He has restored to prominence the conviction that the essence of sin is man's inevitable and universal rebellion against the sovereignty of God, arising out of pride and occasioned by the anxiety generated by the tensions of man's existential situation. Yet, this rebellion is grounded in freedom and not in necessity, despite the fact that it is inevitable in the life of every man. This view of man gives rise to a concept of history as a morally ambiguous process in which each new generation confronts God anew and is forced to decide between faith and unfaith. While repentance and moral renewal are made possible and actual by the grace of God manifest in Christ, the history of rebellion will continue until the end, and only beyond history will the final victory of good over evil be won.[6] Here is an attack upon the center of the liberal outlook from a perspective different from that of Barth, and yet it calls liberalism into question just as decisively.

Both of these men have pointed to serious defects in liberal theology, and both have been instrumental in restoring some of the deeper insights of the historic faith which had been ignored or suppressed in the outlook which they have attacked. This is not to say that these men are without error. Criticism can and has been legitimately made of both. Nevertheless, each of them has exposed errors in the liberal understanding of reality as a whole and of man's place in the scheme of things. This fundamental fault in the overall view of reality in liberalism is at the base of the most serious distortions in the liberal outlook with regard to the main issue of theological concern.

2. THE FUNDAMENTAL ERROR

The heart of the matter is that the liberal notion of an immanent Spirit at work gradually imparting order to nature and by an evolutionary process bringing man to moral and spiritual perfection within history is too simple a version of the relationship between man, the world, and God. To approach the matter from a different perspective, the view that the human situation is best interpreted in terms of a gradual triumph of spirit (the image of God in man which is essentially rational and good) over the drag of nature within (the untamed animal impulses) and without (the impersonal mechanisms of the natural order which produce pain and finally death) misses the deeper truth about man's being and predicament. This understanding of reality does not adequately grasp the full nature of the being of God or of man or of the relationship between God and man in the dramas of history and in personal encounter. The whole series of relations between man, nature, history, and God is more complex, ambiguous, and mysterious than liberalism allowed.

3. THE FUNDAMENTAL CORRECTION

In short, the whole perspective of liberalism needs to be corrected in the light of a better model of reality than that which it appropriated too uncritically from modern culture. This better framework for understanding the nature of God and man and the relationships between them must be derived from a re-examination of the Biblical witness. There is to be found in the Bible a perspective on the fundamental issues of life which focuses upon the relations between the divine Person and human persons on the stage of history. The Biblical way of viewing the divine-human encounter was obscured in liberal theology. A recovery of these neglected insights of the Biblical perspective will point the way to a more adequate theology. Every attempt to interpret the Biblical picture of reality is limited by the historical position of the interpreter and will need correcting by others. Nevertheless, without making absolute claims for the following analysis, it can be stated with some confidence that it points to aspects of Biblical truth which liberalism missed.

According to the Bible, God is related positively to the world as its creator, sustainer, judge, and redeemer, but he also stands over against the world as the Sovereign Lord whose inner being is shrouded in the mystery of his transcendence. His being is expressed but is not exhausted in his dynamic, purposive presence in nature, man, and history. It is this hiddenness and otherness of God that liberalism neglected in its tendency to define God too exclusively in terms of immanence. To say it differently, liberalism had no sufficient place for the holiness of God which defines his freedom from the world and his independence from all that is creaturely and finite. God is the free, Sovereign Person[7] who maintains his self-identity over against the created order and who confronts the world from beyond the world as a transcendent Subject.

Likewise, the liberal understanding of man is inadequate from the Biblical point of view. The deepest truth about the human situation is not the conflict in man between his higher nature and his lower nature but rather the encounter of man and God in personal relations. Man is indeed imbedded in nature, but he also stands over against nature as a free person with power to shape his own destiny by responding to God either in faith or in unbelief. Man's fundamental problem is not his failure to attain the good which he desires in his inmost self because he is hindered by the downward drag of his animal inheritance. Rather, his basic trouble is that his freedom is infected with a mysterious bias toward evil which universally results in a prideful rebellion against God which issues in moral disobedience. In short, the locus of sin is not in nature but in the spirit itself. It was this failure to see that the essence of man's predicament consists in the corruption of the very center of his person that lay at the root of the false optimism of liberalism with regard to the moral possibilities of history.

In summary, the liberal principle of continuity needs to be called into question and corrected in the light of a better understanding of the discontinuity between God and the world, nature and man, and man and God. Liberalism's view of God as the immanent Spirit who is gradually pervading the cosmos with order and meaning obscures the transcendence of God over the world as free, Sovereign Lord. Likewise, liberalism's view of man as an emerging spirit gradually overcoming the drag of nature obscures the transcendence of man over nature as a free moral subject. Liberalism understood neither the freedom of God as Person nor the freedom of man as person. Consequently, it did not understand adequately the relations between God and man in history. The source of these errors is to be found largely in the combination of the principle of continuity with a misinterpretation of the principle of dynamism. The discontinuity between man, the world, and God, which is grounded in the freedom of God and in the nature of human personality, is the basic clue to the way in which the whole liberal perspective needs to be corrected.

5. THE RECONSTRUCTION OF LIBERALISM

A brief treatment here will serve to indicate how this altered outlook will affect the major Christian doctrines which have been dealt with throughout this inquiry. Emphasis will need to be shifted from reason and experience to revelation, now understood in personal rather than in propositional terms. The God who confronts the world from beyond the world as free Subject can be known truly only as he makes himself accessible to men in personal encounter. This does not mean necessarily that no authentic knowledge of the being and nature of God can be derived from an examination of the structure of the world by human reason, but it does mean that God as Person can be known only in personal relations made possible in special revelation. Moreover, the emphasis on revelation does not rule out the subjective factor of experience. Revelation must be appropriated through human response to the divine initiative. However, the focus of attention will now be upon the decision of faith by which men respond to the unique revelation of God in Christ rather than upon religious experience or rational inquiry in general, an emphasis which too easily and simply relates every experience of truth, goodness, and beauty to knowledge of God.

Likewise, the authority of the Bible will be put in the center of attention as the inspired and authentic witness to the mighty acts of God in history in which the divine will and purpose have been disclosed. The focus of the Biblical testimony is upon Jesus Christ in whom God fully dwelt and through whom he has accomplished his redemptive purpose among men. It is not adequate to speak of Christ simply as the perfection of human personality and then through the principle of immanence to identify this perfected manhood with the divine. Instead, it is necessary to speak somehow of a unique entrance of the transcendent God into the world from beyond the world to become personally present in the man Jesus. More attention also needs to be given to the atoning work of Christ whereby the objective situation between God and man is altered, making possible personal reconciliation with God and victory over sin in the life of man.

In the light of what has already been said about the nature of man as a genuinely responsible creature whose destiny is shaped by the way he exercises his freedom in response to the divine will, changes are necessary in the liberal doctrines of sin and salvation. Sin needs to be understood primarily as a prideful rebellion against God which also involves a life of sensuality and a distorted moral orientation toward other men. This revolt against man's true nature and destiny is rooted in free decision which cannot be explained ultimately by reference to any causal factors outside the will itself. Salvation will now be understood in terms of reconciliation to God which at the same time involves a renewal of man's moral behavior in individual and social relations. A new personal relationship emerges between

God and man on the basis of the covenant of grace established in Christ, and out of this reorientation of human existence at its very center flows a life which is capable of indefinite heights of moral and spiritual achievement.

While moral progress in the individual and in the historical process as a whole becomes a genuine possibility for redeemed men and societies, there is no guarantee that forward movement in time will be accomplished by spiritual advance. History is made as men respond to the disclosure of the divine will and purpose either in rebellion and disobedience or in faith and obedience. The level of moral achievement in history depends upon the quality of the responses which men make to the initiative of God in judgment and redemption. Because God and men confront each other as free Person over against free persons, history is dynamic in character. There is forward movement, development, and a certain increase in the range of human powers as men learn from their cumulative social experiences. But since men are genuinely free in their responses to God, there is no way of predicting in advance whether the increased powers will be employed for good or for ill. History, therefore, is morally complex and will remain so until the end.

This means that theology must give renewed attention to eschatology, both with reference to individual destiny beyond death and to the consummation of the whole historical drama. The principle of evolutionary progress which was the key to the liberal interpretation of history and eschatology is too simple. Because of the moral ambiguities of history, the complete fulfillment of life which the Gospel promises must be related more fundamentally than liberalism realized to the consummation which lies ahead of, and beyond, this earthly dimension.

Finally, the liberal doctrine of the church needs revision. Liberalism went too far in dissolving the line between the church and the world and in viewing the church in instrumental terms. The church is a worshiping, witnessing, confessing community of forgiven sinners who rejoice in the grace that has been given them and who proclaim the word of judgment and redemption to those who have not acknowledged the sovereignty of God over their lives. Its relationship to the world is complex. It is in the world as a human institution composed of finite sinful men which never quite escapes the baneful influences of its environment. It is not of the world in that its foundation, its authority, and its hope are in God. There is thus a certain strangeness about the church and a certain tension between the church and the world. Its members take a responsible attitude toward the life of men in the present, and yet attention is focused on the redemption that is now genuinely real but which has not yet fully come.

This kind of outlook, sketched here only in barest outline, has the effect of reviving many of the ancient theological issues which liberalism thought it had overcome once and for all. The relationship between natural, human knowledge and revealed truth, the relation of God as creator to God as redeemer, the problem of relating freedom and responsibility to the notion that men are sinful without exception, the thorny problem of a Christology which takes the deity of Christ seriously, the Trinitarian issue which emerges from a revised view of Christ, the relationship between reconciliation and growth in moral grace, the relation of Christianity to other religions, the problem of relating a more orthodox view of redemption as justification by faith to the complex issue of social salvation, and the problem of relating the church as the Body of Christ to the divided, sinful communities which constitute the empirical churches—all of these problems, to mention some of the more prominent, will now need attention. Many of these issues are, as a matter of fact, in the center of contemporary theological concern as present-day thinkers find themselves wrestling once again with some of the old dilemmas which liberalism had dissolved. The concluding chapter will touch upon some of these problems.

CHAPTER 12

THE RELATION OF LIBERALISM
TO POST-LIBERAL TRENDS

In the years following 1930 a chorus of voices could be heard in America announcing the demise of liberalism.[1] Newer patterns of thought associated with the names of Barth and Brunner in Europe and Reinhold Niebuhr in America were gaining in prominence, and liberal theologians who had just recently been on the offensive against fundamentalism found themselves now on the defensive against a more effective opponent. It is not the purpose of this chapter to review the rise of that movement but rather to raise the question of the relationship of this new theology to liberalism. Is neo-orthodoxy, which is the dominant post-liberal trend, best understood as a repudiation of liberalism, or is it more correctly assessed as a development within the liberal tradition which retains much of liberalism even as it opposes it?

It should be kept in mind that post-liberal theology, like liberalism itself, reflects a wide variety of emphases which cannot be forced into any neat or narrow framework. The mere mention of such names as Barth, Brunner, Aulén, Bultmann, Temple, H. Richard and Reinhold Niebuhr, Ferré, Williams, Horton, Bennett, Calhoun, and Tillich suggests the rich diversity of contemporary theological opinion. Most of the attention of this chapter will be devoted to a consideration of neo-orthodoxy in its various American and European forms. To be more specific, the post-liberal trends that are dealt with do not often move very far away from a broad center that is best represented by Reinhold Niebuhr. However, other perspectives will not be ignored.

One important theological outlook in America is neo-liberalism, which has reacted against liberalism less strongly than neo-orthodoxy and makes an effort to preserve some sort of balance between the two. Such men as John Bennett, Daniel Day Williams, and Walter Marshall Horton fit into this broad group. One should also make mention of an outlook centered largely in Great Britain which can be called modern orthodoxy. It is like neo-orthodoxy in its appreciation of the classical formulations of Christian truth but is not as bound to a Kantian epistemology and an existentialist philosophy as neo-orthodoxy is. It also shares with liberalism a high regard for the rights and capacities of reason. Men like Alan Richardson, William Temple, and Nels Ferré come immediately to mind as examples. In addition, there are the existentialist theologians like Bultmann and Tillich who do not fit well into any of these groups.[2]

No detailed description or classification of this variety will be undertaken here. However, there are certain recurring themes in the thought of most of these men which add up to a broad pattern of thought which contrasts sharply with the classical American liberalism of 1900–1935. While the attempt will be made to take into account some of the differences that exist among the men chosen to represent the dominant post-liberal trends, the main effort will be to discover the underlying principles which are more or less shared by the leading contemporary thinkers and to compare these principles with those which are constitutive of liberalism. In particular, the purpose is to show how the liberal motifs of continuity, autonomy, and dynamism are affirmed, rejected, or modified in some of the major present-day thinkers.

I. The Aim of Post-Liberal Theology

The thesis that is to be explored here is that while the fundamental aim of liberalism was to harmonize the ancient Gospel with the life and thought of modern culture, the basic aim of post-liberal thought has been to discover the distinctive, authentic Christian faith which appears in the Bible and to set it forth in its purity against all other competing faiths both ancient and modern. The effort has been made to cut loose the Christian message from all "entangling alliances" with reason, philosophy, culture, and from any partnership however defined which blunts, distorts, or compromises it. Daniel Day Williams points out that to speak of a theological renaissance in our times means that "there is throughout Christendom a new determination to find out what it is that makes Christianity a decisively different faith from all others. What is it that gives Christianity its own integrity and its independent standard of judgment over all other philosophies and causes which bid for the allegiance of men?"[3] This is perhaps the dominant question of the contemporary theological era. Whatever connection the Christian revelation may have with man's self-directed attempt to discover saving truth and attain the good life—and there are sharp differences of opinion among contemporary thinkers on this score— it is widely affirmed that in the last analysis the Christian message is a unique given which must be understood in and through itself. This is a note which has been sounded in recent years in writings which run the theological gamut all the way from Fosdick's 1935 sermon entitled "The Church Must Go Beyond Modernism" to Barth's *Commentary on Romans*.

The applications of this theme are widespread. Reinhold Niebuhr distinguishes Greek and modern views of man and history from the Biblical view; John Bright points out the uniqueness of the Mosaic faith in the thirteenth century B.C.; Anders Nygren distinguishes sharply between *agape, nomos,* and *eros,* which respectively define the fundamental motifs of Christianity, Judaism, and Greek thought; Hendrik Kraemer sees an absolute cleavage between the Christian revelation and all other religions; Emil Brunner speaks of the long philosophical attempt to define the good life as a "heap of ruins" and sets over against this the Christian ethic; Nels Ferré is attempting to work out a complete philosophical theology on the basis of the *agape* motif, which he maintains is unique among world religions; Karl Barth is striving for a theology based solely on the Word of God; and most recently Richard R. Niebuhr has maintained that the resurrection of Christ provides a foundation for the distinctive Christian view of nature, history, and God. This list could be lengthened indefinitely, but it is clear that in contrast to liberalism the contemporary aim of theology is to discover what is uniquely Christian in relation to all competing truth and value claims. Of course, liberals too knew that Christianity was a distinctive faith, but their idea was that Christianity exhibits in its fullness what is beginning to be discovered elsewhere. The contemporary trend, however, is not to stress the likeness between Christ and other witnesses to the truth but to magnify the difference beween them.

During the last few decades, then, theology has entered a new phase in which the union of Christ and culture fostered by liberalism has been dissolved. The year 1935 is particularly significant in marking the turning point in America in that it saw three prominent thinkers make impassioned appeals for Christianity to disassociate itself from a culture that was waning and to stand on its own independent foundation in historical revelation. H. Richard Niebuhr, in a volume appropriately entitled *The Church against the World,* declared that the "task of the present generation appears to lie in the liberation of the church from its bondage to a corrupt civilization."[4] The church, he said, is captive to nationalism, to capitalism, and to an anthropocentrism which affirms the sufficiency of man. He called upon the church to assert its independence by renewing its loyalty to God and to Jesus Christ. Reinhold Niebuhr claimed that "the adjustment of modern religion to the 'mind' of modern culture inevitably involved capitulation to its thin 'soul.' "[5] He spoke of the need for an independent Christian ethic based on faith in a transcendent, creator God who gives meaning to history by his relevant activity as man's redeemer. Harry Emerson Fosdick, who had been the most outstanding liberal preacher, gave clarity in a famous sermon to his own growing conviction that the Christian message had suffered near dissolution because of its tendency to adapt itself too completely to the relativities of a particular culture. He proclaimed that Christians must go beyond modernism and reaffirm the distinctive foundations of Christianity in the Biblical revelation. "What Christ does to modern culture is to challenge it."[6]

What were the causes of this shift in theological aim and emphasis throughout the Christian world which led to the rejection of the liberal accommodation of Christianity to culture? The sources of post-liberal theology are as complex as those which gave rise to liberalism decades before, but the major one seems clear and may be briefly indicated.

The Christian Century series, "How My Mind Has Changed in the Last Ten Years," published in 1939, included essays by thirty-four prominent religious leaders who described their theological pilgrimage since 1929. Those who indicated a movement away from liberalism in the direction of neo-orthodoxy specified as the primary source of the change in their thinking the impact of the social catastrophes of the twentieth century. Reinhold Niebuhr, in his contribution to this series entitled "Ten Years that Shook My World," spoke of the "rejection of almost all the liberal theological ideals and ideas with which I ventured forth in 1915,"[7] contending that "there is not a single bit of evidence to prove that good triumphs over evil in this constant development of history."[8] Speaking of his experience with the Ford empire in Detroit, he said that "the simple little moral homilies which were preached in that as in other cities, by myself and others, seemed completely irrelevant to the brutal facts of life in a great industrial center."[9] Not all those who indicated a change expressed their disenchantment with liberalism as strongly as Niebuhr did, but his essay was dramatically indicative of the trend.

In summary, what happened was that American theologians began to see that in adapting the Christian message to modern culture, grievous errors had been introduced into theology which did not square either with the profoundest interpretation of human experience or with the historic faith. It was increasingly recognized that liberalism was in large part a cultural faith expressed in Christian terminology and not a genuine reinterpretation of the Christian revelation. Moreover, the culture to which liberalism had accommodated itself was threatened, and it became evident that the Christian faith had to be extricated from the relativities of this culture or perish. The sources of the Christian message in a culture-transcending revelation had to be rediscovered before the church could preach a saving word to a civilization in a state of crisis. This seems to be the major factor underlying the search in this theological generation for the distinctively Christian view of reality, an outlook which can speak to every culture because it is identified with none.

II. The Structure of Post-Liberal Theology

A. *The Rejection of Continuity*

The difference in aim between liberal and post-liberal thought is closely connected with the structure of thought involved in each case. The fundamental motif of liberalism was the principle of continuity, which is neatly reflected in the intent of liberal thinkers to demonstrate the harmony between the permanently valid essence of Christianity and the best aspects of the scientific, democratic culture of the modern

West. The contention of this chapter is that the basic motif of post-liberal thought is discontinuity, which manifests itself in the effort of recent thinkers to distinguish the unique grasp of reality involved in the Christian revelation from all other philosophies and religions. Just as continuity shapes the whole theological perspective of liberalism, so discontinuity is a theme which affects practically every doctrine touched by the most influential thinkers of recent years. This motif, however, is expressed in varying degrees of absoluteness in post-liberal theologians. It is evident mildly in the neo-liberalism of men like Williams, Horton, and Bennett; it is seen more thoroughly in the neo-orthodoxy of men like Reinhold Niebuhr; and it is present in still more radical form in men such as Nygren and Barth. While these important differences must be kept clearly in mind, discontinuity is the best single clue to the understanding of the various types of post-liberal thought.

The foremost cause of the break of theology with liberalism has already been mentioned—the growing awareness that the liberal union of the Christian message with the life and thought of modern culture had led to a false confidence in social progress which was inconsistent with the experience of Western men in the twentieth century. This revolt led to the reaffirmation of the discontinuity between the Christian revelation and all human and cultural attempts to discover the ultimate truth about human existence. Moreover, the sight of the vast evils and injustices of this century, many of them perpetrated by the most highly educated and culturally advanced nations of the world, gave impetus to an emphasis on the universality and depth of human depravity and on the moral transcendence of God in relation to man. Furthermore, skepticism concerning moral progress in history gave rise to a new stress on the metaphysical discontinuity between God and the world, associated with increasing doubt as to the theological value of the facts of natural evolution. The loss of confidence in the historical perfectibility of man also inspired new accents in Christology which recognized the need for a divine redeemer who can save the human race from the corruption of original sin. Finally, a new stress was put upon the church as a distinctive community of faith in an alien world, and a new eschatology was shaped which looks more consistently beyond history than liberalism did for the victory of good over evil. All of these new emphases involve a reassertion of the discontinuity between nature, man, and God.

In addition to the social catastrophes of the twentieth century there are a number of other developments which have contributed to the rise of a new climate of theological opinion in which the liberal principle of continuity has been questioned. In fact, one can detect the convergence of a wide variety of movements in the life and thought of this century which stress discontinuity in the same way that nineteenth-century culture emphasized continuity. In both centuries theology has both participated in, and responded to, these trends. A brief account of some of these factors will be helpful at this point.[10]

1. SCIENCE

Nineteenth-century science was dominated by the notion of a universe operating exactly according to universal laws and gradually developing in all of its parts without any significant breaks anywhere. Chemists set forth the principle of the conservation of matter, and physicists elaborated a doctrine of the conservation of energy. Darwin propounded his theory of organic evolution in which one species gradually and insensibly changes into another. There are no sudden leaps, he said, but only a series of short, slow steps. Anthropology was strongly imbued with the assumption that culture develops through a continuous process in which the complex forms of language, economic life, and religion gradually replace the simple. Practically everywhere the principle of continuity was dominant.

The twentieth century has seen a marked trend in the various sciences in the opposite direction. The picture which recent physics has presented of the world is shot through with discontinuities. The quantum theory seems to make it necessary to regard the orbit of an electron as a "series of detached positions, and not as a continuous line,"[11] thus disclosing the "startling discontinuity of spatial existence."[12] Moreover, "some effects which appear essentially capable of gradual increase or gradual diminution are in reality to be increased or decreased only by certain definite jumps."[13] In one context light appears to consist of waves and in another context to consist of particles. In 1927 Heisenberg set forth his "Principle of Uncertainty," which asserts that it is absolutely impossible to determine precisely the velocity and the position of an electron at the same time. Lincoln Barnett concludes that quantum physics abolishes two foundations of the older science—causality and determination. "For by dealing in terms of statistics and probabilities it abandons all idea that nature exhibits an inexorable sequence of cause and effect."[14] Speaking of the quantum theory and other recent developments in physics, Bertrand Russell remarks that seemingly "all natural processes show a fundamental discontinuity whenever they can be measured with sufficient precision."[15] Cosmologists seem bound to affirm either that the universe began some billions of years ago from some intensely compressed, explosive primordial center and gradually expanded to its present dimensions or that matter is somehow, somewhere, being continuously created. Both the "big bang" theory and the "steady state" theory involve impressive discontinuities, but attempts to escape their implications have not attracted widespread attention.[16] New problems have arisen concerning the absolute conservation of mass or energy.[17] There seems to be an ultimate speed in the universe beyond which it is impossible to go. Biologists now speak of mutations and sudden leaps, as essential to the evolutionary process.[18] Anthropologists are suspicious of the simple evolutionary theories of cultural development dominant in former years and now recognize the importance of crises, impredictability, and quick reversals or shifts in culture patterns.[19]

This discussion of recent science is sketchy and makes no pretense of presenting the complete picture or the most advanced views. Many of the philosophical implications of the new physics remain in dispute. Some scientists would likely regard some of the preceding examples merely as gaps in present knowledge and not as genuine discontinuities in the physical world. One certainly should not fail to mention the attempt of Einstein to arrive at a "Unified Field Theory," which would bring together both gravitational and electromagnetic force in one comprehensive, ultimate law. "Believing in the harmony and uniformity of nature, Einstein has evolved a single edifice of physical laws to encompass both the phenomena of the atom and the phenomena of outer space."[20] Nevertheless, it does seem true that, for one reason or another, discontinuities impress themselves upon the scientific investigator today in a way that contrasts noticeably with the contrary tendencies of the previous century.

It is difficult to determine the relationships that may exist between contemporary science and theology. Many present-day theologians maintain an air of lofty indifference toward the results of empirical science as far as their relevance to theology is concerned. Among the important exceptions in this country is Nels Ferré. While the conscious influence of twentieth-century science on contemporary theology may be slight, it is worthy of notice that both science and theology seem more impressed with the gaps in the world and in man's knowledge of it than was the case in the nineteenth century. The contemporary stress on discontinuity seems to be the manifestation of an undercurrent in the cultural feel for reality, a climate of opinion, in which both science and theology are participating·and to which both have contributed. One must be on guard, however, of making too much of this, for the total intellectual situation of this age is complex and defies any neat schematization.

What is perhaps of most importance for theology is the fact that recent philosophy of science has been dominated by analytical philosophy, which stresses the inherent limitations of man's knowledge. A positivistic and nominalistic attitude prevails among many scientists which is skeptical about the possibility of deriving general patterns of explanation from the study of the physical world which provide the foundation for a metaphysical system. Since man cannot fathom the structure of reality by science or speculative philosophy, he must depend on some sort of subjective commitment or convictional perspective when it comes to religious and ethical issues.

2. PHILOSOPHY, LITERATURE, AND THE ARTS

The same reversal of trends can be seen in the development of philosophy. The dominant philosophies of the nineteenth century, whether idealistic, naturalistic, or positivistic, were all profoundly convinced of the unity of the world. Thinkers as different as Hegel, Schelling, Comte, and Spencer were all philosophers of continuity. Recently the prevailing philosophies have undoubtedly been logical positivism and existentialism. Both of these outlooks are more impressed with the discontinuities of life than with its continuities. Existentialism has perhaps been the most potent philosophical influence on recent theology, and there seems to be a theological trend in the making in America which looks to the latter-day positivists, now called analytical philosophers, for philosophical support of a theological position which is skeptical about the power of human reason to discover the ultimate truth about human existence. William Hordern, for example, argues for the compatibility between recent developments in analytical philosophy and a theological position which is based firmly on revelation.[21]

The positivists of the school of A. J. Ayer see a fundamental difference between empirical statements which are subject to verification by observation and metaphysical statements for which no empirical tests can be specified. The former, along with purely analytical or tautological judgments, constitute the whole range of meaningful statements, while the latter merely give expression to various feeling states or are simply nonsensical. Positivists of this persuasion restrict themselves either to certain observation statements which yield only judgments of probability or to the analysis of language. Anything beyond this is purely subjective and cannot make claims to genuine knowledge of objective reality. This is essentially a skeptical philosophy which leaves a deep chasm, almost completely disconnected, between thought and being. More recently new perspectives have developed in this general school which have broadened the concerns of the older positivism. These men prefer to be called logical empiricists or analytical philosophers, and they define their task in terms of an inquiry into the types of meaning which language has when used in various contexts. This means that philosophy may legitimately investigate the nature and intent of theological language, whereas the older school would have simply declared all non-empirical statements of a religious nature to be meaningless by definition. However, while the newer modes of thought have considerably broadened the range of meaningfulness, it is another question as to whether the range of truth (verifiable knowledge) has been extended beyond the limits defined by the positivists. It is still true that statements made about God must proceed from some faith perspective and that such affirmations cannot be positively correlated with empirical statements which are subject to verification by some sort of observational test and which alone constitute dependable, objective knowledge. Thus, any alliance of theology with positivism or analytical philosophy will involve the assertion of the discontinuity between faith and reason.

The existentialists point to the radical difference between man as a disinterested knower and man as a free, finite self involved in the making of crucial decisions in which the meaning of his personal existence is at stake. As dispassionate spectator man seeks knowledge of the objective world and control over it through theoretical theology, rationalistic philosophy, empirical science, and applied technology. As involved subject he seeks the courage to be—an authentic human existence—in the midst of a life continually threatened by pain, meaninglessness, and death. One cannot move from a detached relationship to the world to a state of involvement in which certain ultimate values and loyalties are affirmed merely by the increase of theoretical knowledge or by simply sharpening one's logical faculties but only by a commitment which transcends the rational processes of thought and deliberation.

The theist Kierkegaard, a nineteenth-century figure who has attained posthumous fame only recently, distinguishes sharply between discovering what Christianity is and becoming a Christian. He describes religious faith as a radical leap of commitment made by the self in a state of subjective passion and in the presence of rational absurdity and objective uncertainty. The atheist Sartre affirms the discontinuity of existence and essence and the priority of the former. Man is radically and inescapably free, but his decisions must be made in the absence of any rational norms, ethical imperatives, natural laws, or religious principles in terms of which his freedom could be structured. Man first exists—surges up, is there—and only then does he become something as he creates himself by his normless freedom. A host of other thinkers join these two in enunciating similar themes.

The leading movements in recent literature and the arts parallel the developments in theology and philosophy in that all these realms reflect the loss of man's faith in himself as a self-sufficient creature. T. S. Eliot's *The Wasteland,* Kafka's *The Castle* and *The Trial,* Arthur Miller's *Death of a Salesman,* Williams' *A Streetcar Named Desire,* Auden's *The Age of Anxiety,* and many other similar works deal with the loss of meaning, purpose, and direction which characterize modern society and the guilt, anxiety, and despair from which men in this age suffer.[22] Camus has developed the category of "the Absurd" to describe the ambiguities, contradictions, and paradoxes of human existence. Surrealism and expressionism in art reflect similar themes. In these movements patterns, essences, and structures are lost or hidden, and reality takes on a distorted, broken, discontinuous appearance. All of these various movements express the doctrine that man is either estranged from his essential nature or lacks any such normative pattern by which his behavior can be guided. Discontinuity, then, is the profoundest truth about life.

3. BIBLICAL STUDIES

Along with the developments in the larger culture there have been new accents in Biblical studies which have contributed to the break with the principle of continuity. In Old Testament studies the Well-hausen theory of evolutionary development has been overcome by a new emphasis on certain crucial events in the history of Israel, particularly the exodus and the making of the covenant, which provided the theological framework in terms of which the Hebrews understood their existence as a people. In New Testament studies the old quest for the recovery of the historical Jesus has been largely abandoned, and attention has been directed to the *kerygma,* which points to the life, death, and resurrection of Jesus as the culminating event in the history of salvation. New Testament scholars no longer speak much of the ideal personality of the man Jesus and his teachings concerning the gradual evolvement of the kingdom of God on earth but instead concentrate on the proclamation of Christ as the supernatural inaugurator of the New Age. Moreover, recent studies have emphasized the extent to which New Testament eschatology is dominated by an apocalyptic dualism which affirms the deep gulf between the Old Age dominated by sin and Satan and the New Age to be established by the sudden, decisive entry of God into history. Furthermore, according to recent interpreters, the apostolic church sees itself existing in tension between the times, remembering that the crucial eschatological event has occurred in Christ and yet hoping for a final consummation that is yet to come. It knows itself to be saved and yet not saved. All of these developments lead to, and are associated with, an emphasis in systematic theology on the discontinuity between the human Jesus and the divine Christ, the message *of* Jesus and the theology of the church *about* him, human society and the kingdom of God, ethics and eschatology, the present age and the age to come, the church and the world, etc.

4. A PARTIAL EXCEPTION

From all these directions have come influences which have converged upon the theological enterprise in recent decades. Some of them, of course, have been more important than others. But the result has been that a new pattern of interpretation has emerged, a new climate of opinion, in which discontinuity has come to be an important theme. The main point at which discontinuity has affected theology is in the reaffirmation of the transcendence of God. This shift of emphasis has implications which affect the whole structure of Christian thought.

However, it should be noted that with regard to one very important issue contemporary theology is generally in agreement with liberalism in affirming continuity. This agreement concerns the nature of finite reality. In the Bible God reveals himself to men through events in nature and history which again and again involve the miraculous. One thinks immediately of the incidents associated with the exodus in the Old Testament and the birth, life, death, and resurrection of Jesus in the New Testament. In addition, the redemptive act of God in Christ is put in what is widely regarded as a mythological framework. Orthodoxy generally has taken the Biblical testimony at face value and affirmed it through the centuries without hesitation. Modern thought, however, has been informed by a conviction that finite reality is a dynamic, causal network which can be studied and known by the methods of science. The dominant view has been that empirical study reveals no break in the sequence of natural cause and effect. Both liberal and post-liberal thinkers, by and large, have accepted this fundamental proposition. Developments in recent science which might qualify this outlook have as yet received little notice among neo-orthodox theologians. Once this view of finite reality is accepted, some way has to be found to relate it to the world view of the Bible.

Essentially, both liberal and neo-orthodox thinkers have been guided by some version of the Kantian distinction between pure and practical reason, which leaves the external processes of nature and history to science and looks to the internal life of persons, which is said somehow to transcend nature, for a basis for faith.[23] Thus, at this point liberalism was forced to compromise the principle of continuity and take refuge in a dualistic epistemology, while post-liberal thinkers generally have agreed that there is no discontinuity in the regular and orderly processes of nature and history. This tension between the picture of the world derived from modern science and that contained in the Bible is the source of the fundamental epistemological and metaphysical issues that modern theologians have had to face. In fact, the relationship between the Christian message and the scientific world view which has dominated Western thought since the seventeenth century is still the great unsolved problem of neo-orthodoxy.

The acceptance of the scientific view of the world means that when neo-orthodox theologians assert the discontinuity between God and the world, they have little intention of reviving a pre-liberal kind of supernaturalism. There is indeed a divine order which transcends the world that science can investigate, but it remains hidden from ordinary human view. Thus, Barth in his early career maintained that the incarnation touches visible nature and history at its edge, like a tangent touches a circle.[24] Bultmann takes the transhistorical and supernatural events described by the Bible in connection with the salvation wrought by Christ and demythologizes them into existential meaning.[25] Brunner affirms that the resurrection of Jesus is not an event in ordinary history but an occurrence in sacred history which transcends the natural order by being above it.[26] The deity of Christ, he says, is veiled so that a scientific historian could not observe any manifestations of the presence of God in him.[27] Reinhold Niebuhr says that the incarnation is a symbol which points to a realm of meaning beyond history, but the symbol is to be taken "seriously but not literally."[28] H. Richard Niebuhr affirms that the revelatory events to which the Christian refers are not unique or supernatural in that they transcend the causal order to which other events belong but differ only from the point of view from which they are seen.[29]

Hence, when contemporary theologians assert that the transcendent God acts in history, they are reluctant to insist that this involves any intrusion of the divine order into the natural order in ways that involve the miraculous. Even those who reaffirm the two-nature doctrine of Chalcedon do not generally intend to imply that the union of God and man in Christ is accompanied by visible manifestations of supernatural power or activity. Rather, they stress the fact that the observable Jesus of history is a completely human person. To say that God acts in history tends to mean that the divine order enters nature and history at the limits of the visible, causal realm without disturbing its regularities, or it may involve the transformation of supernatural existence into personal meaning. This accounts, at least in part, for the reluctance to speak of objective, definable content in connection with revelation and for the use of such terms as paradox, symbol, dialectical thought, and myth, which imply that human language points to a transcendent dimension of being and meaning which cannot be contained in the limited categories at man's disposal. God encounters men largely through the medium of the practical reason, which is the realm of personal meaning and existential decision, and this encounter does not yield much that the theoretical reason can handle.

Closely connected with this is the fact that in many quarters when theologians speak of the predicament of man and of the deliverance which Christ brings, they direct attention not to objective or cosmological or visible realities but to the internal life of persons. The evils from which men suffer because of their nature and their sin are described in terms of meaninglessness, anxiety, despair, and other such existential ills.[30] What the Gospel does for man primarily is to give him a new self-understanding which allows him to face the future unafraid (Bultmann), provide him with the courage to be (Tillich), reveal the meaning of human life and history (Niebuhr), and so on. Bultmann contends that to speak of God acting involves no reference whatsoever to any supernatural interference with the observable processes of nature and history. It simply means that the self comes to have a particular existential understanding of some event or series of events through which the Word of God addresses the ear of faith.[31] Allan Galloway wants to speak of the cosmic effects of the redemption wrought by Christ, but what he says is that the world is understood differently because of the new meaning which personal existence comes to have for the believer. What Christ alters is not the objective structures of the cosmos but the existential self-world correlation of the redeemed person.[32] Those who want to find a place for what Aulén calls the classical view of the atonement can say how Christ overcomes the evil powers that enslave men easier by referring to what he does for the believer than by specifying what he does to the demons. For Bultmann, Tillich, and others eternal life apparently does not involve everlasting bliss beyond physical death but rather seems to be a quality of life gained through personal encounter with the Christian revelation.

In short, there is in contemporary thought, particularly where the influence of existentialism is strong, a pronounced proclivity to interpret the actualities of revelation, judgment, and redemption in terms of the experiences that occur within the self. In this sense, recent thought manifests a more pronounced subjectivism than either orthodoxy or liberalism. Orthodoxy was not afraid to speak of the wages of sin in terms of God-sent pain, sickness, tyranny, early death, etc. Likewise, the providence of God was thought to include special protection of life and limb from danger, accident, and peril, and other similarly objective blessings. Liberalism believed that judgment and redemption are concrete, empirical realities which genuinely change the lives of persons and societies.[33] Jesus, for example, was thought to have made an observable difference in world history in that there proceeded from him the moral power which was to make love dominant in the affairs of men.[34] Liberalism affirmed the meaning of life because of the power it saw at work in history transforming the world into an ideal kingdom. This provided some objective check and validation for the values apprehended in religious experience and revealed in Christ. Neo-orthodoxy affirms the meaning of human existence because of faith's grasp of a transcendent revelation. But faith remains objectively uncertain because the concrete actualities of life provide no clear validation of the meaning which revelation discloses. Hence, the scarcity of any observable manifestations of God's redemptive power intensifies the emphasis upon the subjective elements of the religious life. It is clear that the Gospel relates men to a transcendent realm of being and meaning. But the relationship of salvation to objective events of life and history outside the subjective experience of the believer often remains ambiguous.[35]

The relations between the subjective and the objective in contemporary thought, however, are complex. The emphasis upon faith as a daring personal leap in the presence of practical and theoretical uncertainty is accompanied by the renewal of a doctrine of the sovereignty of God. In a sense both subjectivism and objectivism are, in different ways, intensified. Pointing to the existential dimension of faith as a commitment of the whole self to a Reality beyond every finite power which cannot be proven by human means magnifies the importance of the subjective element, while the doctrine that God rules all things according to his omnipotent will shifts attention from the human discernment of divine activity to the objective reality of God's sovereign rule in all natural, historical, and personal events. H. Richard Niebuhr is a good illustration of this point.[36] He holds to a dualism with regard to the way history is known, stressing the fact that the Christian view of history is affirmed by an existential leap which transcends any rational process of demonstration. But he explicitly denies any sort of dualism with regard to the objective events of nature and history. His radical theocentrism leads him to affirm that every aspect of reality, every event, is comprehended within the universal rule of God. This pattern never becomes transparent to human reason, so that faith retains its subjectivity; but the faith is directed to the objective Reality who is Sovereign Subject.

B. *Post-Liberal Theology and Autonomy*

It has already been pointed out that the primary difference between liberal and post-liberal thought arises out of the break with the principle of continuity. There have also been significant changes with regard to the other two motifs of liberalism. Post-liberal theology stands under many of the influences which originally gave rise to these principles, and there has been a considerable carry-over from liberalism. However, both of these motifs appear in a distinctly different light in contemporary thought, and autonomy tends to be seriously qualified or rejected altogether.

Post-liberal theology is in agreement with liberalism in its rejection of the Biblical authoritarianism of Protestant orthodoxy. No major theologian outside of very conservative circles today insists that the Bible contains a system of doctrinal propositions which are binding on all men for all time. Present-day thinkers subject the world view of the Bible to the criticisms of empirical science and employ the historical-critical method in dealing with its contents just as the liberals did. They are in full agreement that the Bible mirrors the historical and cultural background of its writers. The debate that the liberals began concerning the problem of how an ancient document employing outmoded categories can function as a religious authority in the twentieth century continues, as the frequent use of such terms as "myth" (Reinhold Niebuhr), "method of correlation" (Tillich), and "demythologizing" (Bultmann) reveals. In short, post-liberal thinkers employ the same methods in dealing with the nature and authority of the Bible as the liberals used and are in agreement with them that the Bible is a historically conditioned, human book which must be reinterpreted in modern categories to make it relevant for the needs of contemporary men. Both groups agree that there is a message of permanent validity in the Bible, but they disagree in the way they describe this message and in the way they relate it to the human and cultural attempt to discover relevant truth apart from special revelation.

Moreover, it will be remembered that one of the influences which contributed to the shift of the locus of authority from the Bible to experience was the deterministic, mechanistic outlook of modern science. Contemporary theology inherited this problem and has, for the most part, continued to work out its solutions along Kantian lines. Generally speaking, the position taken is that moral values and religious truth are not primarily discovered by examining the objective processes of external nature and history but are affirmed by a leap of faith involving a special, unique grasp of reality in a personal encounter with God. The very strong influence of existentialism can be detected in most recent interpretations of this sort. There is a wide area of agreement, then, between liberalism and contemporary thought in that both tend to affirm that God is known primarily through the practical reason, although there are important exceptions to this statement among both liberal and post-liberal thinkers.

This concentration on the thinking, believing, and deciding which takes place in the believer is closely associated with the view that God can be known only from the point of view of faith in him. Theologians in both the nineteenth and twentieth centuries have reaffirmed Luther's idea that God and faith go together. H. Richard Niebuhr accepts this view as his own and remarks that "Schleiermacher and Ritschl owed no small part of their success to their observance of the limitation of theology to the point of view of faith in the God of Jesus Christ."[37] It is commonplace for theologians to say today that revelation does not occur apart from the response of the believer. Brunner urges that doctrines are distilled from the encounter of the self with God and are secondary to the personal meeting with God in experience.[38] This approach to revelation is involved in the widespread contemporary view that the decisive events in the history of Israel to which the Bible is witness are revelatory only for that person who appropriates their meaning for himself.[39] Ordinary events in nature and history confined within the causal network which constitutes the realm of finite reality may become *Heilsgeschichte* for the eye of faith. The events, however, do not have a self-evident meaning to the objective observer but must be provided with an interpretation which can be affirmed only by an existential leap. It is only the participant in the community which bears the memory and meaning of the events and not the spectator who finds God at work in them.[40] The Bible becomes the Word of God only when it speaks to the believer existentially through personal response.

But while there is wide agreement between liberalism and post-liberal theology that one can speak of God only on the basis of personal experience or encounter with him, there is a significant difference between the way liberals correlated religious experience with a Christocentric revelation and the way this issue is dealt with in contemporary thought. Theology today, in varying degrees, affirms the discontinuity of faith and reason. No longer is the accent on moral and spiritual intuition which easily unites a universally available apprehension of God with a Christocentric revelation but rather on a daring leap of faith which affirms that God has uniquely disclosed himself in Christ. Faith is an adventurous option, freely chosen, involving a subjective decision fraught with objective uncertainty. The emphasis is shifted from reason and experience to revelation, but revelation is now thought of, not in terms of propositions of doctrine heteronomously imposed, but in terms of a personal encounter with God which elicits an affirmative response of trust and commitment.

However, while the source of truth is now in a special revelation of God, in another sense the subject still plays an important role. He is responsible for deciding between faith and unfaith. It should be kept in mind that the freedom and spontaneity of man is given considerably more importance in contemporary thought than was the case in the classical Protestantism to which neo-orthodoxy often appeals. Luther, Calvin, Zwingli, and Edwards all held a rigorous doctrine of predestination which, despite their impressive protests on occasion, inevitably conflicts with the notion that man is free to affirm or to spurn the call of God to repentance and faith. The tendency in contemporary thought is to emphasize the freedom and responsibility of man and to remain quiet with regard to election in the older Calvinistic sense or to reject it. There is some question as to just how much initiative and spontaneity are allowed to man with Barth and some of the Lundensians like Aulén and Nygren, but the main stream of contemporary thought comes out clearly on the side of genuine freedom for man. Moreover, the notion of faith as a commitment of the whole self made in the presence of objective uncertainty focuses attention on the decisions and acts of the self made in its freedom and magnifies the importance of the subjective. It was not a liberal theologian but Kierkegaard, one of the chief influences on contemporary thought, who said, "Truth is subjectivity."

However, the strong emphasis on the sovereignty of God in much recent theology, along with the converse doctrine that man is a creature who is utterly dependent upon God for truth and salvation, makes it inaccurate to speak of man as an autonomous being. In revelation man confronts an Other who is not at man's disposal, and this Other can be known only as he gives himself freely to man by his own initiative. The radical monotheism of H. Richard Niebuhr, the emphasis of Barth upon God as the sole acting Subject in revelation, the stress of Brunner on the freedom of God as transcendent Lord, and similar themes in a host of other thinkers—all of which magnify the priority of God's act and the purely responsive nature of man's believing— define a distinct break with the liberal tendency to identify, or at least make continuous and harmonious, the knowledge of God available to man as man in religious experience and the unique personal truth of divine revelation. The immanence of God made it possible to hold a view of the autonomy of man in a way that is impossible for con- temporary theologians who make primary in their thinking the tran- scendence and sovereignty of God.

Some contemporary theologians have remained much closer to lib- eralism with regard to the autonomy of man than others. Just as one must distinguish the evangelical liberals from the modernistic liberals with regard to this issue, so one must distinguish between a similar division in contemporary thought. Barth and Nygren represent one extreme which distinguishes radically between the revelation of God given in Christ and all attempts to define any sort of natural theology. Little initiative remains with man as far as the attainment of saving knowledge is concerned. Brunner, Reinhold and H. Richard Niebuhr, Nels Ferré, and William Temple define points along a continuum which move progressively in the opposite direction.

Two prominent theologians of the present day seem to be quite close to the modernistic liberals in one respect. Both Bultmann and Tillich have gone further than most recent thinkers in stressing the idea that revelation must be correlated with the understanding of hu- man existence that arises out of the culture in which men live. Tillich's method of correlation involves the view that while revelation provides the content of the Christian message, the form must be determined by the situation. The theologian may make the analysis of the situa- tion, but it is a philosophical task, and in looking at human existence, "his act of seeing is autonomous, for it is determined only by the ob- ject as it is given in his experience."[41] Bultmann argues that the New Testament message must be demythologized before it can be appro- priated by contemporary men, whose world view is shaped by modern science. Science stands in judgment of the mythological framework within which the *kerygma* is contained and necessitates a translation of the saving message of the Bible into the language of the present day. Both Tillich and Bultmann believe that the Christian message in this generation must be put into the categories of existentialist philos- ophy. In both cases many have argued that, despite their protests to the contrary, their understanding of the world and human existence derived from modern culture is determinative not only of the form of the theology they expound but also of its essential content. However, in fairness to them it should be said that both insist that revelation is the Word of God which comes to man from beyond. As Tillich says, "Revelation is 'spoken' to man, not by man to himself."[42] There is, then, a significant difference between the modernism of Bultmann and Tillich and that of Mathews, Macintosh, and Wieman, all of whom believed that experience in general yields to man's reason all the truth that he needs for salvation.

Generally speaking, then, present-day thought stresses theonomy rather than autonomy, meaning by this that religious truth is God-given in special revelation and not available to men apart from the initiative of God.[43]

It may be said, in summary, that the contemporary approach to the relation of human reason and experience to divine revelation is intimately related both to Reformation theology and to liberalism but is identical with neither. In its stress on the transcendence of God and the priority of revelation post-liberal thought has returned to basic affirmations of the classical reformers. However, between the Reformation and the present stand a number of influences which differentiate contemporary theology from the outlook of Luther and Calvin. Both of them, for example, would no doubt have been horrified at Brunner's treatment of the virgin birth and his rejection of the empty tomb and the ascension. The rise of empirical science and the impact of a mechanistic view of the natural world, the historical-critical approach to the Bible, the influence of Kantian and post-Kantian philosophies, and a variety of related movements have entered into the structure of both liberal and post-liberal thought and bind them together in important ways.

C. *Post-Liberal Theology and Dynamism*

Post-liberal theology has retained the liberal view that nature, history, and all the creative processes of human culture are characterized by development. However, in line with the reaffirmation of the transcendence of God, recent thought has rejected the smooth correlation that liberalism was able to make between natural evolution, historical development, moral progress, and divine purpose. Natural evolution is taken for granted but is not regarded as having much theological relevance or value. Historical development is affirmed but is not believed to produce any sustained movement toward the kingdom of God on earth. God is believed to be active in history, but his purposes are veiled except to the eye of faith and have an ambiguous relationship to the concrete processes of historical development. God is thought to be related to history dialectically and not monistically. He is the Judge who frustrates man with the "No" of his holy will as well as the loving redeemer who says "Yes" to man despite his sin. One must now talk about God's relationship to the world in terms of paradox, mystery, and ambiguity, because he is the hidden, transcendent Sovereign Lord as well as the immanent Savior who has drawn near in Jesus Christ.

It should be noted, however, that the approach to the interpretation of history in present-day thought is complex and reveals a variety of tendencies which cannot be comprehended under any one neat pattern. The summary given in the preceding paragraph is typical of a widespread tendency, but it is perhaps closer to Reinhold Niebuhr and Emil Brunner than to H. Richard Niebuhr. To employ the latter's own categories, H. Richard Niebuhr is a "conversionist,"[44] who sees redemption more consistently as a concrete reality in history here and now than do Brunner and Reinhold Niebuhr, who tend more in the direction of a dualism which speaks in terms of hope for a redemption that is to come beyond history. One must be careful, however, about drawing conclusions as to what the reality of redemption here and now means. The position of H. Richard Niebuhr must be sharply distinguished from a liberal outlook which views history from the human perspective and measures redemption in anthropocentric terms. A complete reversal of point of view is called for which will interpret history consistently and completely from a theocentric standpoint. Niebuhr has a Calvinistic sense of the absolute sovereignty of God in which it is necessary to say that in war or in peace, in life or in death, in prosperity or in peril, God is accomplishing his redemptive will.[45] He rejects the view that one first experiences certain moral values and then affirms God as their source. Rather, monotheism affirms that God is Love and Lord of all things and that whatever proceeds from him is good and is to be accepted with gratitude. This is not a denial of the universal pervasiveness of human rebellion and sin in the world, as though there were really no evil, but it is an affirmation that the final reality is God's overarching redemptive sovereignty and not any evil power other than, or in opposition to, God. From the human standpoint relativity, ambiguity, darkness, and fragmentation always remain, but radical monotheism testifies that all the sound and fury and confusion of history become transparent to a pattern of unity and redemption from God's point of view. This is not to put any limits on the extent to which individuals or societies can be morally transformed here and now, so that love becomes an operative reality, but it is to say that history is not to be judged in the first instance on this basis but is to be seen primarily as the story of God's mighty deeds and of man's response to them.

Involved in the reaffirmation of divine transcendence is the conviction that historical development does not disclose any clear progress toward moral and spiritual perfection which provides the whole process with a self-evident, or at least self-validating, interpretation. The meaning of history must be provided by revelation and appropriated by an existential leap. Thus, while liberal theology maintained that the gradual triumph of the ideals of love and brotherhood among men made it easy to believe that the life and teachings of Jesus provide the clue to the meaning of history,[46] post-liberal theology has stressed the discontinuity between reason's attempt to understand the historical existence of man and faith's grasp of the Christian revelation. H. Richard Niebuhr, for example, refers to the faith which arises out of the life, death, and resurrection of Christ that God is utterly loyal to all created beings as "the absurd thing that comes into our moral history as existential selves" and says that it is irrational "to our existential, subjective, decision-making thought."[47] It is commonplace among recent thinkers to insist that the cluster of occurrences which constitute *Heilsgeschichte* has one meaning for the objective historian who derives his patterns of interpretation from the study of world history as a whole and a quite different meaning for the participant or believer who discovers in these events unique self-disclosure of God.[48]

Various degrees of discontinuity between faith and reason in this regard are affirmed by recent thinkers. Karl Lowith goes so far as to say that the meaning of history must come completely from faith and that the actual course of events furnishes no evidence for its truth.[49] Reinhold Niebuhr argues that while the course of history must remain morally ambiguous to the end, so that its meaningfulness is discernible only to faith, there are tangents of meaning in the rise and fall of cultures which partially confirm the Christian view.[50] H. Richard Niebuhr testifies that the Christian interpretation of history must be appropriated through a personal response of commitment, but he asserts that revelation provides a pattern which "brings rationality and wholeness into the confused joys and sorrows of personal existence and allows us to discern order in the brawl of communal histories."[51] Daniel Day Williams affirms an even closer relationship between reason and faith in that he sees a positive correlation between the dynamic view of nature and history derived from process philosophy and the Biblical testimony to God's redemptive activity among men. This belief in redemption is validated by the genuineness of growth in grace and the reality of moral progress in both individual and social existence.[52]

Christology in recent thought has also been vitally affected by the post-liberal modification of the principle of dynamism, and the new developments in this area are closely connected with the contemporary approach to the interpretation of history. The orthodox doctrine of the person of Christ formulated at Chalcedon asserted that the human nature of Jesus was perfectly united with a divine nature. Liberalism attempted to be rid of the dogmas about Christ and to recover the Jesus of history. The doctrine of the immanence of God allowed liberal thinkers to say that the perfect manhood of Jesus also constituted his divinity. Post-liberal theology has reacted strongly against the liberal reconstruction of orthodoxy and has reasserted the discontinuity between the man Jesus and the divine Christ.

In Biblical studies form criticism has shifted attention away from the attempt to recover the historical Jesus to a concern for the reconstruction of the *kerygma,* which is now asserted to be the heart of the New Testament. The message of the early church, the form critics have urged, showed little interest in the details of the life and teachings of Jesus the man and concentrated on the role of Jesus as the Christ who constitutes the eschatological event by which the New Age breaks into history. The New Testament, then, is not a source for the reconstruction of the biography of Jesus but is rather a witness to the "Christ event," the culminating act of God in the history of salvation. This means that the old quest for the historical Jesus is both historically impossible and theologically illegitimate.[53]

The response of theology to the new situation takes a variety of forms. Sometimes the discontinuity between the human and the divine in Jesus seems to involve not so much a return to the older dualism between two natures as a distinction between two ways of knowing.[54] Jesus stands in two histories: ordinary history, which a secular historian can observe, and *Heilsgeschichte,* known only to faith. The Jesus of history is the completely human person known by means of "objective factual knowledge." The Christ of faith is the divine redeemer whom the believer knows through a "personal grasp of meaning."[55] Contemporary theology, then, has returned to the "paradox of Chalcedonian Christology,"[56] but it manifests a widespread tendency to shift the Christological categories from concern with a dualistic ontology to a dualistic epistemology. This way of viewing the problem involves one series of events which are seen from two different perspectives. H. Richard Niebuhr's distinction between "internal history" and "external history"[57] and Rudolf Bultmann's distinction between *"Historie"* and *"Geschichte"*[58] seem to be of this sort.

Others, however, like Barth and Brunner, share in their own way the distinction between ordinary history and sacred history but seem to think of them as two orders of reality which confront the knower, one of them accessible to the neutral spectator and the other transparent only to faith. Within this context both Barth and Brunner affirm that God is objectively and ontologically present in Christ and speak of him as fully God and fully man.[59] However, the relationship between the causal nexus of nature and history in which the human Jesus appears to the historical critic and the superhistory to which the deity of Christ belongs is not always clear. Brunner seems to say that the divine side of the incarnation does not manifest itself at all in the realm of observable historical phenomena.[60] Barth goes further in affirming that the incarnation is accompanied by the miraculous, that is, events which are not conceivable in ordinary causal terms. For example, the virgin birth and the empty tomb are referred to as "signs" of the visitation of God to man in Christ.[61] Richard R. Niebuhr maintains that Barth professes an ultra-realism which so magnifies the priority of sacred history that all problems of historical causality which present themselves to the critical-scientific reason fade into insignificance.[62] Niebuhr concludes that none of the attempts to interpret revelation and redemption in terms of *Heilsgeschichte* really succeed in anchoring the resurrection, which is the key to the Lordship of Christ, solidly in the ordinary, i.e., real, history in which human beings live. D. M. Baillie seems to be close to Barth and Brunner, although he is highly critical of them in some respects. One must, he says, speak of two objective causal orders, one open to inspection by science and the other known only to personal faith. As a result religious language is unavoidably paradoxical, since God "comes in, as it were, on the vertical line from the eternal world ('senkrecht von oben') to touch the horizontal line on which we inevitably have another explanation in empirical terms."[63]

A number of consequences follow from these new accents in recent thought. Christology among some tends to become identified with Christocentric interpretation of history.[64] Associated with this is an inclination to speak more of the meaning which Christ gives to history than of the power which springs from him to enable men to organize society according to the will of God. Moreover, one can detect on nearly all sides a considerable reduction of interest in the life and teachings of the man Jesus. Georgia Harkness has pointed out that the index to *The Divine Imperative,* Brunner's great work on Christian ethics, contains forty-six references to Luther, thirty-five to Calvin, twenty to Paul, and none to Jesus.[65] Barth has said that the historical Jesus is a quite ordinary, unimpressive Rabbi whose human life is a concealment of God rather than a revelation. Baillie takes Bultmann, Tillich, Brunner, and Barth all to task for insisting that God is uniquely revealed in Jesus Christ, while showing little interest in the form that the revelation actually has in the human life of Jesus. Finally, there is perhaps a greater willingness now among theologians than ever before in the history of the church to take the humanity of Jesus with complete seriousness.[66] All of these developments reflect and magnify the fact that contemporary theology is not primarily interested in the historical Jesus considered as the prophet from Galilee but in Jesus as the Christ, the eschatological event in and through which God has made himself known among men.

These new trends lead theology a long way from the one-dimensional view of history held by liberalism in which the historical Jesus is seen to be the concrete embodiment of the immanent Power and Purpose which is at work transforming the actual structures of historical and social existence into an ideal social order on earth. Contemporary theology has moved toward a two-dimensional view of history in which the human Jesus points to, or is the visible manifestation of, the divine and invisible order which comes to bear on history in and through him in a unique way. Reinhold Niebuhr maintains that the powerlessness of the historical Jesus, best seen in the Cross, points to the sovereign love which ultimately controls history.[67] Paul Tillich contends that Jesus sacrifices himself utterly to the Christ and thus becomes the bearer of a final revelation. He is completely transparent to the mystery he reveals in that he symbolizes in a finite existence the eternal order which stands beyond complete historical embodiment.[68] Rudolf Bultmann speaks of Jesus as the objective, historical focus of the *kerygma*, which becomes the vehicle of the Word of God in present existential encounter.[69] Brunner views the historical Jesus as the visible, human side of the God-man, whose deity or divine nature does not enter into the sphere of ordinary observable history at all.[70] D. M. Baillie interprets the human life of Jesus as a perfect channel through which God manifests himself to the world, so that it can be said that what Jesus does is fully the outcome of his own human choice and yet, paradoxically, the result of the divine power and presence in him.[71] H. Richard Niebuhr holds the position that it is not the morality or personality of the human Jesus as such that is of supreme importance to Christian faith but Jesus as the Son of God who consistently points beyond himself and the world to the Sovereign Father and, in a return movement, instructs men in the way and will of God.[72]

III. CONCLUSION

In brief, it may be said that neo-orthodoxy, which is at the center of post-liberal theology, is a development within the main stream of modern Protestant thought which has reacted sharply against certain fundamental features of the liberal stage of this movement while retaining others. This is to say that neo-orthodoxy is a new phase in that tradition which began with Schleiermacher and which is based on an acceptance of the findings of empirical science, the historical-critical approach to the Bible, and some form of Kantian or post-Kantian philosophy. It is different from the liberalism which preceded it in that it has returned to the main line of the orthodox tradition, particularly the Protestant Reformation, for some of its central insights, and thus it is called neo-*orthodoxy*. But it has appropriated these orthodox emphases on the basis of a methodology and in terms of certain fundamental presuppositions which have been inherited from liberalism, and thus it is called *neo*-orthodoxy. In one sense, then, neo-orthodoxy is a repudiation of liberalism in that it breaks

significantly with the principles of continuity and autonomy and modi-
fies the principle of dynamism, all of which were fundamental to
liberalism. In another sense, neo-orthodoxy is a continuation of liberalism in that in both method and content it is dependent upon liberal
insights. The leading contemporary thinkers began their careers under
liberal influences and have retained the distinct impress of their family
background even as they have criticized their theological fathers.

NOTES

Chapter 1. FORMATIVE FACTORS IN AMERICAN LIBERALISM

1. Henry Churchill King, *Reconstruction in Theology* (New York: The Macmillan Company, 1901), p. v.
2. "After Liberalism—What?" *The Christian Century*, November 8, 1933, p. 1403.
3. Arthur Cushman McGiffert, Jr., "Protestant Liberalism," *Liberal Theology: an Appraisal*, ed. David E. Roberts and Henry Pitney Van Dusen (New York: Charles Scribner's Sons, 1942), pp. 106–120.
4. Frank Hugh Foster, *A Genetic History of the New England Theology* (Chicago: The University of Chicago Press, 1907). See also H. Shelton Smith, *Changing Conceptions of Original Sin* (New York: Charles Scribner's Sons, 1955).
5. Foster, *op. cit.*, p. 543.
6. King, *op. cit.*, pp. 28–29.
7. Arthur Cushman McGiffert, Sr., *The Rise of Modern Religious Ideas* (New York: The Macmillan Company, 1915), p. 184.
8. *Ibid.*, pp. 24–44.
9. See Carl L. Becker, *The Heavenly City of the Eighteenth Century Philosophers* (New Haven: Yale University Press, 1932), p. 102. It will become evident in the discussion that is to follow in the text that liberalism was partly a consequence of, and partly a reaction to, the Enlightenment. The optimism about man and his future, and the rejection of authoritarianism, for example, were carried over into liberalism; the transcendent view of God and the cool, detached rationalism of the Enlightenment were rejected.
10. McGiffert, Sr., *op. cit.*, p. 103.
11. John Herman Randall, Jr., *The Making of the Modern Mind* (Boston: Houghton Mifflin Company, 1926), p. 415.
12. *Revivalism and Social Reform* (Nashville: Abingdon Press, 1957), p. 162. It must be recognized, however, that the nearness of God in revivalism is based on presuppositions different from the liberal principle of immanence. Many revivalists, of course, emphasized the miraculous nature of God's activity.
13. McGiffert, Jr., *op. cit.*, p. 115.
14. "The Nineteenth Century and Today," in *The Vitality of the Christian Tradition*, ed. George F. Thomas (New York: Harper & Brothers, 1944), p. 170.
15. McGiffert, Sr., *op. cit.*, p. 189.
16. Browning, "Aurora Leigh."

17. John Dillenberger and Claude Welch, *Protestant Christianity* (New York: Charles Scribner's Sons, 1954), p. 219.

18. For a fuller discussion of these tendencies, see McGiffert, Sr., *op. cit.*, pp. 187–221, and Dillenberger and Welch, *op. cit.*, pp. 217–220.

19. Cf. the discussion of James Brown regarding the various meanings of subjectivity and objectivity in history and in recent theology. *Subject and Object in Modern Theology* (New York: The Macmillan Company, 1955), pp. 11–33, 168–211.

20. For a detailed account of the epistemologies of religious thinkers see D. C. Macintosh, *The Problem of Religious Knowledge* (New York: Harper & Brothers, 1940).

21. The emphasis on experience played a larger role in revivalism than in orthodox Calvinism. However, this emphasis was by no means lacking in Calvinists of the stripe of Edwards and others, who were both orthodox Calvinists and revivalists. There is, of course, an important connection between the emphasis on personal, direct experience of God in revivalism and the rise of liberal theology.

22. Alfred North Whitehead, *Science and the Modern World* (New York: The Macmillan Company, 1925), p. 24.

23. *Ibid.*, pp. 106–107.

24. Cf. Basil Willey, *Nineteenth Century Studies* (London: Chatto and Windus, 1949), p. 2.

25. For the meaning and significance of these distinctions, for Kant, see Hugh Ross Mackintosh, *Types of Modern Theology* (London: Nisbet and Company, Ltd., 1937), pp. 19–25; for Coleridge, see Willey, *op. cit.*, pp. 27–31; for Bushnell, see H. Shelton Smith, *op. cit.*, pp. 152–154; for Ritschl, see Mackintosh, *op. cit.*, pp. 149–155. These distinctions, of course, work against the principle of continuity, but they seemed necessary under the circumstances in order to meet the challenge of mechanistic science.

26. See Hans W. Frei, "Niebuhr's Theological Background," in *Faith and Ethics*, ed. Paul Ramsey (New York: Harper & Brothers, 1957), pp. 16–40. See also Robert Clyde Johnson, *Authority in Protestant Theology* (Philadelphia: The Westminster Press, 1959), pp. 63–88.

27. For an account of these tendencies in romanticism, see Whitehead, *op. cit.*, pp. 105–133; Randall, *op. cit.*, pp. 389–422; and Willey, *op. cit.*, pp. 1–31.

28. Arthur Cushman McGiffert, *Protestant Thought before Kant* (New York: Charles Scribner's Sons, 1911), pp. 186–254.

29. Cf. Edward Caldwell Moore, *An Outline of the History of Christian Thought Since Kant* (New York: Charles Scribner's Sons, 1922), p. 45.

30. Many thinkers who were influenced by Kant were also influenced by Schleiermacher and the romanticists. While Kant had based his belief in God on the universal necessities of thought, many who came later broadened the basis of religion to include feeling, intuition, and religious experience in general. Thus, there is a kind of objectivity about the moral faith of Kant which was not always preserved by later thinkers who were subject to his influence. However, in an important sense the philosophy of Kant itself is subjectivistic in that the categories of thought, though universal and necessary, are imposed on the raw data of experience from within the mind. The "Copernican revolution" which Kant introduced had the effect of emphasizing the creative role of the knowing subject in a way which previous philosophy had not. This emphasis also had an impact on the way

religious knowledge was understood in that it furthered the tendency to look within the soul rather than without.

31. Thus, Dillenberger and Welch insist that while Biblical criticism posed certain problems for Christian thought, this does not mean that liberalism was a reaction to the conclusions of the critics. "In fact, the situation was more nearly the reverse. It was new conceptions of religious authority and of the meaning of revelation which made possible the development of biblical criticism." Dillenberger and Welch, *op. cit.*, p. 197. Cf. Willey, *op. cit.*, pp. 31–32.

32. In the widespread movement of American Christianity in the nineteenth century directed toward the attainment of the kingdom of God on earth, there were dynamic tendencies which would modify the foregoing statements about orthodoxy, since this movement included the more conservative branches of the church as well as the Unitarians. See H. Richard Niebuhr, *The Kingdom of God in America* (New York: Harper & Brothers, 1935), pp. 127–163. It must be recognized, too, with regard to all the statements that have been made throughout this chapter that orthodoxy, no more than liberalism, was not a monolithic structure without internal diversity. Exceptions could be found in certain types of orthodoxy to much that has been said. Nevertheless, as descriptions of orthodoxy in general, it is believed that the characterizations will hold. They are most true perhaps of orthodox Calvinism in its more institutionalized forms.

33. Randall, *op. cit.*, p. 391. For a detailed account of this new emphasis, see Arthur O. Lovejoy, *The Great Chain of Being* (Cambridge: Harvard University Press, 1936), pp. 242–287.

34. For an account of the contributions of these individual men and others, see Randall, *op. cit.*, pp. 381–385, 454–458; McGiffert, Sr., *op. cit.*, pp. 166–174; Crane Brinton, *Ideas and Men* (New York: Prentice-Hall, Inc., 1950), pp. 368–408; Becker, *op. cit.*, pp. 119–168.

35. Brinton, *op. cit.*, p. 369.

36. Randall, *op. cit.*, pp. 454–482; McGiffert, Sr., pp. 166–186.

37. For an account of the impact of scientific discoveries on religious belief before 1859, see Charles Coulston Gillispie, *Genesis and Geology* (Cambridge: Harvard University Press, 1951).

38. McGiffert, Sr., *op. cit.*, p. 201.

39. Randall, *op. cit.*, pp. 417–421.

40. *Ibid.*, pp. 418–419.

41. McGiffert, Sr., *op. cit.*, pp. 174–175.

42. Randall, *op. cit.*, p. 391.

43. One interpreter found in these dynamic tendencies the explanation of the basic differences between the older theology and the new. See Herbert Alden Youtz, "The Critical Problem of Theology Today: the Problem of Method," in *Harvard Theological Review*, IV (October, 1911), p. 443.

Chapter 2. TYPES OF AMERICAN LIBERALISM

1. This terminology is derived from H. Richard Niebuhr, *Christ and Culture* (New York: Harper & Brothers, 1951), pp. 1–39. Niebuhr says, "When Christianity deals with the problem of reason and revelation, what is ultimately in question is the relation of the revelation in Christ to the reason which prevails in culture" (p. 11).

Paul Tillich speaks to the same general point using the terms "message" and "situation." *Systematic Theology* (Chicago: The University of Chicago Press, 1951), I, 3–8.

2. See *Ibid.*, pp. 3–4.

3. Cf. Tillich, *Ibid.*, p. 7.

4. Harry Emerson Fosdick, *The Living of These Days* (New York: Harper & Brothers, 1956), p. vii.

5. By a "type" here is meant a theological orientation which is held in common by a number of thinkers characterized by a close similarity or identity of perspective with regard to certain basic presuppositions, methods, aims, interests, and content of doctrine.

6. The distinction which is to be made here between these two liberal perspectives is not original. It has been suggested to the writer by Henry P. Van Dusen, in *The Vitality of the Christian Tradition,* ed. George F. Thomas (New York: Harper & Brothers, 1944), pp. 168–169.

7. For a statement to this effect by one of the most influential evangelical liberals, see William Adams Brown, "Seeking Beliefs that Matter," in *Contemporary American Theology,* ed. Vergilius Ferm (New York: Round Table Press, Inc., 1933), Second Series, 80.

8. See Van Dusen, *loc. cit.,* p. 172.

9. Others in the perspective but not to be treated here are William Pierson Merrill, Henry Churchill King, William Newton Clark, Harris Franklin Rall, and Rufus Jones, to mention a few of the better known names.

10. This spirit and the method of modernistic liberalism are well indicated in D. C. Macintosh, "Toward a New Untraditional Orthodoxy," in *Contemporary American Theology,* ed. Vergilius Ferm (New York: Round Table Press, Inc., 1932), I, 277–319.

11. Other examples of modernistic thinkers are G. A. Coe, Edward Scribner Ames, and G. B. Smith.

12. For full-length accounts of the fundamentalist movement see Stewart G. Cole, *The History of Fundamentalism* (New York: Richard R. Smith, 1931); Norman Furniss, *The Fundamentalist Controversy, 1918–1931* (New Haven: Yale University Press, 1954). For briefer discussions, see Walter Marshall Horton, "Systematic Theology," in *Protestant Thought in the Twentieth Century,* ed. Arnold S. Nash (New York: The Macmillan Company, 1951), pp. 111–112; Henry Nelson Wieman and Bernard Eugene Meland, *American Philosophies of Religion* (Chicago: Willett, Clark and Co., 1936), pp. 61–76. For an account of fundamentalism which sets it in the whole context of post-Reformation Protestant orthodoxy, see Edwin A. Burtt, *Types of Religious Philosophy* (New York: Harper & Brothers, 1939), pp. 139–166.

13. *Systematic Theology* (Philadelphia: The Judson Press, 1907), p. x.

14. Walter Marshall Horton remarks that it is a questionable procedure to call Mullins a fundamentalist. He is better described as "modern positive" on the order of P. T. Forsyth. Horton, *loc. cit.,* p. 112. For the theology of Mullins, see E. Y. Mullins, *The Christian Religion in Its Doctrinal Expression* (Nashville: Broadman Press, 1917); for his criticism of liberalism, see *Christianity at the Crossroads* (Nashville: Sunday School Board of the Southern Baptist Convention, 1924). For Machen's point of view and his attack upon liberalism, see *Christianity and Liberalism* (New York: The Macmillan Company, 1923).

15. For brief accounts of humanism see Burtt, *op. cit.,* pp. 350–408; Wieman and Meland, *op. cit.,* pp. 251–271; Edwin Ewart Aubrey, *Present Theolog-*

ical Tendencies (New York: Harper & Brothers, 1936), pp. 166–174; and Douglas Clyde Macintosh, *The Problem of Religious Knowledge* (New York: Harper & Brothers, 1940), pp. 79–146.

16. See Burtt, *op. cit.*, pp. 352–364.

17. This phrase comes from E. A. Haydon and is quoted in Horton, *loc. cit.*, p. 113.

18. For the views of these men, see E. A. Haydon, *The Quest of the Ages* (New York: Harper & Brothers, 1929); John Dewey, *A Common Faith* (New Haven: Yale University Press, 1934); Walter Lippmann, *A Preface to Morals* (New York: Harper & Brothers, 1929). Other important humanists during this period were Max Otto, C. F. Potter, C. W. Reese, R. W. Sellars, and J. A. C. F. Auer.

19. In addition to the works already cited in connection with fundamentalism and humanism, the following volumes contain discussions of the theological situation in America during the period under consideration. A conservative view of twentieth-century trends can be found in Carl F. H. Henry, *Fifty Years of Protestant Theology* (Boston: W. A. Wilde Company, 1950). A liberal perspective is presented in Albert Cornelius Knudson, *Present Tendencies in Religious Thought* (Nashville: Abingdon Press, 1924). A volume by a modernistic liberal who can scarcely be distinguished from the humanists is Gerald Birney Smith, *Current Christian Thinking* (Chicago: The University of Chicago Press, 1928). A popular account can be found in William Hordern, *A Layman's Guide to Protestant Theology* (New York: The Macmillan Company, 1955), pp. 56–98.

20. It must be recognized precisely in what sense this statement is meant. The fundamentalists do not present a theology which contains the pure revelation of God in Christ with no admixture of cultural elements. They do indeed base their theology on the literal teachings of the Bible. Nevertheless, the actual theology which is propounded in fundamentalist circles contains elements which can be traced historically to certain particular historical circumstances. Fundamentalism is culturally conditioned by developments in theology in the post-Reformation period and speaks to modern culture in categories shaped by a previous cultural situation. Cf. Tillich: "Fundamentalism fails to make contact with the present situation, not because it speaks from beyond every situation, but because it speaks from a situation of the past." *Op. cit.*, p. 3.

Likewise, the humanists, while they disavow any conscious dependence on the Christian revelation, do not present a religious philosophy which is a purely cultural creation without any admixture of Christian elements. As Tillich points out, the existential basis of all modern Western culture is historical Christianity. "In this sense all modern philosophy is Christian, even if it is humanistic, atheistic, and intentionally anti-Christian." Tillich, *op. cit.*, p. 27.

21. Since this classification is based on a continuum, it is possible for a thinker to occupy any point between the two poles. Each type defines a broad perspective which allows for variations within each group. Thus, the contrasts between any two types shade off into each other as the midpoint on the continuum between them is approached. This means that the point of view of two thinkers who are classified in different groups, in some cases, may be very slight. It should be kept in mind, therefore, that these types differ from one another relatively and not absolutely.

22. Douglas Clyde Macintosh in *The Problem of Religious Knowledge* (New York: Harper & Brothers, 1940) follows this procedure.

23. Wieman and Meland, *op. cit.*, classify American philosophies of religion in this way.

24. *An Outline of Christian Theology* (New York: Charles Scribner's Sons, 1906), p. 76.

25. See, for example, the strong statement to this effect in A. C. Knudson, "A Personalistic Approach to Theology," Ferm (ed.), *op. cit.*, I, 228.

26. See, for example, his intellectual autobiography, "Why I Enroll with the Mystics," Ferm (ed.), *op. cit.*, I, 189–215. Also, see Wieman and Meland, *op. cit.*, pp. 121–129; Harry Emerson Fosdick (ed.), *Rufus Jones Speaks to Our Time* (New York: The Macmillan Company, 1951).

27. See Brightman's essay, "Religion as Truth," Ferm (ed.), *op. cit.*, I, 53–81. Among his more important books are: *Religious Values* (Nashville: Abingdon Press, 1925); *The Problem of God* (Nashville: Abingdon Press, 1930); *A Philosophy of Religion* (New York: Prentice-Hall, Inc., 1940). For a brief account of Hocking's thought, see Wieman and Meland, *op. cit.*, pp. 108–114. His most important book is *The Meaning of God in Human Experience* (New Haven: Yale University Press, 1912).

Chapter 3. THE OLD GOSPEL AND THE NEW THEOLOGY: WILLIAM ADAMS BROWN

1. The procedure in each case will follow the same pattern. First of all, a brief introduction will be given to the man and to his thought in general terms. Then, the specific teachings of each man will be examined under five headings: (1) general orientation to theology, including a consideration of theological method, (2) the doctrine of God, (3) the doctrine of man, (4) the doctrine of Christ, and (5) the doctrine of the church.

2. *A Teacher and His Times* (New York: Charles Scribner's Sons, 1940), p. 109.

3. *Christian Realism in Contemporary American Theology* (Uppsala: A. B. Lundequistska Bokhandeln, 1940), p. 136.

4. *Christian Theology in Outline* (New York: Charles Scribner's Sons, 1906), p. viii.

5. ". . . there is an advantage in relating our modern statements to the older forms about which historic associations cluster." *Outline*, p. 353. Cf. Arthur Cushman McGiffert, Jr., "Dr. Brown's Contributions to the Literature of Religion," in *The Church through Half a Century*, ed. Samuel McCrea Cavert and Henry Pitney Van Dusen (New York: Charles Scribner's Sons, 1936), pp. 51–54.

6. "Seeking Beliefs That Matter," in *Contemporary American Theology*, ed. Vergilius Ferm (New York: Round Table Press, Inc., 1933), Second Series, 90–91.

7. Hammar, *op. cit.*, p. 138. It should be noted, however, that pragmatism refers both to a method of testing truth and to a theory of the nature of truth. According to the former, truth must be tested in practical action of some sort; i. e., the consequences which follow from acting upon any hypothesis determine whether or not it is true. According to the latter, truth is defined, not as correspondence with objective reality, but as the harmony of an idea with the rest of experience. Cf. William Kelley Wright, *A History of Modern Philosophy* (New York: The Macmillan Company,

1941), pp. 511–513, 519–523. Brown agrees fully with James with regard to the method of testing truth. With regard to the nature of truth, however, Brown seems to lean toward a more objectivistic or realistic view. In other words, he seems to believe that hypotheses which validate themselves in experience are in conformity with the objective realm of being.

8. *God at Work* (New York: Charles Scribner's Sons, 1933), p. 9.

9. In *Pathways to Certainty* (New York: Charles Scribner's Sons, 1930), Brown reveals his inclusiveness by setting forth four ways by which religious beliefs can be discovered and tested: authority, reason, intuition, and experiment. Cf. Henry Nelson Wieman and Bernard Eugene Meland, *American Philosophies of Religion* (Willett, Clark and Company, 1936), p. 167, where the connection between grounding religion in experience and eclecticism is mentioned.

10. Cf. Hammar, *op. cit.,* pp. 138–139. What is here referred to as neo-orthodoxy was then called theological realism or neo-supernaturalism. The term neo-orthodoxy is being used in a very broad sense to refer to the renewed emphasis on revelation, the transcendence of God, and the doctrine of original sin. It is in Brown's writings after 1935 that the tendencies toward the new supernaturalism are most evident. The references to these writings are found in the passage cited from Hammar's work.

11. See the essay on nineteenth-century theology by Hans Frei, "Niebuhr's Theological Background," in *Faith and Ethics,* ed. Paul Ramsey (New York: Harper & Brothers, 1957), pp. 21–32.

12. Frei, *loc. cit.,* p. 26.

13. *The Essence of Christianity* (New York: Charles Scribner's Sons, 1902).

14. *Ibid.,* p. 303.

15. "The Task and Method of Systematic Theology," in *The American Journal of Theology,* XIV (April, 1910), 205–206.

16. Cf. Walter Marshall Horton, "Systematic Theology," in *Protestant Thought in the Twentieth Century,* ed. Arnold S. Nash (New York: The Macmillan Company, 1951), p. 110.

17. See Frei, *loc. cit.,* p. 45.

18. Cf. Emil Brunner, *The Divine-Human Encounter,* trans. Amandus W. Loos (Philadelphia: The Westminster Press, 1943), p. 35.

19. Frei, *loc. cit.,* p. 45. The quotation is from *Die Christliche Dogmatik.*

20. The complexities of epistemology within a theological context are well illustrated in William Adams Brown. Brown adheres to the principle of autonomy in that his theology is rooted in experience and not in an arbitrary, external revelation of God contained in Biblical propositions. Brown, however, qualifies this autonomy by appealing to a normative revelation of God in Christ which validates itself in experience by its inherent worth and reasonableness. Another contrast has now to be made. Brown's theology is weighted on the subjective side in that he appeals to moral intuition as the surest road to religious certainty. Brown qualifies this orientation, however, by insisting that moral experience is rooted in real existence and ultimately upon the power and goodness of God. The objectivity of experienced values, he feels, is guaranteed by the practical results in life which follow when these values are appropriated and acted upon. The first contrast has to do with the relationship between general and special revelation. The second has to do with the relationship between subjective and objective factors in human knowledge and experience. In each case Brown stresses the continuity between the contrasting pairs of factors.

21. *Outline*, p. 21.
22. "The Task and Method of Systematic Theology," *loc. cit.*, p. 213; *Pathways to Certainty*, pp. 197–225; *Imperialistic Religion and the Religion of Democracy* (New York: Charles Scribner's Sons, 1923), p. 188; "The Place of Christ in Modern Theology," in *The American Journal of Theology*, XVI (January, 1912), 44, 50; *Modern Theology and the Preaching of the Gospel* (New York: Charles Scribner's Sons, 1914), pp. 198–199; *God at Work*, p. 225.
23. Hammar, *op. cit.*, p. 13.
24. For an account of recent tendencies see John Baillie, *The Idea of Revelation in Recent Thought* (New York: Columbia University Press, 1956).
25. "The Old Theology and the New," in *The Harvard Theological Review*, IV (January, 1911), 14.
26. Hammar, *op. cit.*, p. 128; see also Horace Bushnell, *Nature and the Supernatural* (1858).
27. Cf. Henry Pitney Van Dusen, *The Plain Man Seeks for God* (New York: Charles Scribner's Sons, 1933), pp. 47–55, 61–63, 72–76.
28. "The Old Theology and the New," *loc. cit.*, p. 16.
29. Wieman and Meland, *op. cit.*, pp. 149–154, 167–170.
30. "The Task and Method of Systematic Theology," *loc. cit.*, p. 213.
31. *Outline*, pp. 128–138.
32. Claude Welch, *In This Name* (New York: Charles Scribner's Sons, 1952), p. 28.
33. *Outline*, p. 157.
34. Welch, *op. cit.*, pp. 293–294.
35. *Outline*, p. 161.
36. *Ibid.*
37. *Ibid.*, 98–99.
38. Here is still another facet of the doctrine of continuity. Brown includes without hesitation in his definition of the Christian view of God an element which he affirms is derived from Greek philosophy. A typical contemporary theologian would be much more likely to call attention to the discontinuity (radical difference) between the Christian and Greek views of God.
39. For Brown's account of the doctrine of God see *Outline*, pp. 81–163; *Modern Theology and the Preaching of the Gospel*, pp. 87–127; *Beliefs That Matter* (New York: Charles Scribner's Sons, 1928), pp. 148–176.
40. *Outline*, p. 243.
41. *Ibid.*, pp. 244–250, 271–279.
42. "The Old Theology and the New," *loc. cit.*, p. 15.
43. H. Richard Niebuhr, *Christ and Culture* (New York: Harper & Brothers, 1951), p. 96.
44. This implies moral freedom (power of self-determination) but not metaphysical freedom (power of contrary choice).
45. *Outline*, pp. 315–316, 182–183.
46. Cf. Reinhold Niebuhr, *Faith and History* (New York: Charles Scribner's Sons, 1949).
47. A. C. McGiffert, Jr., maintains that in later years Brown moved away from the eschatological view of the kingdom of God presented in the *Outline* toward a more utopian conception of future possibilities. He contends that in *Is Christianity Practicable?*, published in 1916, Brown throws away his earlier caution and insists categorically that the Christian ideal for society will one day be realized on earth. (*Loc. cit.*, p. 47.) To what extent this

represents a basic change in the structure of his thought or merely a difference of degree in his enthusiasm will here have to remain an open question. For Brown's view in the *Outline,* see pp. 412–423.

48. *Outline,* pp. 258–260, 419–423.
49. "The Place of Christ in Modern Theology," *loc. cit.,* p. 31.
50. *The Essence of Christianity,* pp. 295–301.
51. *Outline,* p. 330.
52. *Ibid.,* p. 331.
53. "The Place of Christ in Modern Theology," *loc. cit.,* p. 43.
54. Schweitzer's *Von Reimarus zu Wrede* was published in 1906, the same
    year as Brown's *Outline.* However, it is included in Brown's bibliography,
    p. 450. In an article published in *The American Journal of Theology* in
    1912, the element of subjectivism in the Christian's estimate of Jesus is
    stressed even more than in the *Outline.*
55. The awareness of this gap, in connection with a variety of other develop-
    ments, was one of the important factors which led to a virtual abandon-
    ment of the nineteenth-century "quest of the historical Jesus." For an
    excellent discussion of this whole problem see James M. Robinson, *A New
    Quest of the Historical Jesus* (London: SCM Press, 1959), pp. 26–47.
56. "The Place of Christ in Modern Theology," *loc. cit.,* p. 44.
57. *Modern Theology and the Preaching of the Gospel,* pp. 198–199; *Beliefs
    That Matter,* p. 92; *Outline,* pp. 331, 349; "The Place of Christ in Modern
    Theology," *loc. cit.,* pp. 45, 50.
58. In other words, Brown's doctrine of the atonement does not fall under
    either the Latin or the classical view but rather under the subjective type,
    to use the terminology of Gustaf Aulén, *Christus Victor* (New York: The
    Macmillan Company, 1951).
59. Samuel McCrea Cavert, "William Adams Brown: Servant of the Church
    of Christ," *The Church through Half a Century,* pp. 16–33.
60. *Outline,* p. 57.
61. *Modern Theology and the Preaching of the Gospel,* pp. 238–239.
62. *Outline,* p. 320.
63. *The Church in America* (New York: The Macmillan Company, 1922),
    p. ix.
64. Richard Niebuhr, *op. cit.,* pp. 91–101.
65. *Modern Theology and the Preaching of the Gospel,* p. 267.
66. Cavert, *loc. cit.,* p. 33.

Chapter 4. PERSONALITY-CENTERED CHRISTIANITY: HARRY EMERSON FOSDICK

1. See his autobiography, *The Living of These Days* (New York: Harper &
   Brothers, 1956).
2. *Ibid.,* p. 57.
3. *Ibid.,* p. 230.
4. *Ibid.,* p. 231.
5. *Ibid.,* p. 234.
6. *As I See Religion* (New York: Harper & Brothers, 1932), pp. 1–31.
7. Fosdick is closely related to Brown at this point. He relies on experience
   rather than on revealed dogma (autonomy) and within experience stresses
   moral intuition and the immediate apprehension of the divine presence and
   power within the self. Fosdick, of course, believes that one must affirm an
   objective creator of value in order to explain this inner experience, but he

begins with the inner reality and moves outward to God and not vice versa. While there is a continuity between the subjective and objective poles, the stress is on the subjective side, at least in comparison with a more rationalistic approach which bases knowledge of God on argument rather than on experience or with the empirical approach of Wieman and Macintosh.

8. *As I See Religion*, p. 44.
9. *Adventurous Religion* (New York: Red Label Reprints, 1926), p. 305.
10. *As I See Religion*, p. 63.
11. *The Modern Use of the Bible* (New York: The Macmillan Company, 1924).
12. For some examples of how this methodology works itself out with reference to particular issues, see *ibid.*, p. 129.
13. *A Guide to Understanding the Bible* (New York: Harper & Brothers, 1938), p. xiii.
14. *Ibid.*, p. xv.
15. *The Living of These Days*, pp. vii, 66, 244.
16. "Shall the Fundamentalists Win?" in *The Christian Century*, June 8, 1922, pp. 713–717.
17. "Beyond Modernism," in *The Christian Century*, December 4, 1935, pp. 1549–1552.
18. *Adventurous Religion*, p. 5.
19. *The Living of These Days*, p. 265.
20. See particularly *As I See Religion*, pp. 160–189, 64–128.
21. *Adventurous Religion*, pp. 72–73.
22. These are the words of George Hammar interpreting Horton in Hammar's book, *Christian Realism in Contemporary American Theology* (Uppsala: A. B. Lundequistska Bokhandeln, 1940), p. 256.
23. *Ibid.* Some humanists, of course, did adopt a rigorous naturalism and become pessimistic about the human situation, Joseph Wood Krutch, for example. The argument of Fosdick and Horton, then, applies only to the optimistic humanists.
24. *As I See Religion*, p. 81.
25. If this interpretation be correct, then Fosdick has broken out of a Kantian limitation of reason, insisting that at least one theoretical argument does in fact give genuine knowledge of God.
26. *As I See Religion*, pp. 83–84.
27. *Ibid.*, p. 88.
28. *The Secret of Victorious Living* (New York: Harper & Brothers, 1934), p. 167.
29. *The Meaning of Faith* (New York: Associated Press, 1919), p. 70.
30. *As I See Religion*, p. 58.
31. *The Living of These Days*, p. 64.
32. *Christianity and Progress* (Westwood, N.J.: Fleming H. Revell Company, 1922), p. 245.
33. *The Power to See It Through* (New York: Harper & Brothers, 1935), p. 35.
34. *As I See Religion*, p. 49.
35. *As I See Religion*, pp. 32–63, 160–189; *Adventurous Religion*, pp. 30–44.
36. *The Hope of the World* (New York: Harper & Brothers, 1933), p. 130.
37. *Christianity and Progress*, p. 99; *The Power to See It Through*, p. 54.
38. *On Being a Real Person* (New York: Harper & Brothers, 1943), p. viii.

The book, more than any other work of Fosdick's, sets forth the insights which came to him through counseling and psychotherapy.

39. *The Living of These Days*, pp. 72–76.
40. *Adventurous Religion*, p. 43.
41. *Christianity and Progress*, p. 176.
42. *Ibid.*, p. 177.
43. *The Hope of the World*, pp. 204–213.
44. *Ibid.*, pp. 21–38; *Christianity and Progress*, pp. 87–126.
45. *The Living of These Days*, p. 265.
46. *Christianity and Progress*, p. 40.
47. *The Living of These Days*, pp. 237–242.
48. *Christianity and Progress*, pp. 174–175.
49. *Ibid.*, p. 175.
50. *Ibid.*, pp. 177–178.
51. *The Living of These Days*, pp. 241–242.
52. *The Hope of the World*, p. 103.
53. *The Modern Use of the Bible*, p. 261.
54. *The Secret of Victorious Living*, p. 117.
55. *The Modern Use of the Bible*, p. 230.
56. *Christianity and Progress*, pp. 233–234.
57. *As I See Religion*, p. 51.
58. *Ibid.*, p. 22.
59. *The Living of These Days*, p. 191.
60. *Ibid.*, pp. 77–78.

Chapter 5. THE SOCIAL GOSPEL: WALTER RAUSCHENBUSCH

1. See his biography by Dores R. Sharpe, *Walter Rauschenbusch* (New York: The Macmillan Company, 1942).
2. H. Richard Niebuhr, *The Kingdom of God in America* (Harper & Brothers, 1935; reprinted, Hamden, Conn.: The Shoe String Press, 1956).
3. *Ibid.*, p. xii.
4. Waldo Beach and John C. Bennett, "Christian Ethics," *Protestant Thought in the Twentieth Century*, ed. Arnold S. Nash (New York: The Macmillan Company, 1951), pp. 125–126.
5. See Henry F. May, *Protestant Churches and Industrial America* (New York: Harper & Brothers, 1949), pp. 136–160.
6. *Ibid.*, p. 264.
7. *Ibid.*
8. *The Rise of the Social Gospel in American Protestantism, 1865–1915* (New Haven: Yale University Press, 1940), p. 318.
9. Niebuhr, *op. cit.*, p. 150.
10. *Ibid.*, p. 151.
11. See *Ibid.*, pp. 150–163. Cf. Timothy L. Smith, *Revivalism and Social Reform* (Nashville: Abingdon Press, 1957), p. 7.
12. Smith, *op. cit.*
13. *Ibid.*, p. 8.
14. *Ibid.*, p. 149.
15. *Ibid.*, p. 12.
16. This is the date set by John Bennett, "The Social Interpretation of Christianity," ed. Samuel McCrea Cavert and Henry Pitney Van Dusen, *The*

Church through Half a Century (New York: Charles Scribner's Sons, 1936), p. 113. Hopkins suggests that by 1880 the social gospel was a youthful movement. May suggests the dates 1877–1895 as the period of the rise of social Christianity.

17. Cf. George Hammar, *Christian Realism in Contemporary American Theology* (Uppsala: A. B. Lundequistska Bokhandeln, 1940), pp. 146–160.
18. "Systematic Theology," Nash (ed.), *op. cit.*, p. 110.
19. Hopkins, *op. cit.*, p. 216.
20. *Ibid.*, pp. 216–217.
21. *A Theology for the Social Gospel* (New York: The Macmillan Company, 1917), pp. 24, 26, 131.
22. *Christianity and the Social Crisis* (New York: The Macmillan Company, 1907), pp. 1–43.
23. *Ibid.*, pp. 44–65.
24. *Christianizing the Social Order* (New York: The Macmillan Company, 1912), p. 67.
25. *Ibid.*, p. 69.
26. Hammar, *op. cit.*, p. 158.
27. For example, John Bright believes with Rauschenbusch that the kingdom of God is the central theme of Biblical religion, but his interpretation of the meaning of this doctrine is quite different. Bright rejects the liberal interpretation of the kingdom as an evolutionary development toward a perfect human society and views the rule of God in the context of a theology which emphasizes the mighty redemptive acts of the sovereign Lord of history. *The Kingdom of God* (Nashville: Abingdon Press, 1953).
28. *Social Crisis*, pp. 143–210; *Social Order*, pp. 69–82.
29. In *A Theology for the Social Gospel* Rauschenbusch lists ten unfortunate consequences which followed from the eclipse of the kingdom ideal. See pp. 133–138.
30. *Ibid.*, pp. 139–145.
31. This thesis is developed systematically in *A Theology for the Social Gospel*, but by 1912 Rauschenbusch had already pointed out the importance of the doctrine of the kingdom of God for the reformulation of theology. See *Social Order*, pp. 94–95. Vernon Parker Bodein points out that this idea goes back even further, at least to 1892. *The Social Gospel and Its Relation to Religious Education* (New Haven: Yale University Press, 1944), p. 100.
32. *A Theology*, pp. 6–7.
33. *Ibid.*, p. 20.
34. A good example of orthodox thinking in this regard is J. Gresham Machen, *Christianity and Liberalism* (New York: The Macmillan Company, 1923).
35. *A Theology*, p. 21.
36. *Ibid.*, p. 1.
37. *Ibid.*, p. 264.
38. *Ibid.*, p. 193.
39. See Hugh Ross Mackintosh, *Types of Modern Theology* (New York: Charles Scribner's Sons, 1939), pp. 181–187.
40. Cf. the views of Shailer Mathews.
41. *A Theology*, p. 176.
42. *Ibid.*, p. 174.
43. *Ibid.*, p. 177.
44. *Ibid.*, pp. 174–175.
45. *Ibid.*, p. 178.

46. H. Richard Niebuhr, *Christ and Culture* (New York: Harper & Brothers, 1951), p. 83.

47. It ought to be noted that to place a thinker in this category does not mean that he approves everything in a particular culture. Many thinkers who are best identified as culture Christians have tendencies in their outlook which would place them in other categories. Thus, Rauschenbusch sometimes sounds more like a conversionist than a culture Christian. He often stressed the distance between Christ and American culture and worked for the transformation of culture in the light of Christian values. Niebuhr himself is quite aware of the dangers of categorizing thinkers too neatly. *Ibid.*, pp. 43–44.

48. *A Theology*, p. 178.

49. *Ibid.*, pp. 178–179.

50. For the extent to which Rauschenbusch carries the doctrine of immanence, see the following: *Social Order*, p. 6; *A Theology*, pp. 14, 48, 49, 152, 186, 264.

51. W. A. Visser 't Hooft, *Background of the Social Gospel in America* (London: Oxford University Press, 1928), pp. 174–180.

52. Sharpe, *op. cit.*, pp. 340–343, and Bodein, *op. cit.*, pp. 127–134.

53. Sharpe, *op. cit.*, pp. 432–438.

54. As might be expected, Rauschenbusch gives practically no attention to the doctrine of the Trinity. See *ibid.*, p. 322, for an indication of Rauschenbusch's attitude toward this doctrine.

55. Cf. Hammar, *op. cit.*, p. 153, for a similar judgment regarding Rauschenbusch.

56. For example, see John Dillenberger and Claude Welch, *Protestant Christianity* (New York: Charles Scribner's Sons, 1954), p. 223.

57. *Social Order*, p. 61.

58. *A Theology*, p. 61; cf. pp. 5, 147.

59. *Ibid.*, p. 46.

60. *Ibid.*, p. 48.

61. *Ibid.*, p. 49.

62. H. Shelton Smith, *Changing Conceptions of Original Sin* (New York: Charles Scribner's Sons, 1955), pp. 198–206.

63. Evils which are transmitted biologically are listed by Rauschenbusch as follows: idiocy, feeble-mindedness, neurotic disturbances, weakness of inhibition, perverse desires, stubbornness and antisocial impulses. He also refers to the biological background of man as a source of the origin of sin. *A Theology*, p. 58.

64. It should be noted that this conception has its origin in Schleiermacher. See *The Christian Faith*, ed. H. R. Mackintosh and J. S. Stewart, pp. 286–288.

65. *A Theology*, pp. 78–79.

66. John Bennett, *loc. cit.*, p. 120.

67. Cf. Daniel Day Williams, *God's Grace and Man's Hope* (New York: Harper & Brothers, 1949), pp. 35–36, 104.

68. *A Theology*, p. 95.

69. *Ibid.*, p. 5.

70. *Ibid.*, pp. 97–98.

71. *Ibid.*, pp. 98–99.

72. *Ibid.*, p. 117.

73. See *Social Order*, pp. 458–476; *Social Crisis*, pp. 343–422.

74. *Social Order*, p. 460.
75. *Social Crisis*, p. 352.
76. *Social Order*, p. 460.
77. *Ibid.*, p. 462.
78. *Ibid.*, p. 465.
79. Bennett, *loc. cit.*, pp. 115–117.
80. *Social Order*, p. 472.
81. *Social Crisis*, p. 346.
82. *Social Order*, p. 125.
83. *Ibid.*, p. 154.
84. *Ibid.*, p. 127.
85. *Social Crisis*, pp. 421–422. Rauschenbusch died in 1918, but his hopes, too, for the future seem to have been chastened by World War I. *Christianity and the Social Crisis* was written in 1907. At that time he seemed to feel that the rate of progress was increasing.
86. *Social Order*, p. 126.
87. *Social Crisis*, pp. 420–421.
88. John Bennett seems to share this view; *loc. cit.*, pp. 117–118. Rauschenbusch was not so optimistic and Niebuhr not so pessimistic as they are often made out to be. Bennett remarks again in an essay written some twenty years after the one just referred to: "One of the great misinterpretations of Niebuhr is the idea that he is the great pessimist of modern theology." "Reinhold Niebuhr's Social Ethics," in *Reinhold Niebuhr: His Religious, Social, and Political Thought*, ed. Charles W. Kegley, Robert W. Kegley, and Robert W. Bretall (New York: The Macmillan Company, 1956), p. 49.
89. For Niebuhr's views, see *The Nature and Destiny of Man* (One Volume Edition: New York: Charles Scribner's Sons, 1943), II, 244–286; *Faith and History* (New York: Charles Scribner's Sons, 1949), pp. 214–234.
90. See *The Nature and Destiny of Man*, I, pp. 150–300.
91. Cf. Williams, *op. cit.*, pp. 37–38. See Niebuhr, *The Nature and Destiny of Man*, II, 98–126.
92. Cf. Hammar, *op. cit.*, pp. 156–157.
93. Niebuhr, *The Nature and Destiny of Man*, II, 68–97. *An Interpretation of Christian Ethics* (New York: Harper & Brothers, 1935), pp. 3–61, 103–135. For a critical analysis of Niebuhr's interpretation of love, see Williams, *op. cit.*, pp. 73–78.
94. *A Theology*, pp. 223–239.
95. Cf. Robert Lowry Calhoun, *Lectures on the History of Christian Doctrine* (New Haven: by the author, 1948), p. 199.
96. *A Theology*, p. 151.
97. Thus, both of these trends in liberal Christology testify to the powerful impact of Kant upon modern Protestantism. He effected a "Copernican revolution" not only in epistemology but also in theology.
98. *A Theology*, p. 148.
99. *Social Crisis*, p. 48.
100. *A Theology*, pp. 154–155.
101. *Social Order*, p. 125.
102. *A Theology*, p. 154.
103. *Ibid.*, pp. 257–258.
104. *Social Order*, p. 464.

105. *A Theology*, p. 119.
106. *Social Order*, pp. 463–464.

Chapter 6. THEOLOGICAL PERSONALISM: A. C. KNUDSON

1. See Knudson's theological autobiography, "A Personalistic Approach to Theology," in *Contemporary American Theology*, ed. Vergilius Ferm (New York: Round Table Press, Inc., 1932), I, 217–241.
2. *Ibid.*, p. 231.
3. See Walter G. Muelder and Laurence Sears (ed.), *The Development of American Philosophy* (Boston: Houghton Mifflin Company, 1940), pp. 221–222.
4. For a discussion of the personalistic view of nature see Carroll DeWitt Hildebrand, "Personalism and Nature," in *Personalism in Theology*, ed. Edgar Sheffield Brightman (Boston: Boston University Press, 1943).
5. Knudson, *loc. cit.*, p. 234.
6. Knudson himself wrote a volume on personalism, *The Philosophy of Personalism* (Nashville: Abingdon Press, 1927).
7. The discussion that is to follow here is taken almost exclusively from these two volumes. They contain a complete and detailed system of theology and represent Knudson's mature thought. Additional works of Knudson are as follows: *The Old Testament Problem* (Cincinnati: Jennings and Graham, 1908); *The Beacon Lights of Prophecy* (New York: Eaton and Mains, 1914); *The Religious Teachings of the Old Testament* (Nashville: Abingdon Press, 1918); *The Prophetic Movement in Israel* (New York: Methodist Book Concern, 1921); *Present Tendencies in Religious Thought* (Nashville: Abingdon Press, 1924); *The Validity of Religious Experience* (Nashville: Abingdon Press, 1937); *Principles of Christian Ethics* (Nashville: Abingdon Press, 1943). These include the books of Knudson written through 1943.
8. *The Doctrine of God* (Nashville: Abingdon Press, 1930), p. 117.
9. *Ibid.*, pp. 106–124.
10. *Ibid.*, pp. 125–145.
11. While Knudson agrees with liberals in general in grounding theology in reason and experience rather than in revealed dogma, in one sense he gives a more objectivistic interpretation to the problem of knowledge than do any of the thinkers previously discussed. As an idealist and a personalist Knudson gives a more extensive role to the speculative reason than do Brown, Fosdick, and Rauschenbusch, who by and large stand within a Kantian framework in estimating the range of man's rational powers. Christianity, he asserts, is a philosophy, and it can be defended on objective, rational grounds.
12. *The Doctrine of God*, pp. 146–170.
13. *Ibid.*, pp. 175–176.
14. *Ibid.*, pp. 187–199.
15. *Ibid.*, p. 173.
16. *Ibid.*, pp. 84–85.
17. *Ibid.*, pp. 203–241.
18. *The Doctrine of God*, p. 241.
19. The difference between Knudson and these men is, of course, a relative one. However, even Brown, who comes closest to Knudson, in that he does offer a systematic treatment of the attributes of God, reflects a more prac-

tical and less theoretical interest than does Knudson. Brown suggests, for example, that the attributes of absoluteness are not defined abstractly as deductions from absoluteness but concretely; i.e., these metaphysical attributes are just so many ways of affirming that the character revealed in Jesus Christ is the ultimate reality in the universe.

20. *The Doctrine of God*, pp. 285–287.
21. Harry Emerson Fosdick is one of the clearest examples of this.
22. *The Doctrine of God*, p. 294.
23. *Ibid.*, p. 297.
24. *Ibid.*, p. 366.
25. Cf. Claude Welch, *In This Name* (New York: Charles Scribner's Sons, 1952), p. 56.
26. The men described by H. Richard Niebuhr as "radicals" and "dualists" are good examples of Christian thinkers who center attention on the doctrine of redemption. See *Christ and Culture* (New York: Harper & Brothers, 1951), pp. 80–82, 188–189, 191–194. The distinction between a theology based on creation and one based on redemption would not hold as well for those thinkers who occupy the "conversionist" category as described by Niebuhr. These men are in the central tradition of the church but maintain a balance between an emphasis on creation and redemption. See *ibid.*, pp. 190–229.
27. When Knudson speaks of the doctrine of creation as monistic, he means primarily that the world is good, not that it cannot be distinguished from God. *The Doctrine of Redemption* (Nashville: Abingdon Press, 1933), p. 33. See also pp. 27–28.
28. *Ibid.*, p. 34.
29. Knudson is abandoning this distinction only with reference to the phenomenal world. Human persons are free, finite beings, and their free acts do constitute an instance of secondary causation.
30. *The Doctrine of Redemption*, p. 100.
31. Knudson does not indicate what he means by body in this connection. Since Knudson is a metaphysical idealist of the personalist type, he presumably thinks of the human body as a part of the phenomenal realm of nature.
32. *The Doctrine of Redemption*, p. 104.
33. Reinhold Niebuhr, for example, makes a great deal of this. See *The Nature and Destiny of Man* (One Volume Edition; New York: Charles Scribner's Sons, 1949), II, 294–298.
34. *The Doctrine of Redemption*, p. 500.
35. *Ibid.*, pp. 257–258.
36. *Ibid.*, p. 261.
37. *Ibid.*, p. 265.
38. *Ibid.*, p. 260.
39. *Ibid.*, p. 270.
40. *Ibid.*
41. See *The Nature and Destiny of Man*, II, 98–126; *Faith and History* (New York: Charles Scribner's Sons, 1949); and *Moral Man and Immoral Society* (New York: Charles Scribner's Sons, 1932).
42. *The Doctrine of Redemption*, p. 431.
43. See the following for the views of these men: Ramsey, *Basic Christian Ethics* (New York: Charles Scribner's Sons, 1950); Nygren, *Agape and*

Eros, trans. Philip S. Watson (Philadelphia: Westminster Press, 1953); Niebuhr, *The Nature and Destiny of Man,* II, pp. 68–97.

44. *The Doctrine of Redemption,* p. 468.
45. *Ibid.,* p. 472.
46. *Ibid.,* pp. 318–333.
47. *Ibid.,* p. 325.
48. *Ibid.,* p. 332.
49. *Ibid.,* pp. 369–387.
50. *Ibid.,* p. 458.
51. *Ibid.,* p. 465.
52. *Ibid.,* p. 466.

Chapter 7. EVOLUTIONARY THEISM: EUGENE W. LYMAN

1. See his intellectual autobiography, "Christian Theology and a Spiritualistic Philosophy," in *Contemporary American Theology,* ed. Vergilius Ferm (New York: Round Table Press, Inc., 1933), Second Series, pp. 103–131.
2. *Ibid.,* p. 118. Cf. Walter Marshsall Horton, "Eugene W. Lyman: Liberal Christian Thinker," in *Liberal Theology: an Appraisal,* ed. David E. Roberts and Henry Pitney Van Dusen (New York: Charles Scribner's Sons, 1942), pp. 24–25.
3. Horton, *loc. cit.,* p. 8.
4. *Ibid.,* pp. 7–8.
5. "What Is Theology?" in *The American Journal of Theology,* XVII (July, 1913), 330–332.
6. *Ibid.,* p. 342.
7. *Theology and Human Problems* (Boston: Pilgrim Press, 1910), p. 1.
8. *Ibid.,* pp. 41–58.
9. *The American Journal of Theology,* XVIII (July, 1914), 355–377.
10. Horton, *loc. cit.,* p. 11.
11. *The Meaning and Truth of Religion* (New York: Charles Scribner's Sons, 1933), pp. 151–225.
12. "Can Religious Intuition Give Knowledge of Reality?" in *Religious Realism,* ed. Douglas Clyde Macintosh (New York: The Macmillan Company), pp. 255–274.
13. Cf. Horton, *loc. cit.,* p. 20.
14. *Meaning,* pp. 347–414.
15. *Ibid.,* p. 349.
16. *Man as Sinner in Contemporary American Realistic Theology* (New York: King's Crown Press, 1946), p. 13.
17. *Meaning,* pp. 443–444.
18. *Ibid.,* p. 403.
19. *Ibid.*
20. *Ibid.*
21. *Ibid.,* p. 63.
22. *Ibid.,* pp. 342–343.
23. Horton, *loc. cit.,* p. 37.
24. *Ibid.,* p. 42.
25. *Problems,* p. 95.
26. *Ibid.,* p. 106.
27. See his intellectual autobiography, "Why I Enroll with the Mystics," in *Contemporary American Theology,* ed. Vergilius Ferm (New York: Round Table Press, 1932), I, 189–215. See also Harry Emerson Fosdick (ed.),

Rufus Jones Speaks to Our Time (New York: The Macmillan Company, 1951), especially pp. 40–47.

28. *Problems,* p. 193.
29. *Ibid.,* p. 195.
30. "The Place of Jesus Christ in Modern Theology," in *The Journal of Religion,* IX (April, 1929), 203.
31. Horton, *loc. cit.,* p. 30.
32. *Meaning,* pp. 420–421.
33. Cf. William Adams Brown, "The Church," Roberts and Van Dusen (eds.), *op. cit.,* pp. 255–272.
34. *Ibid.,* p. 255.
35. *The Journal of Religion,* III (September, 1923), 449–457.
36. *The God of the New Age: a Tract for the Times* (Boston: The Pilgrim Press, 1918).
37. *Meaning,* p. 439.
38. Horton, *loc. cit.,* pp. 36–43.

Chapter 8. SOCIAL CHRISTIANITY:. SHAILER MATHEWS

1. See his autobiography, *New Faith for Old* (New York: The Macmillan Company, 1936).
2. *The Faith of Modernism* (New York: The Macmillan Company, 1924), p. 12.
3. *Christianity and Liberalism* (New York: The Macmillan Company, 1923), p. 21.
4. "Theology and the Social Mind," in *The Biblical World,* XLVI (October, 1915), 204.
5. *Atonement and the Social Process* (New York: The Macmillan Company, 1930), pp. 11–12.
6. *Ibid.,* p. 20.
7. Mathews gives to experience, at this point, a subjectivistic interpretation in that he stresses experience itself rather than the content of experience. Theology is not the formulation of any kind of system of objective truths, whether derived from revelation or reason. Theology is the interpretation of religious experience. However, this subjectivism is qualified in that theology always reflects, not simply the experience of individuals, but the experience of an age. Theology embodies the understanding of reality and religion held by a group during a particular historical era. Thus, an objective note is added, but the objectivity is relative to the group and to the period of history involved. The result is a kind of social subjectivism. The dominant social mind reflects an understanding, not of objective truths, but of social religious experience. In the modern age the objectivity embodied in the social mind takes the form of a scientific interpretation of the world. It will be seen that a problem arises here as to precisely what sort of truth value this scientific account of the world really has.
8. "Theology As Group Belief," in *Contemporary American Theology,* ed. Vergilius Ferm (New York: Round Table Press, 1933), Second Series, 174.
9. *Modernism,* p. 23.
10. *Ibid.,* p. 49.
11. See "Theology As Group Belief," *loc. cit.,* pp. 186–187.
12. *The Gospel and Modern Man* (New York: The Macmillan Company, 1910), p. 48.
13. *Ibid.,* p. 45.

14. *Modernism*, p. 115.
15. *Ibid.*, p. 118.
16. The term "subjectivist" here means that attention is shifted more to the religious subject and away from the religious object. The meaning intended is intimately related to what H. Richard Niebuhr has called the "anthropocentric" tendency in nineteenth-century religion and culture. "Religious Realism and the Twentieth Century," in *Religious Realism*, ed. Douglas Clyde Macintosh (New York: The Macmillan Company, 1931), pp. 415–416. Mathews in his latest period moves to a pragmatic or functional view of religion and of theology, and this involves beginning with the religious subject and his needs, experiences, and ideas.
17. *The Growth of the Idea of God* (New York: Macmillan Co., 1931), p. 219.
18. *Ibid.*, p. 232.
19. *Ibid.*, pp. 232–233.
20. This conviction appears in *The Gospel and Modern Man*, p. 165. It reappears in *The Faith of Modernism*, pp. 97–98. This conviction is found finally, in the newly developed language employed in *Atonement and the Social Process*, p. 195.
21. *Modernism*, p. 99.
22. *Gospel*, pp. 151–152.
23. *Modernism*, p. 91.
24. *Ibid.*, p. 100.
25. *Contributions of Science to Religion* (New York: D. Appleton and Company, 1924), pp. 413–414.
26. *The Social Gospel* (Philadelphia: The American Baptist Publication Society, 1909).
27. *The Spiritual Interpretation of History* (Cambridge: The Harvard University Press, 1916), p. 210.
28. *Ibid.*, p. 219.
29. *Ibid.*, p. vii.
30. *Ibid.*, p. viii.
31. *Ibid.*, p. ix.
32. *New Faith for Old*, pp. 119–151, 296–299.
33. *Ibid.*, pp. 196–197.
34. *Gospel*, pp. 124–125.
35. *Ibid.*, p. 138.
36. *Ibid.*, p. 160.
37. *Modernism*, p. 143.
38. *Atonement*, pp. 164–165.
39. *Ibid.*, p. 198.
40. *Ibid.*, p. 205.
41. *The Structure of the Divine Society* (London: Lutterworth Press, 1951).
42. A question inevitably arises as to whether or not the individualistic view of the church generally held by liberals is in conflict with the widely affirmed principle of social solidarity. Four considerations suggest themselves in this regard. (1) Social solidarity is more fundamental in the thought of some liberal thinkers than others. (2) Some who stress social solidarity also place some emphasis upon the organic nature of the church, e. g., Fosdick, Rauschenbusch, and Wieman. (3) The solidarity of which the liberals spoke refers primarily to the whole society. Since liberals affirm the continuity between the Christian community and the larger community, they have less need for a doctrine of the church as an organic

body distinct from the society as a whole. (4) There is a kind of theological looseness and lack of systematic precision in liberalism which allows for a variety of emphases which are not always entirely harmonious.

43. *Modernism*, p. 179.
44. *Gospel*, p. 322.
45. H. Richard Niebuhr, *Christ and Culture* (New York: Harper & Brothers, 1951), pp. 83–115.
46. *Gospel*, pp. 322–326.
47. *New Faith for Old*, p. 153.

Chapter 9. EMPIRICAL THEOLOGY: DOUGLAS CLYDE MACINTOSH

1. See his intellectual autobiography, "Toward an Untraditional Orthodoxy," in *Contemporary American Theology*, ed. Vergilius Ferm (New York: Round Table Press, Inc., 1932), I, 275–319.
2. *Ibid.*, p. 306.
3. *Theology as an Empirical Science* (New York: The Macmillan Company, 1919), pp. 7–9.
4. *Ibid.*, p. ix.
5. *Ibid.*, p. 29.
6. *Ibid.*, p. 31.
7. For the development of these views, see *ibid.*, pp. 19–21, 103–123; *The Reasonableness of Christianity* (New York: Charles Scribner's Sons, 1925), pp. 134–160; *Pilgrimage*, pp. 172–179, 272–290.
8. *Empirical*, pp. 143–144.
9. *Ibid.*, pp. 44–45.
10. *The Problem of Knowledge* (New York: The Macmillan Company, 1915); *The Problem of Religious Knowledge* (New York: Harper & Brothers, 1940).
11. *Empirical*, pp. 239–246; *Reasonableness*, pp. 161–244; *Pilgrimage*, pp. 206–229; "Experimental Realism in Religion," in *Religious Realism*, ed. D. C. Macintosh (New York: The Macmillan Company, 1931), pp. 329–383.
12. *Empirical*, pp. 240–241.
13. *Pilgrimage*, pp. 180–205.
14. *Ibid.*, pp. 195–205; *Reasonableness*, pp. 40–56.
15. Max Carl Otto, Henry Nelson Wieman, and D. C. Macintosh, *Is There a God?* (Chicago: Willett, Clark and Company, 1952).
16. *Ibid.*, p. 140.
17. *Empirical*, p. 91.
18. *Ibid.*, p. 148.
19. *Ibid.*, p. 162.
20. *Ibid.*, pp. 253–254.
21. See *Is There a God?* pp. 297–298, *Reasonableness*, pp. 154–155, *Empirical*, p. 193.
22. Claude Welch, *In This Name* (New York: Charles Scribner's Sons, 1952), pp. 50–51.
23. The Chicago thinkers like to call themselves theists. For example, see Henry Nelson Wieman and Bernard Eugene Meland, *American Philosophies of Religion* (Chicago: Willett, Clark and Company, 1936), pp. 272–306.
24. *Reasonableness*, p. 84.
25. *Empirical*, pp. 172–175; *Reasonableness*, pp. 84–119.
26. *Empirical*, pp. 68–71; *Reasonableness*, pp. 53–63.
27. *Empirical*, p. 73.

28. *Reasonableness*, pp. 64–73.
29. *Empirical*, pp. 205–215.
30. *Ibid.*, p. 82.
31. *Ibid.*, pp. 227–228.
32. *Ibid.*, p. 139.
33. *Reasonableness*, p. 138.
34. For Troeltsch, see Hugh Ross Mackintosh, *Types of Modern Theology* (London: Nisbet and Company, Ltd., 1937), pp. 181–217; for Foster, see *The Finality of the Christian Religion* (Chicago: The University of Chicago Press, 1906), pp. xii–xiii, 510–518; *Christianity in Its Modern Expression* (New York: The Macmillan Company, 1921), pp. 7–8, 156–158.
35. *Empirical*, pp. 119–121.
36. *Ibid.*, p. 131.
37. *Ibid.*, p. 155.
38. *Ibid.*, p. 237.
39. *Personal Religion* (New York: Charles Scribner's Sons, 1942), pp. 251–252.
40. *Ibid.*, p. 277.

Chapter 10. THEOLOGICAL NATURALISM: HENRY NELSON WIEMAN

1. See his intellectual autobiography, "Theocentric Religion," in *Contemporary American Theology*, ed. Vergilius Ferm (New York: Round Table Press, Inc., 1932), I, 339–352.
2. Shailer Mathews has a viewpoint similar to that of Wieman, but he does not connect his outlook so explicitly with a world view as does Wieman. As a matter of fact, however, Mathews is no closer in his latest books to traditional theism than is Wieman. Both Wieman and Mathews use the term theism to apply to their thought. However, it seems best in the interest of clarity to restrict theism to those systems of thought which affirm that God is a personal being who is in some real sense distinct from the world and transcendent to it.
3. *The Wrestle of Religion with Truth* (New York: The Macmillan Company, 1927), p. 3; *Normative Psychology of Religion*, co-author, Regina Westcott Wieman (New York: Thomas Y. Crowell, 1935), p. 29; *The Growth of Religion*, co-author, Walter Marshall Horton (Chicago: Willett, Clark and Co., 1938), pp. xii, 273–298.
4. *Wrestle*, pp. v–vii.
5. "Values: Primary Data for Religious Inquiry," in *Journal of Religion*, XVI (October, 1936), 379–405. Cf. *Wrestle*, p. 135.
6. *Wrestle*, pp. 71–73.
7. *Ibid.*, pp. 160–167.
8. "Values: Primary Data for Religious Inquiry," *loc. cit.; Normative*, p. 46; *Growth*, pp. 329–331.
9. *The Source of Human Good* (Chicago: The University of Chicago Press, 1946), pp. 16–23.
10. "Values: Primary Data for Religious Inquiry," *loc. cit.*, p. 394.
11. *Growth*, pp. 331–338.
12. *Religious Experience and the Scientific Method* (New York: The Macmillan Company, 1926), pp. 21–47. See also "God Is More than We Can Think," in *Christendom*, I (Spring, 1936), 433.
13. *Wrestle*, pp. 94–95.
14. *Ibid.*, pp. 83–96.

15. *Experience*, pp. 65–85.
16. *Ibid.*, p. 197.
17. *Wrestle*, pp. 15–16.
18. "Theocentric Religion," *loc. cit.*, p. 347; *Normative*, p. 122.
19. *Experience*, p. 158.
20. *Ibid.*, p. 346.
21. *Growth*, pp. 423–427.
22. "God Is More than We Can Think," *loc. cit.*, p. 438; *Normative*, pp. 119–120.
23. Wieman himself contributed to the volume, which is the best source of the realistic movement in American theology. Wieman's article is "God and Value," in *Religious Realism*, ed. Douglas Clyde Macintosh (New York: The Macmillan Company, 1931), pp. 155–176.
24. Henry Nelson Wieman and Bernard Eugene Meland, *American Philosophies of Religion* (Chicago: Willett, Clark and Company, 1936), p. 7.
25. *Is There a God?* co-authors Douglas Clyde Macintosh and Max C. Otto (Chicago: Willet, Clark and Company, 1932), p. 13; "God and Value," *loc. cit.*, p. 155.
26. *God*, pp. 201–202.
27. Wieman has given a variety of definitions of God in his career which elucidate various facets of this view of God. See *ibid.*, pp. 14, 59, *Methods of Private Religious Living* (New York: The Macmillan Company, 1929), pp. 46–47, *The Issues of Life* (Nashville: Abingdon Press, 1930), p. 162, "God and Value," *loc. cit.*, p. 155, *Is There a God?* p. 13, *Normative*, p. 51, "God Is More than We Can Think," *loc. cit.*, p. 428.
28. "John Dewey's Common Faith," in *The Christian Century*, November 14, 1934, pp. 1450–1452.
29. "Is John Dewey a Theist?" in *The Christian Century*, December 5, 1934, pp. 1550–1553.
30. *Ibid.*, p. 1550.
31. *Ibid.*, p. 1551.
32. *Ibid.*
33. "God Is More than We Can Think," *loc. cit.*, pp. 436–438.
34. This criticism is made by D. C. Macintosh. See *Is There a God?* p. 27.
35. Robert L. Calhoun urges that Wieman's view is a type of "theological behaviorism." "God Is More than Mind," in *Christendom*, I (Winter, 1936), 343–344, 347–348; "How Shall We Think of God?" in *Christendom*, I (Summer, 1936), 593–611. See also Macintosh, *Is There a God?* pp. 24–25.
36. *Is There a God?* pp. 13–15, 88–89.
37. "Faith and Knowledge," in *Christendom*, I (Autumn, 1936), p. 771.
38. *Ibid.*, p. 772.
39. *Ibid.*
40. "Not all events involve mind, but some do; and it may be that what gives the character and creative advance to the whole of nature and every part of nature is that there is operative through the whole of nature a Mind." *Experience*, p. 181. This statement appears in his first published book, but since he later repudiates it, it may be assumed that this represents a temporary conviction which he soon abandoned.
41. "Theocentric Religion," *loc. cit.*, p. 349.
42. *Issues*, pp. 220–221.
43. *Is There a God?* p. 126.
44. *Ibid.*, p. 148.

45. "God Is More than We Can Think," *loc. cit.*, pp. 432–433.

46. *Ibid.*, pp. 441–442; "Faith and Knowledge," *loc. cit.*, pp. 774–775; "God in Emergent Evolution," in *The Christian Century*, October 2, 1935, p. 1242. Calhoun attempts to demonstrate that the denial that God makes mechanisms leads to a Marcionite explanation of the world which makes another God responsible for the physical world. "The Power of God and the Wisdom of God," in *Christendom*, II (Winter, 1937), 32.

47. "Faith and Knowledge," *loc. cit.*, pp. 777–778.

48. *Ibid.*, p. 778.

49. *Is There a God?* pp. 202, 280.

50. *Ibid.*, p. 280.

51. *Ibid.* Calhoun contends against him at this point that the affirmation that God is the source of all good and that integration as such constitutes goodness is a Neoplatonic assumption which can be carried through logically only by a monism which identifies evil with plurality and nonbeing or by a kind of Marcionism which makes another power than God responsible for evil. Wieman indicates no willingness to accept either of these alternatives. "God as More than Mind," *loc. cit.*, pp. 340–341.

52. *Is There a God?* pp. 317–318.

53. *Ibid.*, p. 14.

54. "Faith and Knowledge," *loc. cit.*, pp. 770–774. See Calhoun's criticism of this point. "God as More than Mind," *loc. cit.*, pp. 343–346; "How Shall We Think of God?" *loc. cit.*, pp. 601–605.

55. "Faith and Knowledge," *loc. cit.*, p. 773.

56. *Normative*, pp. 52–59.

57. "God Is More than We Can Think," *loc. cit.*, pp. 435–437.

58. "Faith and Knowledge," *loc. cit.*, pp. 778.

59. *Is There a God?* pp. 14–15.

60. *Wrestle*, p. vi.

61. *Ibid.*, p. 99; see also *Normative*, p. 321.

62. *Normative*, pp. 320–340; *Wrestle*, pp. 83–132.

63. *Wrestle*, p. 109.

64. *Ibid.*, p. 110.

65. *Normative*, p. 148.

66. *Wrestle*, pp. 123–124.

67. *Normative*, pp. 153–163.

68. *Is There a God?* p. 279.

69. October 1, 1930, pp. 1181–1184.

70. May 2, 1934, pp. 589–591.

71. *Ibid.*, p. 590.

72. *Issues*, pp. 39–40.

73. *Experience*, p. 246. See also *Wrestle*, pp. 128–129.

74. *Methods*, p. 140.

75. *Normative*, p. 504.

76. *Ibid.*, pp. 513–514.

77. *Methods*, pp. 64–65.

78. See also *Normative*, pp. 501–504; *Growth*, pp. 308–309.

79. January 25, 1939, pp. 116–118.

80. *Ibid.*, p. 117.

81. *Ibid.*

82. *Source*, p. 269.

Chapter 11. THE ESSENCE OF LIBERALISM AND ITS VALIDITY

1. Cf. Reinhold Niebuhr: "Modern culture is always an essentially temporalized version of the classical answer to the problems of human existence. Anaxagoras had said: 'In the beginning everything was in confusion; then Mind came and ordered the chaos.' The modern version is: 'In the beginning everything is in confusion; but Mind grows progressively to order the chaos." *Faith and History* (New York: Charles Scribner's Sons, 1949), p. 30. It is evident that idealism and evolution have contributed most to this outlook. It needs to be noted, however, that the modern world is not unanimous in affirming an idealistic position. Nevertheless, many nonidealistic perspectives share the belief that history is a redemptive process, e. g., Marxism and the optimistic versions of naturalistic humanism. In short, while there are dissenting voices of one sort and another, it can be said as a general principle that Niebuhr's thesis with regard to the fundamental orientation of modern culture holds.

   Thus, even those liberal theologians who are oriented more from a naturalistic than from an idealistic outlook are in agreement that there are forces at work which are leading to the perfection of moral personality. Mathews and Wieman would not speak of Mind or Spirit as a power distinguishable from nature as a whole, but they affirm that there are personality-producing forces in the world process which perform a progress-making function.

2. "After Liberalism—What?" in *The Christian Century*, November 8, 1933, p. 1403.

3. *God Was in Christ* (New York: Charles Scribner's Sons, 1948), pp. 9–10.

4. *The Epistle to the Romans*, trans. Edwyn C. Hoskyns (New York: Oxford University Press, 1933), p. 10.

5. *Ibid.*, p. 28.

6. For the views of Niebuhr, see particularly *The Nature and Destiny of Man* (One Volume Edition, New York: Charles Scribner's Sons, 1949) and *Faith and History*.

7. There are, of course, difficulties in speaking of God as a Person, and it must be recognized that this concept is used as a symbol. Person cannot mean precisely the same thing when applied to God as when applied to man. Nevertheless, since it is necessary to use language derived from human experience in speaking of God, it is better to refer to God in personal terms than in some alternative way. Despite Tillich's protest there are strong Biblical and theological reasons for referring to God as a Person. See Millar Burrows, *An Outline of Biblical Theology* (Philadelphia: The Westminster Press, 1946), p. 60; Emil Brunner, *The Christian Doctrine of God*, trans. Olive Wyon (Philadelphia: The Westminster Press, 1950), p. 139.

Chapter 12. THE RELATION OF LIBERALISM TO POST-LIBERAL TRENDS

1. See John Bennett, "After Liberalism—What?" in *The Christian Century*, November 8, 1933, pp. 1403–1406; Walter Marshall Horton, *Realistic Theology* (New York: Harper & Brothers, 1934); and Mary Francis Thelen, *Man as Sinner in Contemporary American Realistic Theology* (New York: King's Crown Press, 1946), p. 2.

2. Cf. William Hordern, *A Layman's Guide to Protestant Theology* (New

York: The Macmillan Company, 1955), for a similar classification of recent trends.

3. *What Present-Day Theologians Are Thinking* (New York: Harper & Brothers, 1952), p. 12.
4. *The Church against the World,* co-authors Wilhelm Pauck and Francis P. Miller (Chicago: Willett, Clark and Company, 1935), p. 124.
5. *An Interpretation of Christian Ethics* (New York: Charles Scribner's Sons, 1935), p. 15.
6. "Beyond Modernism," in *The Christian Century* (December 4, 1935), p. 1552.
7. April 26, 1939, p. 542.
8. *Ibid.,* p. 544.
9. *Ibid.,* p. 545.
10. This next section is heavily dependent on an unpublished lecture by L. Harold De Wolf, "Themes of Continuity and Discontinuity in Recent Thought and in the Christian Faith."
11. Alfred North Whitehead, *Science and the Modern World* (New York: The Macmillan Company, 1925), p. 190.
12. *Ibid.,* p. 51.
13. *Ibid.,* p. 181.
14. Lincoln Barnett, *The Universe and Dr. Einstein* (New York: William Sloane Associates, 1948), p. 27.
15. Bertrand Russell, *The ABC of Relativity* (New York: The New American Library, 1959), p. 51. The original hard-cover edition of this book was issued by George Allen and Unwin, Ltd. of London in 1925.
16. See Barnett, *op. cit.,* pp. 96–104; Milton K. Munitz (ed.), *Theories of the Universe* (Glencoe, Ill.: The Free Press, 1957), pp. 390–412, 419–429.
17. Rudolf Ernst Peierls, *The Laws of Nature* (New York: Charles Scribner's Sons, 1956), pp. 30–31, 245–249.
18. George Stuart Carter, *A Hundred Years of Evolution* (New York: The Macmillan Company, 1957), pp. 95–126.
19. E. Adamson Hoebel, *Man in the Primitive World* (New York: McGraw-Hill Book Company, Inc., 1949), pp. 484–494; Melville J. Herskovits, *Cultural Anthropology* (New York: Alfred A. Knopf, 1955), pp. 430–442.
20. Barnett, *op. cit.,* p. 107.
21. *The Case for a New Reformation Theology* (Philadelphia: The Westminster Press, 1959), pp. 27–30.
22. See Paul Tillich, *The Courage To Be* (New Haven: Yale University Press, 1952), pp. 126–154.
23. Cf. Paul Tillich, *The Religious Situation* (New York: Meridian Books, 1956), p. 45. See also Richard R. Niebuhr, *Resurrection and Historical Reason* (New York: Charles Scribner's Sons, 1957), pp. 72–89.
24. *The Epistle to the Romans,* trans. Edwyn C. Hoskyns (New York: Oxford University Press, 1933), pp. 27–32.
25. *Jesus Christ and Mythology* (New York: Charles Scribner's Sons, 1958); "New Testament and Mythology," in *Kerygma and Myth,* ed. Hans Werner Bartsch, trans. Reginald H. Fuller (London: SPCK, 1954), pp. 1–44.
26. *The Mediator,* trans. Olive Wyon (Philadelphia: The Westminster Press, 1947), pp. 573–584. Cf. *The Christian Doctrine of Creation and Redemption,* trans. Olive Wyon (Philadelphia: The Westminster Press, 1952), pp. 328, 368.

27. *The Theology of Crisis* (New York: Charles Scribner's Sons, 1929), pp. 41 ff. See also *The Mediator*, pp. 303–308.
28. *The Nature and Destiny of Man*, One Volume Edition (New York: Charles Scribner's Sons, 1949), II, 35–96. Cf. *Reinhold Niebuhr: His Religious, Social, and Political Thought*, ed. Charles W. Kegley and Robert W. Bretall (New York: The Macmillan Company, 1956), p. 446.
29. *The Meaning of Revelation* (New York: The Macmillan Company, 1946), pp. 74–76.
30. See Paul Tillich, *Systematic Theology* (Chicago: The University of Chicago Press, 1951), I, 49. See also Vol. II (1957), pp. 44–78.
31. *Jesus Christ and Mythology*, pp. 60–85; *Kerygma and Myth*, pp. 196–211.
32. *The Cosmic Christ* (New York: Harper & Brothers, 1951).
33. See, for example, the criticism of Reinhold Niebuhr by Williams and Wieman to the effect that redemption is seen by him primarily in terms of the meaning which Christ gives to life (justification or forgiveness) and not sufficiently or clearly enough in terms of the concrete transformation of personal and social existence in the empirical realm of history. Kegley and Bretall (eds.), *op. cit.*, pp. 205–213, 345–348. See also the criticism of Williams against neo-orthodoxy in general on this score, *God's Grace and Man's Hope* (New York: Harper & Brothers, 1949), pp. 27–32.
34. Cf. Karl Lowith, who explicitly denies that world history is observably any different now than before Christ came. *Meaning in History* (Chicago: The University of Chicago Press, 1949), p. 190.
35. For example, Brunner cannot even be sure what realities, if any, lie behind the eschatological symbols which Niebuhr uses to refer to the fulfillment of life beyond history. Kegley and Bretall (eds.), *op. cit.*, pp. 31–32.
36. *The Meaning of Revelation*, pp. 86–88, 185–187; *Christ and Culture* (New York: Harper & Brothers, 1951), pp. x, 190–256; "Is God in the War?" in *The Christian Century*, August 5, 1942, pp. 953–955.
37. *The Meaning of Revelation*, p. 23.
38. *The Divine-Human Encounter*, trans. Amandus W. Loos (Philadelphia: The Westminster Press, 1943), pp. 107–136.
39. See Bernhard W. Anderson, *Understanding the Old Testament* (Englewood Cliffs, N.J.: Prentice-Hall, Inc., 1957), pp. 1–10, 38–50.
40. See Lowith, *op. cit.*, pp. 182–190.
41. *Systematic Theology*, I, 64.
42. *Ibid.*, p. 65.
43. One should be careful not to confuse the use of autonomy and theonomy here with the meanings given to them by Paul Tillich.
44. See *Christ and Culture*, pp. 190–229.
45. See note 36 above. Cf. Thelen, *op. cit.*, pp. 148–163.
46. See Shailer Mathews, *The Spiritual Interpretation of History* (Cambridge: The Harvard University Press, 1916).
47. *Christ and Culture*, p. 254.
48. Cf. Richard R. Niebuhr, *op. cit.*, pp. 81–89.
49. *Op. cit.*, pp. 1–19, 191–203.
50. *Faith and History* (New York: Charles Scribner's Sons, 1949).
51. *The Meaning of Revelation*, p. 109.
52. *God's Grace and Man's Hope.*
53. James M. Robinson, *The New Quest of the Historical Jesus* (London: SCM Press, Ltd., 1959), pp. 26–47.
54. See Hans W. Frei, "The Theology of H. Richard Niebuhr," in *Faith and*

Ethics, ed. Paul Ramsey (New York: Harper & Brothers, 1957), pp. 104–116.

55. Williams, *What Present-Day Theologians Are Thinking,* p. 103. See pp. 100–107 for an excellent discussion of these new tendencies in Christology.
56. Niebuhr, *The Meaning of Revelation,* p. 90.
57. *Ibid.,* pp. 59–90.
58. See Richard R. Niebuhr, *op. cit.,* pp. 51–62, 81–84. See also Bultmann, *Jesus Christ and Mythology,* pp. 60–85.
59. Barth, *Church Dogmatics,* trans. G. T. Thomson and Harold Knight (New York: Charles Scribner's Sons, 1956), I, 2, pp. 122–171; Brunner, *The Mediator,* pp. 232–327, and *The Christian Doctrine of Creation and Redemption,* pp. 322–378.
60. *The Mediator,* p. 308, note 1.
61. *Church Dogmatics,* I, 2, pp. 172–202.
62. *Op. cit.,* pp. 42–51, 72–89.
63. *God Was in Christ* (New York: Charles Scribner's Sons, 1948), p. 110.
64. *Ibid.,* pp. 71–79.
65. *Christian Ethics* (Nashville: Abingdon Press, 1957), p. 29 n.
66. Baillie, *God Was in Christ,* pp. 9–20, 34–39, 48–54.
67. *The Nature and Destiny of Man,* II, pp. 70–76; *Faith and History,* pp. 139–150.
68. *Systematic Theology,* I, pp. 132–137.
69. *Jesus Christ and Mythology,* pp. 78–83; *Kerygma and Myth,* pp. 22–35, 117.
70. *The Mediator,* p. 343, note 1.
71. *God Was in Christ,* pp. 114–132.
72. *Christ and Culture,* 11–29.

INDEX